Harrington O'Reilly

Life Among the American Indians

Fifty Years on the Trial a True Story of Western Life

Harrington O'Reilly

Life Among the American Indians
Fifty Years on the Trial a True Story of Western Life

ISBN/EAN: 9783337061739

Printed in Europe, USA, Canada, Australia, Japan

Cover: Foto ©ninafisch / pixelio.de

More available books at **www.hansebooks.com**

LIFE AMONG THE AMERICAN INDIANS

Fifty Years on the Trail

A TRUE STORY OF WESTERN LIFE

BY

HARRINGTON O'REILLY

*WITH OVER ONE HUNDRED ILLUSTRATIONS
BY P. L. FRENZENY*

London
CHATTO & WINDUS, PICCADILLY
1891

Copyrighted in America] *[All rights reserved*

PREFACE.

AN author who writes a long preface is a bore. I trust I shall not be voted an offender in this respect if I ask for a few moments the attention of my reader before he plunges into the story of John Y. Nelson, the man who is the subject of it.

Living on the fringe of civilisation as he has for over forty-five years, during the period of what may be termed its transition state, he has taken part in scenes and episodes such as could only have existed under the exceptional circumstances of the opening up of a new country, and especially such a country as the Western States of America.

Many of these scenes and episodes have been far from creditable to the persons concerned in them, and some of them not creditable to John Nelson personally. I make no apology for him; if any can be found, let it be in the fact that nearly every man's hand has been against him, and his, doubtless, more than it should have been, against every man.

My object has been merely to give an unvarnished and circumstantial account of the existing events which have occurred to an individual whose position was no better than that of a "social outcast," a position he had sought of his own free will, not a position forced upon him by the violation of any of the laws of his country.

In giving expression, or what may be better termed "local colour," to most of the incidents enumerated, I have adopted, as far as possible, my subject's own phraseology. Any attempt of mine to convert it into pure English, and thus deprive it of its idiosyncrasy, would only have resulted in a dire failure.

This book is really a chapter in American Frontier history. The spots where villages, townships, and even cities now stand were familiar to Nelson as camping-grounds long before the march of civilisation had penetrated the vast tract of country lately marked on the map of the United States with the word "Unexplored."

One of these maps side by side with one of to-day will explain far more eloquently than words the wonderful changes that have taken place during the period of which this book treats.

Few men have run more risks in life than John Nelson, and few can congratulate themselves upon having had more lucky escapes. He complains that he was born under an unlucky star. He that reads this story of his career will assuredly declare that this is ungrateful; for if ill-luck really had pursued him, the first few chapters of his life would be all that would have been written, and I should have been spared a task which, although it has cost me much time and trouble, has also given me as much delight.

One great disadvantage I have had to contend with. John Nelson's memory is very erratic with regard to dates. This is, doubtless, due to an accident that happened to him some two years ago. From the explosion of a revolver a bullet passed through his left wrist, took an upward course through his mouth, and finally lodged in the frontal bone, from which it was expelled in an effort of sneezing. This bullet Nelson now wears suspended round his neck as a memento of his lucky escape.

If dates are missing here and there, or even if an incident is misplaced, I ask the indulgence of my reader on this count. He who is familiar with the march of events of American Frontier history will readily dovetail anything into its proper place that may be somewhat out of it; he who is not, will never know the difference.

With disjointed narratives, disjointed dates, disjointed sequences of events, incoherency, prolonged sittings, and a thousand difficulties which few can understand, such as sitting with a loaded revolver in my left hand whilst I wrote with my right; and on another occasion, when similarly engaged, having bullets whizzing round my head, I have at last finished my task in as coherent a manner as possible.

But whether this book is found interesting or otherwise, or whatever diversity of opinion exists as to its literary merit, there will be but one verdict as regards its illustrations.

A weak librettist bolstered up by a brilliant composer has been known ere this in the theatrical and musical world; why not a *simile* in literature? What this book may lack in one respect, always assuming that any hypercritical reader finds it lacking, is amply atoned for in the other.

Few living artists can paint an Indian as Paul Frenzeny, and fewer can depict scenes and character in the West as he can. With him this is a gift enhanced by long residence amongst these people. Had I sought the wide world through, I could not have found a more able pictorial exponent than he.

Illustrating this book, he writes me, "has given me more pleasure than any work I have ever undertaken; for it is so graphic that it recalls, without any effort on my part, scenes which I am able to draw, not from imagination, but from personal observation."

To Mr. Edward Badoureau I am also indebted for the trouble he has taken in the printing and preparation of this work.

One word more. I must not omit to state that in one instance I have availed myself of the help of Mr. Arthur Robottom, who was a personal friend of Porter Rockwell, and received his information from Rockwell direct. Mr. Robottom supplied me with some details concerning the number of persons who accompanied Brigham Young on his first trip to Salt Lake. Beyond this, and a portrait of "The Lion of the Lord," with which this gentleman has kindly furnished me, I have depended entirely upon John Nelson himself for the facts herein mentioned.

HARRINGTON O'REILLY.

May 1889

CONTENTS.

CHAPTER I.
Boyhood—A Bolt for Freedom—Slinging Dishes around—Wrecked on the Missouri—Life on a Farm—Scared away—A Friendly Caravan—Boonville—Uncle's Ranch 1

CHAPTER II.
Cattle-herding—A Trading Party—The Boundless Prairie—First Hunting Experiences. 14

CHAPTER III.
Bound West—Arrival at the Platte River—An Indian Encampment—Civilisation forsaken—The Ogallala Band—Adoption by "Spotted Tail"—An Initiatory Ceremony—Christened Cha-sha-sha-opoggeo—A Few Words about Buffaloes—An Adventure with them—Winter on the Solomon River 24

CHAPTER IV.
Habits of the Indians—Their Religion—The Sun Dance—Personal Mutilation 39

CHAPTER V.
Matrimonial Suggestions—Wom-bel-ee-zee-zee—An Inexplicable Squaw—Mother-in-Law—Patience rewarded—Trapping Beaver—Notes on their Peculiarities 46

CHAPTER VI.
Fighting the Pawnees on Little Blue River—A Bloodthirsty Massacre—Wom-bel-ee-zee-zee vanishes—A Scrimmage on the Rickaree Fork—The Sioux Method of Warfare—Only one left to tell the Tale—Rickaree Tornadoes—Born Thieves 60

CHAPTER VII.

Early Traders—Two Buck Elk's Gratitude—Zint-calla-wee-ah—More Matrimony—Cotton-wood Springs again—A Strange Caravan—First Meeting with Brigham Young—Spotted Tail's Resolution . 76

CHAPTER VIII.

Among the Mormons—Fort Laramie—*En route* for the Promised Land—Green River—Passage of the Rockies—First Sight of Salt Lake—Is it Snow?—Establishment of Salt Lake City—Arrival of the Mexican Contingent—Return of the Pioneers . . . 86

CHAPTER IX.

Farewell to the Mormons—Trapping with Canadians on the Platte River—First Scalping Experiences—A Bear Story—Arrival at St. Verain's Fort—Homeward Bound—Two Buck Elk's Greeting—Exit Zint-calla-wee-ah—New Matrimonial Experiences—Cong-he-sapa-wee-ah 99

CHAPTER X.

Camping on the Republican River—Drunkenness amongst the Brûlés—A Death in the Family—Indian Grief—Cong-he-sapa-wee-ah fillets herself—Two Buck Elk's Commiseration—A Trip to the Wajajas—Meeting with a Party of Emigrants—News of Thomas Atkinson—A Tragic Occurrence 115

CHAPTER XI.

Arrival at Laramie—Valaundrie and Joe Jewitt—Crossing the North Platte River—Tarantula Juice—The Raw Hide Butes—Crazy Woman's Fork—Trading with the Wajajas—Disagreement with the Canadians—Wee-ah-pee-ta-cha-la—First Gold-find in the Black Hills—Rejoining the Ogallalas—Return to the Brûlés on the Republican—Exit Cong-he-sapa-wee-ah—Gathering Clouds—A Government Commission to Laramie—Official Peculation—Dissatisfaction of the Indians—An impending Calamity . . . 124

CHAPTER XII.

Establishment of Fort Kearney—The Spark that fired the Train—Massacre of Twenty-nine Soldiers—Spotted Tail on the War-path—General Harney to the Rescue—The Battle of Ash Hollow—Engagement as Interpreter at Kearney—Spotted Tail sent to Fort Leavenworth—Building the New Fort—An Indian Surprise—A Flight for Life—A Tarantula Incident—Trapping with Hal Gay. 136

CONTENTS

CHAPTER XIII.
Dog Town—The "Robbers' Roost"—A Roving Saloon—Capture and Burning of the Shanty—Return to Dog Town—"Skinned out"—Trading for Alec Constance—A Trip to Fort Leavenworth—General Albert Sidney Johnson—A Few Words about the Mormons—The Government Expedition to Salt Lake—Engagement as Scout and Guide 145

CHAPTER XIV.
Breaking-in Mules—*En route* for Utah—A Startling Incident—Winter at Hams Fork—Starved out—Passage of the Rockies—Arrival at Salt Lake—Camp Floyd 155

CHAPTER XV.
The Mountain Meadow Massacre—Arrival on the Scene—Discovery of the sole Survivor—Return to Camp Floyd—Life in Dobie Town—A Disagreeable Adventure—A First White Life—Tracks for Provo City 163

CHAPTER XVI.
Meeting with Daniel Spencer—Bull-Whacking to California—Disagreements in the Outfit—Severance from the Party—Five Hundred Miles on Foot—Scaring a Caravan—Fallen amongst the Utes—A Painted Mormon Renegade—Started again—Arrival at Beal River 171

CHAPTER XVII.
Meeting with Billy Cameron—Return to Salt Lake City—Introduction to Joshua Alpin—Hunting for Work—Pony Express to Winty Valley—"A Narrow Squeak"—Conversion to Mormonism—Brigham Young again—Brother Nathaniel Jones—Appointment as Major-Domo 183

CHAPTER XVIII.
Life in a Mormon Home—Sister Annie—Rebecca's Jealousy—A Sisterly "Mill"—Brother William Godby to the Rescue—Peace again—Treacherous Indications—A *Dénoûement*—A Refuge with Godby—An unlucky Incident—Pete Dotson—Farewell to Salt Lake City 195

CHAPTER XIX.
Nemesis, or the Destroying Angels—Enemies in the Camp—A Discovery—A Surprise—The Prisoners and their Sentence—Another Bear Story—St. Verain's Fort—A Big Drunk—Arrival at Denver

—A good Resolution—Tracks for Civilisation—A Passenger for Omaha—Teamstering again—Ill-luck once more—A Raving Maniac—Death of the Mule—Under Arrest—Escape—The "Waggon Boss" shot—Swimming the Platte River—Arrival at John Young's Ranch 208

CHAPTER XX.

A Lucky Meeting—*En route* for Omaha—Tracked by the Dutchman—A Scene with the Coach—Omaha at Last—Old Farmer Keats—Arrival of the Caravan—Meeting with the "Waggon Boss"—Robbed by a "Bunkey"—Life at Keats's Ranch—Cord-wood Chopping at Florance—Teamstering to Fort Desmoines—Loading with Flour for Denver—From Teamstering to Hunting—Buckskin Jo's Gulch—A Hunt for a Job—Contracting for Venison—"Hold, enough!"—Gambling Forsaken—Return to the "Glory Hole" . 221

CHAPTER XXI.

Desperadoes in Denver—"The Rocky Mountain News"—A Scene at the Denver Hall—A Resolution to quit—Ackley's Ranch—Engagement as Bar-tender and Factotum—Pining for Freedom—Cotton-wood Springs again—At Billy Hill's—First Meeting with Dan Slade—The Story of Jules Berg—A Close Shave—A Brave Britisher—Death of Billy Hill—Tracks from the Ranch . . 232

CHAPTER XXII.

With the Brûlés on Cotton-wood Springs—A new Squaw—Rage—Consolation—"Hu-pa-sap-pah-wee-ah"—An Impracticable Mother-in-Law—Engagement with the Gilman Brothers—The Californian Telegraph Line—Exit "Hu-pa-sap-pah-wee-ah"—Trading with Spotted Tail and Two Buck Elk—Building Fort Macpherson—John Gilman Marries—Amongst the Cheyennes—Trading at Laramie—A Visit to the Ogallalas—"Op-an-gee-wee-ah"—Married once more—Cheyennes on the War-path—Return to Gilman's Ranch—Engagement as Scout, Guide, and Interpreter at Fort Macpherson—Carrying Despatches to Fort Hayes—A Lynching Episode—Two Years of Guerilla Warfare 246

CHAPTER XXIII.

The Treaty of 1866—The Firstborn Halfbreed—Independent Trading—Frozen Buffalo—White Antelope again—Lone Wolf to the Rescue—Out of the Frying-pan into the Fire—Massacre of Twenty Soldiers—Captain Egan and Party saved—Back again at Macpherson—"More War"—Colonel Brown's Expedition—Duties of a Guide—Camp on the Republican—"A thousand dollars for a

CONTENTS xiii

village "—A Reconnoitre with Beldon—The Kentucky Racer—
Into a Hornet's Nest—Escape—Six Days and Nights' Fighting—
A Driftwood Fire—Lassoing a Cavalry Horse—Return to Camp . 261

CHAPTER XXIV.

Mutiny in Camp—Attempt on Col. Brown's Life—A Skirmish at
Medicine Creek—Return of the Expedition to Fort Macpherson—
General Bradley's Arrival—Scouting with his Expedition—Catching
a Pony—The Result—Alarm—Danger—Victory—Row with Lieu-
tenant Whaling—The Broached Keg—Return to Headquarters
Camp—Reported to the General 284

CHAPTER XXV.

Responsibilities of a Scout—Indian Cunning—Sent to the Rickaree
Fork—Massacre of Col. Forsyth's Scouts—Following the Indians
—Return to General Bradley—A Strange Voice—"Superstition".—
No. 280 Siding—Shot through the Thigh—In Hospital—Jennie's
Arrival—Married by the Reverend John Robinson—Thieving
Squatters—A "Run Out" with Bill Cody—The Lost Horses—
Alone on the Prairie—Rescue by Six Pals—Return to the Fort . 298

CHAPTER XXVI.

Discharged from Hospital—Guarding Gilman's Ranch—Hay-making
under Difficulties—Departure of the Gilmans—A Trip to Nebraska
—Death of the Firstborn—Cast into Prison—General Duncan's Expedition—The Lone Squaw on the Plains—Appointed Master of
Transports at Omaha—Recognised as an Indian by the Government
Treaty—Back to the Reservation—Trading Whiskey for Horses
with the Cliffords and others—A Fight in Camp—Escape—Thirty-
two "pass in their Chips"—Return to the Agency . . . 313

CHAPTER XXVII.

Buffalo-Hunting for the Chicago Market with the Cliffords—Hank
Clifford goes to Omaha for Whiskey—Trading with Che-wax-sah—
A Difference of Opinion—Departure—A Fiendish Revenge—The
Prairie Fire—Arrival at the Rendezvous—Arrest by Order of the
Commandant—Hank Clifford sent to General Augur—Rele..se—
Departure for Red Cloud Agency--Meeting with Frank Wheeling,
Broncho Bill, Slim Jim, and Self-raising William—A Marauding
Expedition—Following a Trail—Capture of 300 Horses—Charac-
teristics of Companions—A Cheerful Surprise—Fighting against
Odds—Frank shot in the Shoulder—Recapture of the Horses by
the Enemy—Dejected Return to the Fort 326

CHAPTER XXVIII.

Squatting on Medicine Creek—Building the first Ranch—A new Speculation—Collapse of the Project—"Save us from our Friends"—Buffalo Meat for the Soldiers—Conversion of Pleasant Valley into Frontier County—The Jack Bratt & Co. Swindle—Pulling up Stakes for Pine Ridge—Trading with the Indians on the Reservation—Differences with Dr. Seville—The J. W. Dear Trades Union—"Wanted for Illicit Trading"—The Raid on the Village—"Hunting for John Nelson"—The Deputation to General Mackenzie—A Narrow Squeak for "Three Bears"—Peace with the General—Seville and Dear kicked off the Reservation—An Indian Famine—Rascality of Government Officials—An Intimation to clear out 340

CHAPTER XXIX.

A Trading Spec to Deadwood—Objections of "Sitting Bull" to Mining in the Black Hills—General Crook acts as Mediator—A General Exodus ordered—Establishment of the Record Office—A Winter in Sidney—Return in the Spring—The last Claim—Appointment as Chief of the Sidney Police—Notes on Outlaws—Lynching of "Fly-speckled Billy"—Advantages of Practical Law—Doc Middleton kills a Soldier—"Rushlers" and Desperadoes—A Street Fight with the Military—A Resolution to quit—Joining Clifford and Ruff on the Running Water—The Ranch Post-office—Jennie sent to Pine Ridge 353

CHAPTER XXX.

The Cheyennes on the War-path—Rejoining the Government Service—Expedition to the Sandhills—Water everywhere, but not a drop to drink—Saved by the Snake River—Frank Wheeling carries a Despatch and trudges Twenty-five Miles on Foot—Death of another Child—Erection of Pine Ridge Agency—Teaching the Indians to drive—Reprimanded for thrashing a Redskin—Mr. Agent Macgillicuddy—Appointment as Chief of Indian Police—Erecting a Telegraph Line—The Agent's Peculations—Robbery of 200,000 Dollars a Year—President Cleveland to the Rescue—A few Words on the Indians—A few more on myself—Predestination—At last a "Globe-trotter"—A List of Officers fought under 367

INTRODUCTION.

IN WRITING indirectly this history of my life I am prompted by no feeling of vanity, by no desire to have my name handed down to posterity as that of a man whose deeds have entitled him to this form of recognition. It is, in short, by no wish of my own that I now find myself in print.

The day has long since passed for me when the notoriety achieved by publicity could possibly be of any benefit.

I am in the sere and yellow leaf, and it does not matter to me how or where my remaining years are passed.

A man stricken in years does not care to sit down and rack his brains to recall everything that has occurred through a long and—yes—a misspent life.

Why I should have allowed myself to be bullied and cajoled into doing what I have always fought against—*i.e.* giving the history of my life—I am at a loss to understand. I frankly confess that all my good resolutions vanished before the pertinacity of the author of these pages, who has succeeded in worming out of me many incidents in my career which, in my opinion, would have been best untold.

Since, however, he has learnt my secrets, and will use such of them as he thinks fit, I have but to say I vouch for the accuracy of everything I have told him. I have not drawn upon my imagination in any way, but merely stated facts, which have occurred just as I have related them. In a word, this book is a true story of my life.

John Y. Nelso

FIFTY YEARS ON THE TRAIL.

CHAPTER I.

BOYHOOD—A BOLT FOR FREEDOM—SLINGING DISHES AROUND—
WRECKED ON THE MISSOURI—LIFE ON A FARM—SCARED AWAY
—A FRIENDLY CARAVAN—BOONVILLE—UNCLE'S RANCHE.

I WAS born on August 25, 1826, at Charleston, Virginia. My father and mother were both Americans, so I may claim to be of the true Southern breed. My mother's maiden name was Young, and I take my second Christian name from her.

My father for many years occupied the position of overseer of the saltworks at Malden. Malden is about twelve miles from Charleston. A large number of negroes were slaves there, and of these he had charge.

The South was the ruling power in the United

States at this time, the slave interest being predominant. My early experiences were those of niggers and pickaninnies, who were my playmates and companions. It was little thought in those days that the bugle would ever sound that would plunge the elements of brotherhood into bitter strife. Yet thirty-five years later this was the case, and, strange to say, I who was reared in a perfect hotbed of slavedom, and regarded it as one of the laws of nature, knew little or nothing at the time of the struggle that was taking place. Perhaps it was better for me I did not, for my lot would most assuredly have been thrown in with the Confederate cause, with the probable result that I should have met a soldier's death.

I can carry my mind back to six years of age. I remember a small white dog I used to set at the niggers when they beat me. This was by no means an unusual occurrence when no one was looking. At length my dog—his name was "Peep,"—was found one morning in a boiling salt-pan. My antipathy for niggers took root that day. It has been growing ever since.

Young as I was, I determined to have my revenge. I took it on a nigger boy who was a trifle bigger than myself. My father had always told me never to fight with a nigger, but if I did to be sure and come out victorious.

Besides bossing the salt business, my father made tubs on his own account for storing the salt, and he owned a cooperage, where he had some sixty slaves at work.

About three miles from the salt-works was a coal-mine. This supplied the works with fuel, run down in cars on a laid track every fifteen minutes. I took my young nigger out on the track, and started fighting him right in front of my father's cooperage. The nigger got me down, and I was getting the worst of it, when my father came out with a hickory hoop in his hand. He walked up to us, and said to me :

" Didn't I tell you never to fight with a nigger unless you licked him ? Now you've fought and got the worst of it, I'm going to give you some more."

With this he started whacking me and the negro boy. We were both still fighting and clutching. One moment I would be uppermost and get the hickory, and the next it would come down on his hide.

I couldn't stand getting thrashed both ways, so I grabbed a piece of iron that had been splintered off the rails, and came within my reach as I rolled over. With this I almost cut the young nigger to pieces before my father discovered what I was up to. When he realised the position he separated us, and gave me the worst hiding I ever had. I don't believe the nigger bled half as much as I did after my father had done with me.

This performance, I think, showed a pretty blood-thirsty temperament for a youngster. I little thought then what after years had in store for me.

I was sent to school, but I was always larking about and playing pranks on my school-fellows, instead of attending to my books and trying to learn anything. My mother said I was the most mischievous boy in Virginia. I believe she was right. Before I was twelve I had become the terror of the neighbourhood.

My hidings about this time became frequent; something unpleasant was always occurring, not through any fault of mine.

There was an orchard at the back of the cooperage, fenced in with cedar posts, which were very difficult and expensive to procure. People, at some time or another, had been shooting in this orchard, and, instead of hitting anything alive, had buried their bullets in these posts. I discovered this, and, thinking lead more valuable than cedar, I chopped the posts up to get the bullets out. I had destroyed a dozen in this way, when my father was called upon to pay for them. Of course I got a hiding. It was to be in twelve lessons, one for each post. After the third I bolted. They got hotter each time, and as I began to wonder what the twelfth would be like, I thought it better to skip before it was due.

In the middle of the night I stole out of the house, and tramped up to Charleston. A friend of my father's, named Aaron Whittaker, had a store there, and to him I went and unburdened all my grievances. He took me in, and I stayed with him a month before my father found out where I was.

At length he came over with a black snake whip, and, making me run in front of his horse, with a rope round my waist and fast to his saddle, tanned me all the way home.

Never shall I forget that whacking! I was one mass of weals. I swore I would run away again, and, waiting until a favourable opportunity occurred, I availed myself of it a few months afterwards.

There was no particular row this time. I had made up my mind to go, and nothing would deter me.

I had often heard my father speak of his brother-in-law, who lived up in the state of Missouri. His name was Thomas Atkinson, and he had married my mother's sister. I had no idea of distance, or I should probably never have undertaken the journey.

I set about it by running off to an aunt, a sister of my father's, who lived about fifty miles from Malden. This distance I did on foot, and, arriving safely, was put up comfortably. But my aunt insisted upon writing to my mother to say I was there.

In about three weeks an answer came from my father, saying he was coming over to fetch me.

This was quite enough to scare me out of my wits. I had not forgotten the last time he had taken this trouble on my account. Instead of going to bed that night, I slipped out of the house, and, starting off by a circuitous route, made my way to Charleston.

On the terrors of that journey I will not dilate. In each shadow I saw, or fancied I saw, the stalwart form of my father, whip in hand, ready to tan me every step of the way home again.

At length I arrived, footsore and weary, feeling like a hunted dog, and not daring to show my face more than I could help. For three days I hung about the quays and warehouses, sleeping at night on bales of cotton, or secreting myself in any out-of-the-way corner where I could rest unobserved.

I had a little money—enough to last me about a week—and laid it out principally in gingerbread and crackers, upon which I lived.

Fortunately, when funds were getting pretty low, I made pals with a man who was taking a "candle" coal boat down to New Orleans, and he shipped me as an odd boy, to cook, make the beds, wash up the crockery, and do anything that was useful.

My new life suited me admirably. There was a feeling of independence about it that just dovetailed in with my ideas.

Neither my captain nor his crew had any qualms of conscience about appropriating other people's property. We had a small boat in which we would row to the shore, and steal geese, turkeys, fowls, pigs, anything eatable we would spot as we drifted down the river. As I was small and particularly active, I was of great assistance on these expeditions, especially in grabbing ducks and chickens, in which sport I became quite an adept Fresh vegetables we would secure at night, and be miles away in the morning before our depredations were discovered.

In due course we reached New Orleans, and I stayed

on board the boat until our cargo was disposed of. My skipper wanted me to go back with him, but I knew better than that, and, having on the quiet found out a passenger steamboat that was going up the Mississippi to where the Missouri falls into it, I got a billet as cabin-boy, and slipped on board just as she was starting. My duties were to wait upon the passengers and make myself generally useful. This I did to the complete satisfaction of the steward, and also of many of the passengers, who presented me with tips. These, added to my pay, small as it was, gave me a few dollars in hand when we arrived at our journey's end. That end came some three weeks after we left New Orleans.

My next move was on to a small steam-packet which was running up the Missouri River as far as Boonville. This time I shipped as a junior waiter, in which capacity I could sling dishes around with the best of them.

Some six or seven days after we had been out our boat struck on a sunken snag, or rock, or something, and foundered, and some twenty people were drowned.

The crew took care of themselves, and never thought about me. When I found I was left with a lot of screeching, yelling, cursing, and praying passengers, who were rushing madly about not knowing what to do, I just slipped overboard and struck out for the shore. The distance was about two hundred yards, but I could swim like a duck, and after drifting with the stream for some time I struck the bank and clambered out. When I looked around for the steamer, she had disappeared.

Some of the saved were landed on the Illinois side of the river, and the others on the Missouri. I was on the latter, and, the others joining, we went in a body to a farm, where we were taken in and hospitably treated.

I had only the clothes I stood up in, such as they were, for I had thrown off my coat and vest, hat and boots as I jumped into the water. My little store of money I had not had time to save, so, taking it all round, I suppose I was as badly off as any beggar on the face of the earth.

The day following a lot of country people came down to our farmer to take the saved off his hands until they could be forwarded on by another boat.

One old chap took a fancy to me, and offered me twelve dollars a month to go and work on his farm. I jumped at this, and he took me to his homestead, some six or eight miles in the country.

The old fellow's name was Jack Fisher. He was a well-to-do farmer, and had quite a large house, and plenty of land under cultivation. He was exceedingly kind to me, and gave me everything I wanted, both clothes and money.

I stayed with him all through the summer; and when the winter came on, as there was no farm work to be done, he sent me to school. This I attended regularly, and worked as hard as I could in order to please him. Although he had two boys of his own, he looked upon me quite as one of his sons.

It was a mixed school—boys and girls—that I was sent to, presided over by an old whiskey drinker, who disseminated knowledge for the entire country round. Amongst the pupils was a girl of about fourteen years of age, who was a trifle silly. She could remember nothing, and was a great trouble, not only to the master, but to all the scholars, on account of her stupidity.

One day the old chap was more than usually cross with her. I fancy his liver or something must have been out of order, as he started bullying her the first thing, and kept it up all the morning.

In the afternoon he took to whacking her because she could not pronounce some word, and the more she tried to do as she was told, the more he confused her. I stood it for a long time, until he gave her several severe cuts with his cane across the shoulders and arms. This was more than I could stand, so I went for him with my slate, and broke it over his head.

We had only log benches to sit upon, some of which were fixed upon pieces of wood let in to serve as legs. Seizing one of these, I gave him the soundest hiding I was capable of, and, knocking him down, nearly killed him as I thought, for when I left off he was stretched motionless on the floor.

There was a regular stampede in the school; and when I saw what I had done, I became a little frightened, and running off to old Jack Fisher, told him all about it.

"All right, my boy," he said; "we'll see about it in the morning. Go to bed now."

I went, but I could not sleep. I thought I had killed the old man, and should be hanged or sent to the penitentiary.

For hours I tossed about, scared out of my life, waiting for the morning to come. About 3 A.M. I could stand it no longer; so, getting up, I sneaked away from the house, and as fast as I could run I started off across the country. One of my greatest regrets through life has been that I did not say "Good-bye" to the old farmer, who was the first real friend I ever had.

I was a pretty good runner; few boys about the country were able to beat me. I only stopped to take a drink from a stream here and there, and have a short rest in a wood, until I had put at least twenty-five miles between old Jack Fisher's place and myself.

Mounting a hill, I came across a caravan of six waggons, containing a party of settlers bound West, and they took me in.

I had some money with me, about twenty dollars, so I felt pretty independent.

They were very kind to me, and I went with them for three days, until we reached a small town on the Missouri River.

There I left them, and waited for the first boat that came along bound up river. On this I went, and paid my passage (twelve dollars) to Boonville.

The journey lasted about six days, and I arrived at my destination feeling as fit as a fiddle. This time the cabin-boys had to sling the dishes around for me, and as I knew the business as well as they did, I just made them skip when I wanted anything.

I found upon inquiry at Boonville that my uncle, who was one of the first settlers in that part of the country, and was well known there, lived in Moniteau County, about seventy-five miles off.

I had no spare cash left to hang about with, so I lost no time in setting out to tramp the distance. It had been raining heavily for several days, and the mud, knee deep, made it very difficult going. I, however, plodded on, and, sleeping the first night in a barn and the two next in a wood, arrived at my uncle's place the third day just about sundown.

There was no mistaking the ranche, for there was no other near. I felt rather queer when I got in sight, and speculated upon what reception I should have. Pulling myself together, I marched straight up to the door, and, giving a good loud rap with a thick stick I carried, inquired if Thomas Atkinson lived there.

My uncle opened it, and said, "Yes."

I asked if I could stay all night, as I had walked a long distance and felt very tired.

To which he replied, in a long drawling tone—

"Wal, I guess you may. Come in."

There was no one in the room but a young boy, and, telling me to sit down, my uncle began asking me various questions as to where I had come from, whither I was bound, &c.

I gave him evasive answers. I was afraid to tell him who I was, as he looked such a cross-grained sour old chap. Presently the door opened, and in came my aunt.

I gave a start when I saw her, for she was the image of my mother, in appearance, voice, everything.

She walked up to me, and, looking hard at me, said to her husband;

"Tom, who is this boy? Where did he come from?"

My uncle replied, "That's just what I'm trying to find out."

My aunt then went to the other end of the room, and, sitting down, stared at me for a minute or two whilst I was talking to my uncle. Suddenly she started up, and, coming straight over to me, took my head between her hands and looked in my face.

"Tom," she said, "you can't deceive me. That voice and those eyes are my sister's; this boy is her son."

I had made up my mind not to tell them who I was at first, but could hold out no longer after this; so I got up, threw my arms around my aunt's neck, and said:

"Aunt, you've guessed who I am. I'm the eldest son of your sister, Catherine Nelson."

She drew back for a moment, and said, "Where's your mother?"

"She's well," I replied; "I left her in Virginia."

Then we went in for explanations. I sat up half the

night answering questions. Before I went to bed I was enrolled a member of the family.

In a few days I was made to write to my parents, who, we heard later, thought I was dead. My father did not give me a very good character, as may be imagined. When he did write, he told my uncle that I was a very bad boy, and required holding in an iron grip.

I had two cousins, one older than myself, and the other about my own age, and I got along capitally with both. With the younger one I was fighting all the time. Sometimes he would lick me, and sometimes *vice versâ*, but through it all we were firm friends.

I was first put to hauling wood, farming, and agricultural pursuits generally. My work subsequently developed into minding cows and seeing that they did not stray all over the country.

However the boys and I might disagree at times, we were unanimous about one thing, and that was in our dislike for my uncle. He was a mean, psalm-singing, contemptible specimen of a man, and would skin a flint in everything he did.

My aunt was just the opposite in every respect. She was liked just as much as he was despised by the squatters all round about the country.

CHAPTER II.

CATTLE-HERDING — A TRADING PARTY — THE BOUNDLESS
PRAIRIE—FIRST HUNTING EXPERIENCES.

Y uncle's ranche was on the direct route to the prairie lands of Kansas, Nebraska, Wyoming, &c., which were then known under the general term of the "great American desert." It was not often that we had a party of traders, "bound West," passing our place. Still, these did come along at times in bands numbering from twenty to fifty, a force strong enough to cope with any little difficulty that might arise between them and the Indians, with whom they traded knives, beads, &c., in exchange for furs. But this business was carried on many hundred miles from Boonville.

Some ninety miles above my uncle's place the boundless prairie began, and extended no one in our part knew where. Even the traders were ignorant of its illimitable expanse, for they only visited certain locations, to which at stated times of the year they knew the Indians would come in order to unload their stock.

The time I am now speaking of was before Kansas

attracted the attention of Missouri and the other Southern States, and the question arose as to whether it should be made a slave State. This finally resulted in the border warfare between the slavists and free-soilers, terminating in the victory of the latter. Students of American history, keeping this period in their minds, will be able to form a general opinion of the condition of this portion of the country at the time I arrived there.

When I had been with my uncle a little over a year and a half, one May morning I was looking after the cows. Presently I spied in the distance a convoy of "prairie schooners," as they were called, coming towards the ranche.

I rode out a few miles to meet them, and found they mustered about fifty-five men. They were on a trading expedition, and said they were bound for Nebraska. That night they corralled close to my uncle's ranche.

In a waggon corral all the waggons are drawn long-ways into position so as to form a circle, the front wheels of one being drawn up to and placed alongside the hind wheels of its predecessor, and so on until a complete circle is formed. The wheels are then chained together. In a peaceful country the mules or cattle would be left with their heads towards the circumference of the circle, but in a fighting corral their heads would be turned towards the centre, and the forage unloaded and packed as high as the wagon boxes, so as to make a very substantial fort.

I was decidedly of a wandering disposition; the

gipsy nature was in my constitution, although not in my blood. I knew that I should do no good where I was. Herding cows all day did not give me that element of excitement for which I had run away from home. Apart from this, young as I was, I had been my own master, earned my own living, and the feeling of independence strong within me was often checked by my uncle, who persistently set me to do things he knew I hated.

Looking after cows I found particularly monotonous, and I lessened the tedium of it by making practice with my gun. In this way I became an expert shot.

As a horseman I could hold my own with any of the men on my uncle's ranche or near it. My reputation in this respect spread around, and any squatter with a particularly unruly horse sent it to my uncle's for me to break in. I never found any difficulty with horses, and never yet came across an animal that I could not stick on to.

In most things required round about a ranche I was an adept for a youngster of seventeen, and as I was strong and well set up, I was just the sort of youth likely to recommend himself to a party of traders. It was not surprising, therefore, that they "spotted" me, and asked me if I would like to go along with them.

I was willing enough, but my uncle did not quite see it. He knew what my value was to him, and did not care to part with me. However, I prevailed upon him, saying that if he did not give his consent I should go without it.

Eventually he condescended to remark that I might do as I pleased; so, putting all my belongings together—they did not amount to more than I could conveniently carry in a side pocket—and bidding good-bye to my relations, I mounted a mustang my uncle had given me, and the following day joined the caravan after it had proceeded some ten miles on its journey.

I was not to receive pay for my services, but merely to make myself useful, and in return for my grub be allowed the privilege of picking up what knowledge I could of the business of a trader.

It was not many hours after I had joined before I made myself useful in several small matters, and gained a position far above that of many men in the company more than double my age.

I knew the country well for some miles in the direction we were going, and that knowledge was useful to the "boss," particularly in his selection of suitable camping ground, close to both timber and water.

Nothing much occurred to upset the even tenor of our way; one day was the same as another, and in a few days we had reached the confines of the so-called desert. It was with a feeling of extraordinary pleasure that I entered the mystic regions. Away from civilisation and its surroundings, my spirits rose as those of some of my companions fell. The country seemed to open out a vast expanse. At first it was scattered here and there with patches of timber, but these disappeared by degrees as we advanced, until nothing but the open country met the eye.

The approaches to a prairie are very like a gigantic park, intersected by running streams and small ravines, that vanish at last as the timber disappears. A prairie is not necessarily flat. It may be covered with hills or rising ground, so far as level is concerned. Its principal feature is the total absence of all semblance of timber. Nothing but stunted grass and scrub bush is visible.

On the confines of Missouri where we were now, crossing into Kansas, the country was almost flat for hundreds of miles, with only a slight undulation here and there to break the monotony. The further we penetrated into the great land-sea, the more a feeling of devilment seemed to possess me. The vast expanse, with its peculiar vegetation waving with every breath of air, had for me an immeasurable attraction. We seemed to be entering an unknown land, not knowing what fate had in store for us; not knowing whether the Great Spirit, that in the intense stillness seemed hovering around us, would guide our footsteps to luck or to the reverse.

I say "we," but there was one in the assembly who already longed to be free and away from his companions, and that one was myself.

As we went onward this feeling grew upon me. I would absent myself from the camp when we halted for the night, and wander far away into the solitude. There for hours I would follow the mysterious paths traced by the steps of wild animals, or tether my horse, spread my blanket, lie down, and sleep.

This last, however, could not be done in a hurry. It required a certain amount of preparation. As thus : I would first take my lariat made of horsehair, without which no man ever travelled on the plains, and coil it in an oval about four feet wide and seven or eight feet long. No snake will pass over a horsehair coil. Having thus secured immunity from these venomous reptiles, I would next spread my blanket, step within the magic ring, lie down, and sleep in perfect security.

I never ventured to light a fire, for fear of attracting the attention of the Indians, who, if they did not actually see it, would probably notice the reflection in the sky This, in that wonderfully clear atmosphere, would be seen for miles round, and I had no desire to be found on the plains alone by any wandering band of these gentry.

In the early dawn I would ride back to the camp, take my morning meal, and then ride several miles ahead to scout the country, sometimes alone, but more frequently in company with two or three of the men, and select the best halting place for the midday meal, and later in the day the best camping-ground for the night. I was a good rider, and well fitted for this work, and I was in consequence usually employed in carrying messages between the "boss" and what may be termed the advanced scouting party.

We had been out some few weeks when, on my

return one morning from one of my usual midnight rambles, a discussion arose as to how the camp larder should be replenished.

Meat was getting low, and we had been compelled to kill and eat one of our steers. We had been unfortunate so far in securing game, save a few prairie chickens that had crossed our path. I was asked whether I had seen any trails of larger animals, such as buffalo or antelope. I had, but not of recent date. It was necessary, however, to secure something, whether large or small, and foraging parties were accordingly organised to start out each day and beat up the country.

We had plenty of flour and meal, so there was no fear of an immediate famine. It was only the luxury of fresh meat that was required; and the more difficult it was to obtain, the more eager every one became for it.

Day after day the hunting parties returned without bringing in anything. Many times I felt that if the one to which I was attached had only gone in a certain direction and done certain things our luck would have been different; but I was a youngster, and any suggestions I made were only pooh-poohed.

One day I determined to go on my own hook. So I sneaked out of camp to follow up certain tracks I had seen leading in a north-easterly direction the previous day. Following these for about five miles, I suddenly came upon a herd of nearly five-and-twenty antelopes browsing in a small valley two miles ahead of me. By degrees I worked up to within range, and taking careful aim fired. To my great delight, I saw an animal fall; but my astonishment was greater when, instead of the entire herd running away, as I thought they would, they all trotted up and sniffed at their dead companion.

I lost no time in grassing another, and I believe I could have shot them all; but two were quite as many as my mustang could carry, and I saw no fun in killing animals simply for the wolves and vultures to feed upon.

From after experience I am confident that if others had adopted this principle of never killing more game than they could carry away there would at the present moment be thousands of buffalo and other animals on the western plains, where not one now is left. Galloping up to the herd, by screeching and yelling I scared them off, then, picking up and slinging across the mustang's back my two prizes, I wended my way leisurely back to camp.

The excitement my return caused was so great that I was at one bound elevated into the position of a little hero, and by universal acclamation voted huntsman to the caravan. I was particularly reticent as regards my hunting experiences, and took my honours with as much *sang froid* as if I had been accustomed to receive them all my life. As a matter of fact, I had never seen an antelope before, and until I arrived in camp did not actually know the name of the animals I had shot. The most curious thing was, that there were men amongst the party who had been hunting all their lives, or professed to have been, and who, so far, had not even succeeded in bringing in a coyote. These men, although they were envious of my good luck, did not throw cold water on my exploit, but encouraged me to continue to study the craft of a huntsman, for which one and all agreed I was eminently fitted.

I listened with attention to the various narratives that my exploit called forth whilst sitting over the camp fire, and I decided before I turned in that night that I might just as well follow this calling as any other as a means of livelihood. One thing I determined, and that was, come what may, nothing should induce me to live a humdrum existence in a settlement.

My only real enjoyment was in solitude, and I was never so happy as when following the bent of my own thoughts and wandering across the plains in search of anything that chanced to come within range of my rifle.

In my position as chief huntsman to the caravan I

started out on excursions every day, and very rarely returned without some addition to the larder. I owed to my uncle much of my success in this respect, for the mustang he had given me was a particularly swift one. It had been sent from some distance by a squatter for my uncle's "young man" to break in, with an intimation that if it was found not worth wasting time on, no trouble need be taken to return it.

My uncle—good man!—had promptly replied that the pony was not worth its hide and hoofs, and this before I had mounted it. Even the prospect of securing a few dollars for these trifles was more than he could resist. I however begged it might be given to me, and succeeded in breaking it in to be a very serviceable animal. At first sight no one would have given five dollars for it; but I knew its worth, for when we were out on the plains alone we simply flew through the air.

Each day I started out on my hunting excursions, and rarely returned without bringing in some supply or other of fresh meat. Thus I steadily rose in the estimation of my companions. How the good resolutions I formed of becoming a hunter were dissipated, will be seen in the next chapter.

CHAPTER III.

BOUND WEST—ARRIVAL AT THE PLATTE RIVER—AN INDIAN ENCAMPMENT — CIVILISATION FORSAKEN — THE OGALLALA BAND—ADOPTION BY "SPOTTED TAIL"—AN INITIATORY CEREMONY—CHRISTENED CHA-SHA-SHA-OPOGGEO—A FEW WORDS ABOUT BUFFALOES—AN ADVENTURE WITH THEM—WINTER ON THE SOLOMON RIVER

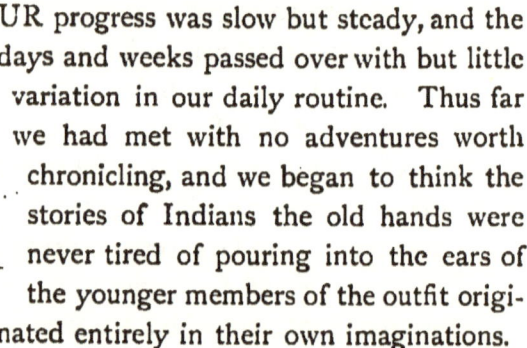

UR progress was slow but steady, and the days and weeks passed over with but little variation in our daily routine. Thus far we had met with no adventures worth chronicling, and we began to think the stories of Indians the old hands were never tired of pouring into the ears of the younger members of the outfit originated entirely in their own imaginations.

The country through which we were now passing was *terra incognita* to all of us. Our course was steered simply by the compass and the stars, and we could form no idea how long it would take to reach the Indians of whom we were in quest, or what the country would be like in which we found them.

About three months had elapsed since we first struck the prairie when we at length arrived upon the banks of the Platte River. We followed its course for about two weeks. Suddenly, one afternoon, at a bend in the river, we came upon an Indian encampment of about four hundred tépees, or tents,

and, as far as we could judge, about two thousand Indians. There was much consternation amongst our party at first, when we discovered the magnitude of the band, but as there was no chance of turning back we put on a bold face, and determined to see the thing through. We, however, found the Indians peaceably disposed, and bent upon trading with us.

This was my first introduction to redskins, and I felt much interest in them. From the moment they came into camp they exercised a charm over me, and I determined before the day's trading operations were over to make a study of their habits and customs, and become more intimately acquainted with them. This I knew was only to be done by living amongst them, and I determined at all risks to do that.

I was utterly sick and tired of our caravan life, and its continuation had no attractions for me.

We traded with this band for about a fortnight, and secured everything they had to dispose of. At length the negotiations were concluded, and orders given that we should continue our journey the following day. I had made up my mind what to do, and accordingly, before sunset on the last day, I slung my rifle over my shoulder, and, bidding farewell to my faithful mustang, left our corral unobserved, and walked down to the Indian encampment. No one molested me, so onward I strolled amongst the tépees, when, making straight for a decent-looking one, I lifted up the flap, entered, and sat down.

There were five squaws present and a chief. They were astonished to see me, and I thought the chief meant coming at me with a knife which he had in his hand, but, assuming all the *sang froid* I was capable of, I took no notice of either of them.

Immediately I squatted down they all began to chatter away, the construction I put upon their remarks being that they admired my darned impudence. Anyway, I stayed where I had planted myself, and smiled approvingly upon them. Of course I could not understand a word they said, nor they a word I said.

I looked around, boy-like, and was much interested in what I saw. In the centre of the tépee a wood fire was burning. The smoke from this curled upwards, and found its way out where the tépee poles clustered together at the top. The tépee itself was made of skins sewn to-

gether with raw hide, and ranged longitudinally around this were several long-looking basket boxes made of willow, all painted different colours. In each of these was a buffalo robe, which led me to suppose that they were the beds of the chief and his squaws. I also noticed at the back of each a sort of valise or bag, also made of skin, and covered with beads.

In the corner of the tépee was a pile of flat-looking packages, which I subsequently ascertained contained dried meat. Various rough-looking stands were arranged here and there about the apartment, and these were filled with bows and arrows.

The inside of the tépee was gorgeously painted with pictures of wild animals and human beings. Spread on the floor were several buffalo robes, on which the squaws were seated, beading mocassins, whilst the chief was busily occupied whittling a stick he was converting into an arrow.

After sitting thus for some long time, I made them understand by signs that I was hungry. They were very hospitable, and gave me some buffalo meat. This I ate, and enjoyed immensely.

As time wore on they endeavoured to make me understand that I was wearing out my welcome but I pretended not to comprehend them. I knew very well that they wanted me to go, but I meant stopping. The ingenuity they displayed and the little tricks they adopted to get me out were most amusing.

When they waved me to the entrance I never moved. Then one would sit down next to me, and, attracting my attention, would get up and solemnly walk out. Finding this had no effect, they would endeavour to lead me to the entrance; but I was stolidly indifferent to everything they did.

I kept this up all through the day, and when night

had come on apace there I still sat stoically, not having budged from my original position.

Lots of the young bucks had been in and out to have a look at me, but as it grew later their visits became less frequent, and eventually ceased altogether.

There was now evidently a great deal of consternation in the chief's home as to what was to be done with me, and I felt, to say the least of it, that my presence was becoming somewhat embarrassing; still I sat and smoked on, and the old chief and his squaws sat and looked at me.

About midnight they seemed to realise that it was useless attempting to get me out, and the chief said something to this effect, with the result that one of the women brought me a buffalo skin to lie on and another one to cover me with. I stretched myself out by the fire, and when they saw by this that I fully meant staying, the women turned into their respective baskets, with the exception of the favoured one, who accompanied the chief.

For my part, I rolled myself well up in the warm skin, and in a few moments was fast asleep.

The caravan I had left moved off at daybreak the following morning. So far as they knew or cared, I was dead, for they never took the trouble to inquire after me, and I never saw any of them again.

My first move was to make the Indians understand that as I had been left behind they must take care of me. This was rather a difficult matter, and necessitated a great deal of ingenuity on my part; but they finally understood what I was driving at, and seemed pleased at the thought of my staying with them. A tépee was given me, and before the next night came round I was quite a favourite, each one doing his little best to teach me the language. This they managed by bringing various articles into my tépee, and making me repeat the names given them.

I thought at first that I should never acquire the pronunciation, but after a few days my ear seemed to become accustomed to the guttural sounds, and within a week or two I had made such progress as to render my demands for food, water, &c., fairly intelligible.

It was necessary to christen me, and they soon hit upon a name which, if not euphonious, had the effect of making me known throughout the tribe. This was "Cha-sha-sha-opoggeo, or "Redwood-fill-the-pipe."

There is a description of red willow out of which the Indians make arrows. When dried it becomes very hard and brittle. This wood is also ground into powder and mixed with plug tobacco, to which it imparts a pleasant flavour and aroma. I had displayed a great partiality for the mixture, as I found it excellent smoking, and in consequence gained this mellifluous cognomen.

It appeared that I had struck two bands of the Sioux, viz. the Ogallalas and Brûlés. "Spotted Tail" was the chief in command, and it was his tépee I had entered.

Their number as estimated by the people in the

caravan—viz. 2,000—was rather under than over the mark. There were various other bands of the Sioux roaming about in different parts of the country. At that time (1843) the Sioux nation must have numbered nearly 200,000, but now (1888) they have been reduced to less than 30,000.

After I had been with them about three months a meeting of the tribe was called, and a resolution passed that I should be adopted into it. This, however, could not be done until another chief, named Ma-ca-ha-ma-ney, or "Walk under the Ground,' had been consulted. Accordingly, we went south about two hundred miles and joined his band, and when his consent was obtained, a general council of the chiefs was called, and I was duly initiated.

This function was a feast of buffalo tongues and a roasted dog, of which I had to eat. After the banquet I was presented with six horses, a saddle, bow and arrows, a quiver, a pair of canvas trousers, and other articles.

I could not understand what it all meant at first, but I gradually learned that I was now considered a full-blown Indian.

The various bands, after having fixed me up to their complete satisfaction, separated. The Ogallalas, to whom I belonged, in virtue of Spotted Tail having stood sponsor to me, started off on a buffalo hunting expedition.

We took the district watered by the Little Solomon

river, a tract of country covering a very wide area. The buffalo were very plentiful down there, and we killed large numbers of them, drying the meat in the sun, or, as it is commonly called, "jerking" it. This meat was then packed away for winter use in flat

packages made of the skin of the animal with the fur taken off.

The process of jerking consists in cutting the meat into long strips, as thin as it is possible to cut raw meat. These are then hung upon poles to dry, and when dry are exceedingly brittle, breaking readily into chips. In the process of drying, and before the meat becomes too hard, it is lapped over into flat packages or bricks, which in turn are so arranged as to form a large flat package, which is finally wrapped up in the raw hide or skin.

The buffalo is a most intelligent animal; it seems

to know by instinct where to find the best pasturage. I have known buffaloes travel one hundred to one hundred and fifty miles in search of it, and always in the right direction. On the table lands the food of the animal is a peculiar kind of grass, which is called buffalo-grass. This grows from one to three inches high, and is as thick as the hairs on a dog's back. It is particularly rich and sustaining, and affords the staple food of the animal during the winter. When the snow is very deep the roots are still green, and these the buffalo will grub up by scraping the snow away until he gets at them. In the summer the tall grass on the prairie is the special delicacy of the buffalo, and in this he will hide, and eat to his heart's content.

At a certain time of the year the herd will change their localities, seeking a part of the country to winter in totally different from that in favour during the summer months. Once located they do not, as a rule, change about much, unless there is urgent necessity for doing this. In summer—e.g. a drought—when the grass is all dried up, or in winter, exceptionally cold weather, will make them shunt.

One peculiarity of the buffalo is that it rarely, if ever, selects a timbered country; it sticks to the plains. Occasionally I have known buffaloes take to a small copse of cotton-wood, but only when heavy snow is impending. In such cases they go far out of their way to find this shelter.

At the time I am now speaking of the number of

buffaloes on the plains was marvellous. I have sometimes mounted a slight elevation and looked over a level plain, on which as far as the eye could reach they would be seen in one solid mass. When in motion it would appear as if the whole earth were moving up and down, or like the waving of a field of grass under a heavy wind. The noise of their feet and their bellowing could be heard for miles.

Another curious feature in connection with the buffalo is the way in which the old bulls are turned out of the herd by the younger ones. Whenever a bull is no longer of any use a dead set is made upon him, with the result that he has to skip off and wander around by himself until he dies or the wolves make an end of him. I have met these solitary animals sometimes as much as fifty miles away from a herd, and was always glad to do so, for it was a sure indication that I was on the right track for the main body of whom I was in quest.

As a rule, I never used to shoot these wanderers unless I was very hard pressed for food. They were too tough even for a redskin to get his teeth through them. There were only two possibly edible portions—the tongue and the inside tender loin, just over the kidney. Curiously enough, no matter how ancient a buffalo may be, this loin is always as tender as a chicken, although every other part of the animal may be as hard as nails.

In one of my early experiences of buffalo hunting I nearly lost my life. I was out with Spotted Tail, a regular sportsman, and several of the young bucks, when we made an attack upon a young bull, who was particularly ferocious. I was the only one of the party who was armed with a gun, all the others having bows and arrows. My ammunition had run short, and I had practically given up operations for the day, when, seeing that the Indians had detached the young bull from the herd and were having some fun with him, I rode

up to look on and enjoy the sport. Somehow, just as I cantered up, and within a few yards of the bull, my pony slipped one of his legs into a hole and, falling, threw me under him. The bull grasped the situation in a moment, and, although he had half-a-dozen arrows sticking in his hide, gave up the Indians and devoted himself entirely to me. I was powerless to extricate myself, and, looking up, saw the bull with his head down charging full at me. I thought my last moment had come; but even in death the love of life and of taking life was strong within me, and with an effort I drew my hunting-knife, and, holding it over my head, determined that in killing me the buffalo should impale himself at the same time. The few seconds before he was on me seemed minutes; I saw his horns approaching and felt his hot breath on my face, when suddenly he crashed down, the impetus of his charge carrying him right on top of me. My death from suffocation was now almost as near as my approaching end from goring; but this was soon rectified by the Indians, who dragged the animal off so much of me as was uncovered by my horse, who was making things still livelier by kicking and struggling his utmost.

When rescued I was almost as flat as a pancake, and every particle of wind was knocked out of me. Spotted Tail was my deliverer; he had sent an arrow right into the animal's heart, just at the critical moment. An error of judgment in distance, even of a foot, would have been fatal to me, but, as I have said, he was too good a sportsman to make mistakes.

In the use of the arrow and also in throwing the dart the Indians were very strong. They would hit a bird on the wing easily, and a surface as large as the palm of the hand at any distance within range. Their knowledge of the vital parts of animals was also extensive; they knew how to tease a victim and drive it nearly mad, and then with one well-directed shot put it out of its misery.

I had to stand a great deal of chaff about my gun,

and listen to the merits of arrows and darts as compared with it, but I had more faith in my "old Bess" than in all their javelins and shooting apparatus; and I think they had too, when in chaff I now and then turned it against them, for they would then run a couple of miles without stopping. The want of ammunition was the only thing that bothered me. When I ran out of this I had myself to fall back upon bows and arrows, in the use of which before long I became as proficient as the Indians themselves. My powder had to be fetched from one of the forts many miles away, or to be got in exchange from other Indians, some of whose chiefs were the possessors of antiquated flintlocks, warranted to burst at the first discharge, and rarely if ever used on that account. Later on, a better class of weapon found its way into the country, as the United States troops learnt when, years later, they had to meet the Indians upon their own ground.

After collecting meat sufficient to last us through the winter months, we struck our camp and moved up some hundred and fifty miles to the head waters of the Solomon River, to a place named by the Indians Little Turkey Creek. There we built some tépees of saplings, and made ourselves snug and comfortable for the winter.

The Indian method of passing the winter months is very simple. They go out after the buffalo once or twice a week, make what is termed a surround—i.e. chase the animals all together—then ride in a circle round them, shooting down those they required. I have known from 1,000 to 1,500 head killed at a time in this manner. The waste of good meat when these *battues* were going on was very great. All that would be taken for eating purposes was the tongue, whilst the skin would be preserved for barter, and the rest of the carcass be left as carrion.

No one has any conception of the immense number of these animals that were on the plains at the time of which I write. I have already said that a single herd made a compact moving mass as large as the eye could take in. There were hundreds of similar herds roaming about the country.

Our camp amusements were primitive, but, nevertheless, not utterly devoid of excitement. During the day the young men would usually sleep, and night would be made hideous by their singing, dancing, and making love to the girls. I threw myself completely into the vortex of general amusement, and had as good a time all round as any of them.

CHAPTER IV.

HABITS OF THE INDIANS—THEIR RELIGION—THE SUN DANCE
—PERSONAL MUTILATION.

THE Indians are a race of people the reverse of the white man in every respect. The former wishes to become rich, the Indian prefers to remain poor.

He who gives away the most is considered the best and bravest among the Redskins.

The Indians are a nomad race, ever on the move. They believe in travelling about for their health's sake, and this is the principal reason why they never remain long in one place. I have known them even to leave the buffalo, which they follow as the magnet turns to the north, simply because their restlessness prevented them from keeping still. From a year to eighteen months old they are inured to hardships of every description. At this age I have seen them running about barefooted in the snow without any ill effect.

The principle of their rearing consists in making them undergo hardships that would kill a white child.

The sole idea an Indian has, is to excel in the art of war. This is a sort of creed with them, and the trouble and patience they expend in teaching their papooses war is worthy of a better cause.

Almost as soon as a youngster can run alone a bow and arrow are put into his hand, and he is taught to shoot at objects, such as a rabbit, a wolf, or a dog. These he will torture in a manner in which cruelty in its worst form is displayed.

Every living thing he is taught to kill. Even the cattle around the camp are not free from this pernicious precocity, and it is no uncommon thing to find the cows that supply them with milk stuck all over with these baby arrows, which the youngsters have only sufficient power to send into their hides without doing any internal injury.

As a rule, the Indian is a pretty cleanly being, the Sioux being the best in this respect; but taking all Indians generally they do not seem to think cleanliness next to godliness, as we understand it. They are fond of the water in the summer-time, but in the winter avoid it like the plague.

During the warm weather they seem almost to live in the river, if their camp is anywhere near one, and most of them can swim like ducks.

Swimming is an essential part of a youngster's education, and, next to riding, is the most necessary, for it frequently happens that in crossing streams both rider and horse have to battle for their lives.

The usual method of crossing a river is for the lodge poles, which are very light, to be tied together in the form of a raft, upon which the camp gear, utensils, &c., are placed, and this is then towed by

thirty or forty bucks, harnessing themselves to, and swimming across the river.

The squaws do all the work about the camp. A young Indian buck would disdain to touch anything—it would be an insult to ask him to. He will look placidly on and see the squaws struggling over a heavy load, and not move a muscle to help them. He is quite a superior being in his own opinion, and under the impression that his only mission in life is to hunt and fight. Squaws are given him to do the work, and slave on his behalf.

As a rule he will not do the most simple thing for himself. He is essentially lazy.

The only redeeming trait about the Indian is his religion. In this he is an example to the white man.

Their Great Spirit up above is the one they worship, and for him they will undergo any torture. For instance, in their sun dance, which occurs every year, usually in June or July, the pains they undergo are surprising.

Then some thousands of them will meet at a certain place, previously appointed, and where wood, water, and grass are plentiful. The tépees are arranged in a great circle, sometimes over a mile in diameter, and in the centre is a smaller one of posts interwoven with brush and able to hold about a thousand persons. This is roofed in, about thirty feet from its circumference, with the tépee poles, and thus a large open space is left in the centre. In this space is a large drum, the sun dance drum.

Proceedings are opened with a feast, in which everybody participates, the bucks having previously been hunting the buffalo for the purpose.

After the feast, an Indian maiden, 16 to 25 years old, previously selected, rises, and having given three blows on the drum, says, "If there is any man in this assembly who knows 'better,' let him here step forth and say so."

Should there be an affirmative response, very rarely the case, the girl is spurned and treated to every kind of indignity, spat at, pelted with mud, and finally turned out of the community. All that is left her then is to hang or drown herself.

If there is no response the entire assembly rise and follow her. She leads them to a large tree some sixty feet high with forked boughs, and into this she plunges an axe which she carries with her.

The tree is cut down, stripped of its branches with the exception of the two forks, and is dragged on waggons tied together, or, if this can be managed, pulled by some hundreds of men to the centre of the inner circle. A large hole is then dug, and in this the tree is set upright. About a dozen lassos or lariats are then tied to the forks, and the principal ceremony of the function begins.

Those of the braves who have been called upon in a dream, cut a slit in their chests, insert a rope in it, throw themselves backwards, and try to wrench the rope through the skin. In this way their flesh is sometimes stretched half a yard before the skin will give way. Immediately this happens they are free; but it is very unusual that it is so. As a rule they dance around the tree three days without food or water, and until they faint from exhaustion.

When their lives are considered to be in danger they are released, and the ceremony is at an end. This is looked upon as an offering to the Great Spirit, as well as a test of bravery.

The squaws do not take part in all this, but they force a gouge into the upper part of the arm, and, extracting a lump of flesh, throw it into the hole in which the tree is planted.

At a sun dance also a brave can divorce his squaw, or she can divorce him.

This is done by the one that wishes to be free giving one loud tap on the drum and saying, "I throw my squaw away; anyone can have her who wants her," and *vice versâ*. Should no one step forward and take the squaw she goes back to her friends and relatives.

The ear-piercing of children also takes place on these occasions. This is a religious ceremony. The child is thrown on a block, a large incision is made in the ear, and in this a piece of lead is fixed to prevent the parts uniting.

It is not uncommon to find holes in an Indian's ears through which the little finger can be thrust.

One characteristic of the Indians is their generosity. This has especially shown itself at the sun dance. It is then for the sake of their religion that they help their poor. Horses and everything else they possess in the way of goods, furs, blankets, &c., change hands in the most ungrudging manner. The young braves, as a rule, recommence the year after the function with simply the clothes, such as they are, that they stand up in.

When a warrior dies he is buried, so to speak, "up in the air," with all his war implements. His corpse is placed on a scaffold, and under this his horse is killed, so that he may have it ready to accompany him in the happy hunting grounds.

Years ago, before the whites came amongst the Indians, and taught them lying, stealing, drinking, and gambling, the Indians were the happiest and best people to be found on the face of the earth, and their virtue was of the highest standard.

This was practically the state in which I found them that fine evening I left the white camp on the banks of the Platte River, and cast in my lot, for better or worse, with the Redskins.

CHAPTER V.

MATRIMONIAL SUGGESTIONS—WOM-BEL-EE-ZEE-ZEE—AN INEXPLICABLE SQUAW—MOTHER-IN-LAW—PATIENCE REWARDED—TRAPPING BEAVER—NOTES ON THEIR PECULIARITIES.

AMONG the Ogallalas the time passed pleasantly enough. Spotted Tail was chief of the Brûlés, and on this hunting expedition accompanied our band merely as a guest; but as he was a chief of renown there was a tacit understanding that he was in command.

One morning, as I was starting with some of the young bucks on a trapping expedition, Spotted Tail called me into his tépee, and, looking at me steadily, said, "Cha-sha-sha-opoggeo, I think it is time you took a squaw."

"It is very kind of you to think of my comfort," I replied.

"I and my squaws," he continued, "together with my friends have been talking over this matter, and we have come to the conclusion that a squaw will be good for you. You are now one of our nation. You need some one to keep your home and cook your food instead of my squaws doing it for you."

Since I had first walked into Spotted Tail's lodge that memorable morning his squaws had always looked after me, kept my tépee in order, and done everything necessary for my comfort. I suppose they had begun to kick at this, and probably with some cause, doubtless thinking it was high time I was taken off their hands.

"My friend," I replied, "I am young and foolish yet. I think this little matter had better be deferred until I am older and have more sense."

"No, my son," said Spotted Tail. "We have decided that a squaw is good for you, and a squaw you must have. She will help you in many respects; you will learn the language more quickly and better, and, above all, you will have some one to look after you."

I saw at once that the chief was determined, and that it was no use my objecting, so I remarked:

"Well, chief, since you wish it, so let it be. Whose daughter do you propose?"

"My niece, Wom-bel-ee-zee-zee" (Yellow Elk), was his answer.

"Good," I replied, "I will endeavour to render myself worthy of her."

A long conversation then ensued in which Spotted Tail's squaws took part. It was finally arranged that I should pay my court to the young lady (with whom, by the bye, I was only slightly acquainted), and woo her in the manner prescribed by the customs of the Sioux nation. These manners and customs were explained to me as follows:—

"You must," said Spotted Tail, "go down to the stream at twilight, sit on the bank, and wait for my niece to come down and fetch water. You will find other young men waiting for her, and probably one or two of them will jump up and throw their blankets over her head and talk to her. You must watch, and when you see the first sent away by her, and the second, and perhaps also the third, you will try your luck. I am inclined to think you will succeed where others have failed. When you have thrown your blanket well over her head, and popped your own beneath it, you can tell her all, and I will answer for it she will listen. You can tell her you love her, that you admire her, and that if she will marry you, you will give her every comfort and necessary—in fact, tell her all the nonsense young men tell girls when they want to marry. You will go down to the stream, go through the same performance, repeat the same words, every evening for ten evenings. At the end of that time you will return to me and report the result. Go now, my son; I do not wish to speak to you on the subject until then, so be good enough not to refer to it again."

"Your wishes shall be carried out," I replied, "and I will return to you a victor or not at all."

"Well said, my son. May good luck attend you," said the chief, as I left him and started off at once on my first experiences in love-making.

First I went to my tépee, and, selecting one of my largest and best blankets, threw it over my head, and wandered down to the river-side. Here I planted myself on a convenient spot pretty high up on the river bank, down which I knew Wom-bel-ee-zee-zee must pass.

There were several young bucks squatting about waiting for various girls, and probably, as the chief had said, some of them waiting for Wom-bel-ee-zee-zee; but I had discounted their chance by the strategical position I had taken up, and knew that at any rate I should get hold of her first. I did not see any fun in allowing my future bride to be mauled about under a blanket by a parcel of Redskins, and as when I made up my mind to do a thing I always did it, I determined to see this through.

None of the other fellows there knew who I was, as I had my blanket well over my head; and even had they known, Indian etiquette would have prevented their taking any notice of me.

I had waited about an hour, and the sun had sunk behind the hills, when in the stillness I heard a light footstep, and turning my head I saw Wom-bel-ee-zee-zee tripping along, her bucket, made out of the paunch of an antelope, in her hand.

As she approached me I had time to take in all her points. She was short in stature, only about 4 feet 3 inches in height, somewhat stout, weighing about 125 pounds, thirteen years of age, features finely chiselled and, in a word, the prettiest girl in the camp.

As she passed by me I jumped up, and slinging my

blanket over her head popped mine in and did as I had been told.

I thought that it was no use beating about the bush, so I let off straight away that I loved and admired her, and had always done so; that the feeling had been growing on me so long I could not sleep at nights for thinking of her, and I was now obliged to come and tell her. She listened attentively to all I had to say, and did not struggle to get away as I had seen some of the other girls. I delivered my finest speech, and stopped to take breath. She merely turned her eyes up and looked at me, so I went on and said that if she would be my squaw, I would work for her and get her plenty of beads, blankets, and everything she wanted. Finally, I wound up by saying, "I know that I am a white man, but I am formally adopted into the tribe, and am just the same as an Indian. I feel sure that I can make you as happy as any buck in the crowd can. Say, Wom-bel-ee-zee-zee, shall it be or no?"

All I could get from her in reply was, "I don't know," "I don't know." To all my pleadings this was her stereotyped answer.

Finding there was no further progress to be made that day, I released her and went into a thicket. There I sat down, had a smoke, and thought what peculiar cattle women were. I flattered myself I was quite as good as any Indian, both in colour and looks, and it rather riled me to think that a girl should tell me "She didn't know," when from my point of view she ought to have just jumped at the honour, and said "Yes," almost before I asked her.

The next day I tried my luck again, with precisely the same result, I letting off the same speech, and she giving me the same answer. We kept this up for nine consecutive nights, by which time I knew everything I had to say off by heart. If it had been necessary to do this ninety-nine, or even nine hundred and ninety-nine times, I would have done it; for the longer it continued, the more interested I became to see what the end would be.

However, on the tenth occasion, after I had mechanically rehearsed my part, to my surprise she said, "I will marry you if my mother is willing." I stood speechless for a moment, and before I had time to grasp what she really had said, the perpetual "I don't know" ringing in my ears, she had slipped from under the blanket, and bolted off as fast as her legs could carry her.

When I had regained sufficient composure to fully realise the situation, I thought I had better report progress: so I pulled myself together, strolled off to Spotted Tail, and told him the result of my wooing.

He listened to all I told him, and said, "It is good, my son. You have succeeded where others have failed, as I said you would; but all is not finished yet. You must next send two, three, four, five, or as many horses according to your means, and in proportion to the amount of love you have for her, to her parents' tépee, tether them at the entrance, and leave them there. If you are accepted, the horses will be herded with the family stock; if you are rejected, they will be brought back and tethered outside your own tépee. In the latter case you will perhaps try again by sending more, but if whatever you send is continually returned to you, you will know that you are not considered an eligible suitor, and may as well save time by thinking no more of the matter. On the other hand, if you are accepted, the sending back will cease when it is thought you have given sufficient evidence of your affection."

With this advice I went down to where my little herd of ten horses was tethered, and, selecting two of the best, sent them by an old Indian, telling him to tether them at the entrance of my lady-love's abode.

I crept to a convenient spot, where I concealed myself and where I could keep watch.

There was a great deal of commotion in the family circle when the horses first made their appearance, and messages were sent to all the relatives to attend a council. I watched for over three hours whilst this was going on. Then a man came out, and my two horses were taken away and herded with the family stock. So I knew that I had been accepted.

The next afternoon the mother, accompanied by another daughter, brought my squaw over to my tépee with three horses and all her bag and baggage. They fixed up a willow wicker-work basket bed for us, put everything in order, and left.

I had been out with some of the boys trapping, and when I returned in the evening, much to my surprise, found my squaw in possession. She was a peculiar girl when I found myself alone with her, and as nervous as possible. She reminded me very much of a small wild bird caught and held in the hand. Her heart was going pit-a-pat; I could hear it beating all over the tépee.

We did not make much progress at first. She would wrap herself up in a blanket and tie thongs of buffalo hide all around her. I stood this for about a week and then had quite enough of it. I said to her, "Why do you do this"? but the only reply I received was, "I don't know." At length I said, "Well, if you don't, I jolly soon will," and thereupon bounded out of the tépee and over to her mother's.

"Look here, mother," I said: "Wom-bel-ee-zec-zee and I do not get along at all; I think you had better take her back again."

"Why, what is the matter?" inquired the old squaw.

"Everything is the matter; she ties herself up in blankets and buffalo thongs, and there she is, she won't come near me. For a whole blessed week have I been gazing upon this bundle of frightened rags. I have had enough of it. Take it away from me. I can stand it no longer."

"You are young and inexperienced and do not understand, my son," said my mother-in-law. "Wom-bel-ee-zee-zee is also young and perhaps silly, but you must humour and be kind to her, and it will be all right."

"I know I am young and inexperienced," I replied, "and I told Spotted Tail so before I married your daughter. But I also know that I did not take a squaw to have her shrink away from me every time I go near her. Pale-face women don't do it. They frisk around and dance and jump about, saying what a mighty fine thing it is to be married, and I want Wom-bel-ee-zee-zee to do the same. You had better tell her so."

"My son, you must not be impatient; Wom-bel-ee-zee-zee does only the same as any other Indian maid. You are too impetuous. Go and do as I tell you, and all will yet be right."

I did not feel very cheerful or very amiable when I returned to my tépee with my respected relative's advice. There was my squaw still squatting on a buffalo robe, looking the picture of misery. I cast one glance at her, and a feeling of devilment overcame me.

I rushed out of the tépee and went and joined all the bad society round the encampment, for, strange as it may seem, we had both fast and steady members of our community.

For days I kept this up, all the time fully expecting to have an arrow sent through me by one of my squaw's injured relatives. But no one appeared to take any notice of my doings. All they did was to pass me by without seeing me.

I would return to my tépee very late at night and never take the slightest notice of Wom-bel-ee-zee-zee. After about the tenth night of this reckless dissipation I noticed that the buffalo thongs had disappeared, but I said nothing.

A few nights later the blanket had also vanished, but still I was stoical. Four nights following this she became quite cheerful and began to chat with me; but the blood of the Nelsons was up, and I refused to have anything to say to her.

It was my turn now, and I kept up a stolid indifference for quite a fortnight before I would give in. At length, finding I had brought her completely to her senses, I condescended to smile upon her and pat her on the head. The effect was magical, and we became like a pair of turtle doves in a cage. Being young, she was full of fun, and kept me pretty well amused. She was always larking about and preparing various surprises for me. I never did anything about the tépee, as she attended to all the domestic arrangements. All I had to do was to go out hunting and bring in anything I could kill, when we would have a feast and invite all her relatives.

One of my principal amusements was trapping the beaver, in which I would engage with three or four of the Indians. We went out on all the streams round the creek, and watched the signs and indications for the coming winter. If the weather was going to be severe, the beaver would be seen biting down cotton-wood trees and dragging them to their quarters. This they do by gnawing them into lengths of from two to six feet. These, three or four of the animals push and drag to the banks of the stream and pile up in front of their houses. Some of the pieces they stick up on end, so as to support the others, using their tails as shovels for the mud which they plaster round the base for a foundation. These logs constituted their supply of winter food. When the streams are frozen, so that the beaver cannot come out through the water entrance, they use the land end, and, securing these logs, drag them one by one into their holes, where they live upon the bark.

Their holes or rooms are made right on the banks of a stream, usually above high-water mark, and built at an angle of 45° with the stream. There are always six inhabitants in a beaver family, viz.: two old ones, two kittens, and two yearlings, provided they are all alive.

If the winter is to be open and mild the beaver do not trouble to prepare their food, but travel from one stream to another in the untroubled pursuit of enjoyment.

The indications we had seen denoted a severe winter, and we made our preparations accordingly. When the frost did set in we had enough to do in setting our traps and securing the skins.

The flesh of the beaver is excellent eating, especially when boiled with wild turnips. These grow plentifully on the prairies, and the squaws gather them in the spring, dry them in the sun, and then string them on twigs. The feet of the beaver are also a delicacy. They are prepared by rolling them in hot embers; this enables the tough skin to be easily removed. When boiled or roasted, the feet are a great improvement on pigs' trotters. The tail, served in the same way, is also capital eating.

A beaver weighs from 45 to 60 pounds, and the skin is very valuable. At the time I mention, the price was a dollar and a half per pound, the skins averaging about two and a half pounds each. Of late years, however, the price has increased to five dollars per pound.

The way we caught them was simple enough. Each of us would be supplied with eight steel spring snap-traps —the number a man could conveniently carry. These we would peg down with long sticks in convenient places near to the runs, from four to six inches under the water, baiting them with a twig dipped in musk. The beaver would smell the musk from any distance and swim up to it. Then their feet would be caught in the trap. When the streams were covered with ice our method was to cut holes and set our traps below them.

Out of eight traps set at night, if five of them had not secured a prize it would be considered very bad business. We had to be very smart in getting to our traps the first thing in the morning, so as to secure the animals before they wriggled away. This they would often do, leaving only their feet behind them.

As we worked out the intermediate streams, we penetrated further up the Solomon River, and went several days' journey after our game. On these occasions we took two or three tépees and two or three squaws with us. Wom-bel-ee-zee-zee always accompanied me. We still got along capitally together, and I began to find the advantage of having a nice little squaw

None but those who have tried it know how comforting it is to return to camp after a hard day's work, and find a good-natured young woman preparing the supper. All the hunter has to do is to squat down and eat, then pull out his old pipe, have a good smoke, talk over the events of the day with his squaw and companions, and speculate as to what luck the day following has in store.

I know the difference between this and having to set to work, light a fire, and cook your own meat when you are footsore, weary, and aching from many hours in the 'saddle. Matrimony has its advantages at times, whatever scoffers may say against it. My matrimonial experiences have been far from limited, as the reader will ascertain as he goes along. I do not purpose writing a record of the advantages of wedded bliss, so at present I content myself with saying that when hunting the beaver under the circumstances in which I was then placed, I have often mentally thanked Spotted Tail for the acumen he displayed in providing me with my first matrimonial partner.

CHAPTER VI.

FIGHTING THE PAWNEES ON LITTLE BLUE RIVER—A BLOOD-THIRSTY MASSACRE—WOM-BEL-EE-ZEE-ZEE VANISHES—A SCRIMMAGE ON THE RICKAREE FORK—THE SIOUX METHOD OF WARFARE—ONLY ONE LEFT TO TELL THE TALE—RICKAREE TORNADOES—BORN THIEVES.

BREAKING our camp in the spring of the following year, we moved east, and travelled down the Republican River about two hundred miles, to fight the Pawnees. They were on the head water of the Little Blue River. Reaching a part of the country through which we knew our enemies must pass, we pitched our camp and remained there three months, watching for them.

Buffaloes were plentiful in our vicinity, and for sixty miles east of the point where we established ourselves.

We knew exactly where the Pawnees would go for their summer hunt. They would require white skins, such as buckskin, antelope, and elk, and buffalo cow skins for the purpose of making tépees and mocassins.

In the summer, the Indians as a rule do not trouble to secure buffalo robes; the fur on the skin of the animal is then very short, and does not become long and woolly until about the second week in October. All skins taken after the latter date, and until the 1st of May the ensuing year, are religiously set aside as robes. On the 1st of May the tépee or mocassin season commences. It will be seen that good robes can only be obtained during about six months in the year.

In August, the animals travelled north or northwest. We knew this, and also that the Pawnees would follow them as soon as they began to migrate. We discussed the exact locality of the enemy, and secreted ourselves so as to give us a great advantage over him when he came tripping merrily into our ambuscade. We had scouts continually watching his movements, and trying to find out his strength.

Three or four of the smartest and bravest of the Sioux would hide themselves close to the Pawnee camp during the daytime. At night they would crawl into it and count the number of the tépees. In this way they calculated the number of warriors, reckoning that there would be five to each tépee. I have always been able to tell the number of Indians in a camp by this means.

About the 5th of August the enemy made a move, and approached within five miles of where we lay, in a thick grove of cotton-wood timber.

Our scouts came running in, and reported he was close at hand, and that he had encamped for the night. A hurried consultation was held, and it was resolved that, instead of waiting for him to fall into our trap, it would be better sport for the young men to attack him where he lay. Consequently, at twelve o'clock at night, I, in company with all our warriors, except a few old men who were left to guard the camp, sneaked as close up to the Pawnees as we could, and then waited for daybreak.

As the first streaks of early dawn shot across the horizon, the enemy's squaws got up and turned the horses loose to graze. This was just what we were waiting for. A few of us made a dash for the herd. Our main body lay concealed in a ravine close by, and it was arranged that the horses should be driven into the ravine for the purpose of drawing the Pawnees thither.

Everything happened as we had anticipated. I was one of the horse-stealing party, and helped to drive off the herd. We chyiked them into the ravine and clean through it like a streak of lightning.

Directly the Pawnees saw what was up, and so few of us engaged in the daring robbery, they yelled with rage, and came tearing after us right into the trap.

After driving the herd into a place of safety, I returned to see how the fun was going on, when I discovered that my Sioux had killed 125 men, women, and children as they fled in all directions.

It was an abominable slaughter, but I personally could have done nothing to prevent it. The only reflection was that if the boot had been on the other foot, we should have met the same fate.

This was the first hard fighting I had witnessed between

Indians, and it impressed me considerably on account of the cold-blooded butchery with which it was conducted. "Kill everything that has life," seemed to be the motto of the conflicting parties, and they carried out their principles. The most ghastly part of the business was the mutilation of the corpses. These were treated to every indignity conceivable, and with an extraordinary ingenuity of purpose. I never was particularly squeamish, but my "first fight" nearly settled me from a stomachic point of view.

The Pawnees and Sioux were sworn enemies from birth, and whenever they met would fight like cats. Strategy and cunning were practised by both and in this respect they were pretty equally matched.

We captured over two hundred head of ponies and the Sioux presented me with several of them as a reward for my assistance in helping to drive them up. The part I took in the little escapade was favourably commented upon by the chiefs in council, and I was accordingly classified from that time forth as a "brave." I suppose I may say that it was in this battle I first won my "Indian spurs."

After commemorating our victory with befitting pomp and solemnity, collecting the property of the vanquished, admiring and distributing their scalps to their present owners, and doing all that was necessary to cover ourselves with the glory we conscientiously believed we had earned, we broke up our camp and devoted ourselves entirely to hunting the buffalo, following them up in their northern peregrinations for many miles.

There were no enemies anywhere around to interfere with our sylvan enjoyment, and by this we profited by securing such an immense number of skins that we found the greatest difficulty in transporting them.

At length, absolutely satiated with our spoil, we settled down and wintered at a place called the Big Timbers. This is a locality much favoured by the Indians on account of the young cotton-wood tree, the bark of which is excellent food for horses, and very fattening. This place was about a hundred miles from our previous pitch. Dotted about the Republican River were other encampments of various bands of the Sioux.

Our time was passed pleasantly enough in trapping and hunting elk and deer. Sometimes in following game we would be absent from camp for ten or twelve days, sometimes longer. Another mode of passing the time would be for small parties to go off and visit some of the other bands, and we in turn would receive friendly visits from them.

Upon one occasion I went off with a party of ten young bucks on a hunt after elk, and was out about twelve days. Upon my return I experienced my first matrimonial sorrow. We were laden with game, and I had a beaded buckskin dress, for which I had traded the skins of some of the animals I had shot with a party of other Indians we came across on our way home. This I thought would be a nice present for Wom-bel-ee-zee-zee, one that she had told me she wanted. It was rather heavy and had caused me some trouble to carry. It was with feelings, therefore, not unmixed with joy that I rode into camp and up to the locality of my tépee to present it to her.

My astonishment was great when I rode round and

F

round and could not find my abode. At length I inquired of some of the young bucks who were watching my proceedings, where Wom-bel-ee-zee-zee had moved the lodge. They all began to laugh at me, and said "she had gone."

"Gone where?" I asked.

"Oh, yonder," was their reply, pointing their thumbs over their shoulders into the open country.

"Yonder—what do you mean?"

And then they told me that an Indian named Standing Elk, a member of another band which was located

some 85 miles distant, had come into camp on a visit, and had departed, taking with him my squaw, the tépee, and all my horses and other belongings.

"Then this," said I, looking at the four or five pegs

that were still sticking in the ground, " is all that is left of home, sweet home ? "

"Yes, all."

I went over to my mother-in-law's to inquire what it meant, and she tried to persuade me that my squaw had gone off on a visit to one of her uncles. I affected to believe this, but knew better.

The fact was, I had come back rather too soon, for I afterwards learnt that my mother-in-law had sent after her daughter, and if she had succeeded in getting her home before my return, I should never have heard of her unfaithfulness.

In every Indian encampment is a soldiers' lodge. In this the young bucks, and even the very old ones, meet at night, and smoke and chat and pass the time away. In fact, it is a sort of club.

The squaws in the camp all help to cook for these soldiers, and at a certain hour bring in the food. The proceedings, however, are usually opened with a dance, and a drum is placed on one side, on which any one wishing to say anything publicly makes an appeal, somewhat after the manner of the sun dance. For instance, an Indian will in the excitement of the dance show what is termed his bravery by giving one tap on the drum, and then publicly give away a horse, or anything else he wishes, to a friend or poor relative.

The dancing had just commenced when I made my appearance, so I lost no time in joining in. When the proper moment arrived, and after one or two announce-

F

ments had been made, I got hold of the drum-stick and gave one loud tap on the instrument. In a moment all was silence, when I exclaimed in stentorian tones:

"My friends! My squaw has gone off with Standing Elk. I now give Zint-calla-sappa (or the Black Bird) my bay horse, and I have done for ever with Wom-bel-ee-zee-zee."

It is compulsory, as I have hinted above, when making an announcement on the drum to accompany it by giving some one a present. Otherwise the announcement is not valid. Zint-calla-sappa was an old hag whom I spotted sitting in the corner of the tépee, and as she was very poor I thought this "act of bravery" on my part would have a good effect upon my audience, and the answer from all present was:

"That is good, friend; will you stand by it?"

"Yes," said I.

Thus terminated my connection with Wom-bel-ee-zee-zee, and I left the lodge once more a gay and festive young bachelor.

This habit of stealing women by Indian bucks is common. Standing Elk, who was a particularly fine-looking fellow, rather prided himself upon the conquests he had made. He had appropriated many squaws, and after a while turned them adrift again. Wom-bel-ee-zee-zee was no exception to this, for in less than two months she found her way back again to her mother's lodge.

I asked her one day how she had liked her new man, but she pulled her blanket up over her face and would not answer me.

I never spoke to her again after that. The young bucks twitted me about not having gone after Standing Elk and killed him, but Spotted Tail would not allow me to do that. He said, "If you kill him you will always have to be on the look-out for all his relatives, who will be after you for years, and they are so numerous you are sure to get wiped out by one of them in the end. Whereas if he kills you it will engender bad blood between all my young men and his friends, and that will end in one perpetual quarrel between them. Let well alone, my son. There are as fine fish in the rivers and buffalo on the plains as ever came out of either, and there are plenty of young girls who will supply Wom-bel-ee-zee-zee's place."

So I made myself comfortable in the tépee of Two Buck Elk, a Brûlé warrior, a great friend of mine, who generously took me into his family. In the spring of the following year the Pawnees again came up into our country on a return visit to try and steal "our horses," or, as they no doubt looked upon it, to get their own again. They met the same fate as their comrades, but, unfortunately, we lost some of our braves.

The fight upon this occasion was a running one, extending over some twenty miles. I was not in it all the time, so I cannot say how many Pawnees the Sioux killed. Our party returned a great many short, but as the enemy had vanished the victory may be fairly claimed as falling to the Sioux.

Our next bellicose move was to embark fairly on the war path, to the head waters of the Republican River, where a small tributary existed known as the Rickaree Fork, and where, " from information received," we expected to have a chance of wiping out a lot of unsettled scores with our old enemies. We had frittered the summer away somehow, and eventually arrived at our destination in the month of September.

One day, while amusing ourselves with a game of ball, some of the young men came rushing into camp and reported Pawnees.

To the uninitiated no idea can be conveyed of the intense excitement prevailing in an Indian village when it expects an attack. The only thing comparable to it is a wasps' nest disturbed, or a hive of bees turned over.

Imagine 2,000 men, women, and children running about in all directions, tearing down the lodges, packing goods and chattels together, ready to fly at a moment's warning; while 20,000 head of horses are coming into camp on the dead run, with young boys behind them shouting and waving their blankets to frighten the animals in.

I have often mounted a hill and watched all this sometimes under circumstances of extreme danger And in all my career I have never witnessed anything half so exciting. Even the dogs set up the most awful howling and add their quota to the general din.

It can be imagined that when the scouts came in with this news there was no quarrelling as to who had won the game so suddenly interrupted. All the warriors mounted their horses and were off. They rode up to a piece of high ground a short distance from the camp, massed their forces, and awaited further instructions from the chief in command, Spotted Tail. When he said " Go," they started in the direction the enemy was reported to be, each trying his best to outride the other and obtain the lead.

There is very little military discipline or tactics in one of these battles. It is every one for himself and the Devil take the hindmost. On approaching the Pawnees, we found them a small party about fifty in number. They were armed with flintlocks, smoothbore guns, and bows and arrows.

In point of numbers we were about ten to one, but the advantage was discounted by the superiority of their weapons. We had only bows and arrows. All my ammunition even was expended, and I was armed with one of the primitive implements of warfare.

The Pawnees had taken up their position on rising ground, and, having doubtless reconnoitred and ascertained our strength, had dug rifle pits with their hands and knives, entrenching themselves in such a way that it was most difficult to get at them.

We tried all the tactics within our knowledge to

draw them, but they were too wily. On the other hand, every time we came within range, a volley would be fired which would despatch a few of our young bucks to the happy hunting grounds, and kill several horses.

At length the entertainment became monotonous, and we none of us would venture near the little band unless we were under cover. Still we managed to keep them well in check, and fired our arrows at each one who showed himself.

They no doubt thought that when we found we could not dislodge them, we should go away and leave them in peace. But Spotted Tail was not a warrior of that sort. He simply laughed and said, "Have patience, and all their scalps shall be ours." I wondered what plan he had in his mind, but after two or three days this was apparent.

There was a stream within a few hundred yards of the hill where the Pawnees were, and although they could see the beautiful clear water running by, they could not touch a drop of it, for every time one would make an attempt to come out, we shot him.

We used to go down to the stream and drink our fill, then taunt them by holding up the water in our hands and splashing it about. They fired at us in return, but they held out.

For days and days we kept this up. The weather was very hot, and their agony must have been something fearful. Four or five would now make a rush out at a time and try and get down to the stream, but long before they had covered half the distance, a dozen arrows would be sticking through each of them.

In this way we despatched them, all but the last man, whose life was spared so that he might return home to his fellows and tell them the story.

The locality of this fight is known to the present day as Pawnee Creek. It is to be found marked by that name in the Ordnance maps.

Our loss over this business was by no means small. . Many of my friends lost their lives, amongst them a brother of my present wife, and we had quite a large number wounded.

On the scene of this incident, the Rickaree Fork, the country is very hilly and broken up by the heavy rains. The district is noted for the very severe hail and rain storms that occur once a year—usually in July or August These are accompanied by waterspouts, which deluge the earth and sweep everything before them.

The Indians will not camp near the streams or in the valleys for fear of one of these tornadoes. They always select the highest ground they can find.

I remember a company of soldiers, some years later, who encamped in one of these valleys. During the night a flood came on, and washed away tents, men, and horses. Many of the men and all the horses were drowned. Some of the poor fellows were washed out of their beds, carried two hundred yards, and lodged amongst the branches of trees, thirty feet from the ground. Here they had to cling on for four hours, with nothing to cover them but their night clothes; some not even having these to protect them from the heavy hail falling in torrents. Others, swept along in the whirlpool with logs and trees uprooted by the storm, were mangled and torn to pieces, and were never to be found afterwards.

The Pawnees have been the most successful horse-thieves on the American Continent. Over and over again they have made treaties with the Sioux, who would give them three hundred head of ponies as an earnest of their good intentions, and after the Pawnees had left the camp they would sneak back and steal as many more. This is why they were always at war with other tribes to whom they behaved in a similar manner. Thieving is born in them.

At the present date, 1888, the Pawnees are very few in number, have settled down, and are self-supporting. The Government allows them twenty dollars per head per annum, but does not give them rations as it does to the Sioux. The result is, that as they are dependent upon their own resources, they turn them to account by farming and raising stock. In the latter pursuit they are very successful.

I have known some good horses come out of the Pawnee Reservation, and for choice would rather have one of their breeding than many others. As different people excel in different industries, so these Indians excel in the quality and stamina of their stock. The various points of man's best friend seem familiar to them from birth, and in fact the knowledge is born in them. With their antecedents this is not surprising. There is an old aphorism, " Set a thief to catch a thief," and if any one can do a Pawnee over a horse he deserves a pension from the United States Government.

CHAPTER VII.

EARLY TRADERS—TWO BUCK ELK'S GRATITUDE—ZINT-CALLA-WEZ-AH—MORE MATRIMONY—COTTONWOOD SPRINGS AGAIN—A STRANGE CARAVAN—FIRST MEETING WITH BRIGHAM YOUNG—SPOTTED TAIL'S RESOLUTION.

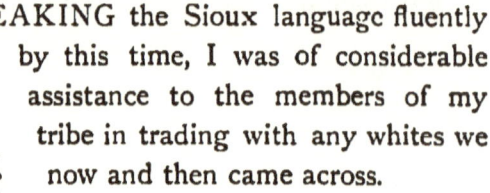

SPEAKING the Sioux language fluently by this time, I was of considerable assistance to the members of my tribe in trading with any whites we now and then came across.

As a rule it was very exceptional for us to meet any of these roving traders. They had too much respect for their scalps to penetrate into the remote regions where we were.

In journeying to and fro we used to meet one old fellow, a Canadian Frenchman, pretty well known on the plains, and barter with him some of our buffalo robes for old flint muskets, lead, powder, beads, blankets, knives, anything handy he might have.

I was still living with Two Buck Elk, and the more I was with him, the more he seemed to like me. He was a man about forty years old, very brave, and very fond of whiskey. It was not often we could get hold of any of this, and when we did it was the most horrible compound imaginable. Fire-water was a mild term for it. It was made out of grain of any kind, and so strong it would take the skin off one's throat in swallowing, whether mixed with water or not. I have seen an Indian take a big drink of it, and in less than ten minutes lie down and die.

The old Canadian Frenchman was never known to have more than a gallon of the spirit along with him. He would bury the rest in a place that he himself only knew, and when he had bartered off his portable supply, go and dig up another gallon. This was a pretty cute move on his part, for it was not worth the Indians' while to kill him for loot, as it would only have been killing the goose that laid the golden eggs.

I think some of Two Buck Elk's love for me arose from the way in which I got the whiskey out of this old trader. As I was a white man, he would let me have it rather than the Indians, and many is the time I have secured it for my friend over the heads of Indians, who offered even better bribes than I. Somehow the old chap imagined that by my influence with the tribe I could guarantee his safety, and I encouraged him in the belief in order to obtain his pernicious poison.

At the same time I verily believe that I did him many a service with the tribe, for I always spoke up for him, and pointed out that if any harm happened to him we should be in a pretty fix for anything we wanted. Also that no other white man would be likely to follow in his footsteps if he were killed.

It was upon one occasion, after I had secured a gallon of this whiskey for Two Buck Elk, that in a moment of generosity, and in return for the service I had rendered him, he asked me if I would not like to marry one of his nieces, and suggested the eldest, one named Zint-calla-wee-ah.

I said I should be very pleased to do so, but pointed out that I had no horses. I only had two left when I returned from that hunting expedition and found Wom-bel-ee-zee-zee gone, and one of these I had given away when I divorced her.

He said, "Never mind that; we will make it up for you." The following morning I found ten ponies tethered outside the tépee.

I went through the same formality as before, and started my wooing down by the stream, but on this occasion no time was lost, and in two days I was fixed in a tépee of my own, with Zint-calla-wee-ah my blushing bride.

She was a fine, tall girl, of pleasing appearance, rather thickset, but thin compared with my former squaw, and fifteen years of age.

As she was the eldest daughter of her tépee, in accordance with Indian custom I had the right of exercising a claim upon all her three sisters, none of whom could be mated without my consent. I thought it would simplify matters at once by claiming the whole outfit, which I accordingly did, as a compliment to the family.

I got along with Zint-calla-wee-ah all right, and about a month after my marriage with her, took her next sister into my wigwam.

I found having a couple of wives very pleasant, and, after three months had elapsed, increased my responsibilities by taking in the third.

The fourth was hardly big enough to be bothered with at present, so I left her to grow a few years older. I was now quite a respectable member of the community, and could hold my own in point of importance with any of the chiefs of the tribe, both in the turn-out of my establishment and the orderly way in which it was conducted.

My three squaws, being sisters, knew each other's little ways and peculiarities. The harmony existing amongst them was delightful. Altogether they presented an example which might with advantage have been copied throughout the tribe.

We wandered about from one place to another, replenishing our stores when necessary, until finally the tribe worked round to Cottonwood Springs, the place where I left the caravan and first joined the Indians.

It seemed ages to me since the day I marched into their camp. Five years had elapsed since then, during which I had wandered far and near for hundreds of miles in a gigantic circle, of which this spot may be said to have been the centre.

Situated on the Platte River, this was a very convenient and favourite place with both the Ogallalas and Brûlés. Here they usually met about once a year, and, joining forces, went off together to meet other bands of the Sioux, or attend the great religious ceremony of the sun dance.

It is in this district that the Platte River branches into the North and South Plattes, and situated at the base of the angle formed by these is Cottonwood Springs. This point in after years became better known as Macpherson. It was from here that the California route branched off from the Platte and took a direct course. The tide of emigration to the Pacific had not set in at the time of which I am writing, for it was only in the year 1847 that this country was ceded by Mexico to the United States.

A caravan on the plains in these days was a rare sight. Those that did come out were only traders of the Hudson Bay or the American Fur Companies. It was, therefore, a matter of considerable surprise to me when one morning our scouts brought in the information that a large train of whites were moving along the bank of the river towards us. During the afternoon they arrived and encamped within half a mile of where we were.

A long time had now elapsed since I had seen or spoken to any of my fellow-countrymen fresh from civilisation, and accordingly I thought it would be a good opportunity to polish up my mother-tongue before I forgot it, as well as to learn a little news of what was going on in the outer world. Accordingly I talked to Spotted Tail, with the result that he and I, with several of the young bucks and my three squaws, went over to the corral with buffalo robes, buckskins, and mocassins, for the purpose of trading them off for anything the strangers might be disposed to offer in return.

We were well received and did a general deal, and I took the opportunity I wanted of talking with some of the party, and asking where they were going, whence they had come, and so forth.

They told me they had left Florance, a small town four miles west of Omaha in Nebraska, on May 7, and were going to find the Promised Land, but where it was they did not exactly know. I further ascertained that they were simply prospecting for a larger party of whites, and that wherever they settled, that would be the place where a big city would be subsequently established.

The party were 147 in number, and made up of 143 men, three women, and one child. The active captain and waggon-master of the outfit was a man named Porter Rockwell, but the chief of the expedition was Brigham Young.

I had never heard of Mormons at this time, and did not know what they were. They told me they were Latter Day Saints. I looked around for their halos, and, not seeing any, said to them—

"What sort of cattle is that?"

To this they replied, they were the chosen people of the Lord.

Said I : " Well, I am very pleased to meet you, for there are mighty few of them about these parts."

Brigham Young said he was the Lion of the Lord.

I looked at him in astonishment, but did not say anything further, particularly as I was not in a position to deny his statement. I thought they were all crazy, and the sooner I skipped over to our camp with Spotted Tail and my squaws the better.

Just as we were packing up our skins, &c., to move off, Brigham came to me and said :

" See here, stranger! Have you ever been as far as the Rockies ? "

I replied that I had been as far as the Black Hills, but never beyond them.

He then asked me various questions about the road, and what sort of country they had to pass through.

I told him to the best of my ability. Then he inquired if I would like to go and show them the way.

I said I had never met any people like them before, and that for choice I preferred to remain with my Indians, who did understand me, and whom I understood.

He asked if my home was with Indians.

My home, I replied, was anywhere where I had my hat on.

" Well," he continued, " then you may just as well

wear it in one place as another, so come along and show us the way.'

It finally ended by his offering me forty dollars a month to pilot them to the Black Hills, or to any place beyond to which they wanted to go.

I thought the matter over for a few minutes and calculated the time the trip would take, and the prospect it offered me of seeing a country I was unacquainted with. Then I went over to Spotted Tail and consulted him upon the matter. He tried hard to dissuade me—saying he did not like the looks of the party, and that possibly they would kill me. They had nothing to trade with. That was the basis of his estimate of them.

I was undecided what to do. I looked at Brigham and his followers, and could not help thinking that it would only be a Christian act to see them through. They seemed to me like children lost on the plains. Up to this point their route had been simple, but after they crossed the Platte they would be in a terrible muddle if they were not put in the right direction.

At length I said to Spotted Tail, "These people are my white brothers, of my flesh and blood. They evidently don't know their way. I think it only right I should take them part of their journey, at least as far as Fort Laramie" (about 300 miles distant).

"Very well, my son," he replied, "do as you like; but if you go, in the event of your not returning by the fall, I shall come and hunt for you, and if I find any harm has befallen you I will settle with these white men." Thereupon he called all the young bucks together we had brought with us, and made them take a long look at all the members of the outfit, that they might be able to recognise them again.

My next difficulty was with Zint-calla-wee-ah and her sisters, and I asked Spotted Tail what was to become of them.

"They can live with their people," he replied. " I will see that they are taken care of."

So I told them what I wished them to do.

They demurred at first, but I smoothed matters over by promising to bring them each all sorts of presents when I returned. Then I gave them all the horses I had, about ten or a dozen, keeping only two of the best for myself, and they went off contentedly with the chief and the others.

There was an old guide with the party named Leon, half Mexican, half Indian. What little confidence Brigham and Rockwell had in him was not increased by the fact that he could speak very little English. He had started out to pilot them the whole route, but, somehow, there was a breakdown when I joined. The old chap seemed to have no idea of distance, and I fancy it was this that annoyed them more than anything else.

All this was explained to me, and I understood I was not to displace the old man, so far as the working details were concerned, but to act as the confidential friend and adviser of the outfit.

I said I was perfectly willing to do as they desired,

provided I did not fall foul of the Mexican. There could not be two guides wishing to take contrary routes. I knew every inch of the country up to the Black Hills, and, at any rate, would take them as far as Laramie, and they could then determine whether I could perform my part of the contract or not.

Finally it was arranged that I should instruct Rockwell as to the road we were to follow, and leave him to settle it with the Mexican.

We struck camp the following morning, and started off at a rate of from twenty to twenty-five miles a day.

CHAPTER VIII.

AMONG THE MORMONS—FORT LARAMIE—EN ROUTE FOR THE PROMISED LAND—GREEN RIVER—PASSAGE OF THE ROCKIES—FIRST SIGHT OF SALT LAKE—IS IT SNOW?—ESTABLISHMENT OF SALT LAKE CITY—ARRIVAL OF THE MEXICAN CONTINGENT—RETURN OF THE PIONEERS.

THE Mormon caravan consisted of twenty waggons drawn by mules. Some of the teams for the heavier waggons were six in number, and those for the lighter ones four. We had plenty of ammunition and guns, a brass cannon, agricultural implements, a smith's forge, iron for making saw-mills, hawsers with pulleys for crossing streams, whilst the commissariat was well provided.

The first thing that struck me was the sermons Brigham delivered directly we corralled at night. He would declaim for an hour, and we had to sit around and listen. Sometimes he would be followed by others, and the ranting would be kept up for two or even three hours.

I never paid much attention to what they said. It was all about the Lord, with whom they seemed to be on intimate terms of acquaintanceship. I felt at once that I was not good enough, and never should be, to belong to their denomination. So I used to squat down and smoke, and build castles in the air, whilst their services were going on. These always wound up with lots of quaint hymns, which, as a rule, awoke me from my reverie.

This life became very monotonous after a time, and when no one was

looking, the old Mexican, who turned out to be a very decent chap, and I would crawl under the wheels of a waggon and have a game at euchre.

After service was over Brigham and the rest of them would laugh and chaff in a jolly, convivial way that made me take quite a fancy to them.

Many a time have I skinned Brigham out at euchre, and many a time he has turned the tables, but as a rule he was very hard to beat at that game.

The followers generally seemed to me an ignorant lot of people, drawn from the lowest classes. The religious mania had a decidedly strong grip upon them, and I believe if these lengthy services had not been held every day somebody would have been killed. They would have thought as little about murdering me as they would one another.

By the time we arrived at Fort Laramie I had become quite accustomed to my new life. There I met some Indians I knew. I stayed with them two days whilst the tyres of some of the waggons were being repaired.

Brigham Young came to me and asked me to go on with them. He said that both he and Rockwell were thoroughly satisfied with me; and they felt they would never arrive at their destination unless I remained with them and took them across the desert.

I said I had no objection, and the existing agreement was continued.

There was an old Frenchman at the fort with a half-breed daughter; to her Brigham took a great fancy, and he tried hard to get her to join the party. But *le père* would not consent. Curiously enough it was here I saw for the first time the father of my present wife, Old Smoke, then chief of the Sioux nation. I little thought that his daughter would one day be my squaw.

After the repairs were fixed up we started off again. But before this I sent a message to Spotted Tail, telling him not to be uneasy about me; that I was all right, was going on with the whites as far as the Black Hills, and would return as soon as I was able.

At Laramie we picked up about a dozen people whom the Mormons had managed to inveigle into joining their community. They had a good hard try to get me into the fold, and held out as an inducement the bait of half a dozen wives. I said that was good enough for me, but I would reserve my decision until later on, especially as I had matters concerning their welfare and safety on my mind that were more important for the moment. So they agreed not to pursue the subject further, and left me unmolested for quite a considerable time.

Our route was now across the North Platte, leading straight for the Rocky Mountains. Here for 150 to 200 miles on the plains we saw hundreds of thousands of buffalo. Of these we killed as many as we required for food, carrying along with us a lot of the meat, which we dried in the sun.

In this part of the country, as we went onwards, we came upon several streams and rivers. These streams mostly came from the mountains, were as cold as ice, and ran as swiftly as a cataract. The river beds, moreover, were full of large boulders, and on all sides were precipices.

Crossing these streams—too deep to ford—was always a matter of much danger.

The way we set about surmounting the difficulty was as follows. We felled a large pine tree and started a good man's saw-mill—that is, with a whipsaw divided the timber into lengths and stood it on end to dry. This, in that climate, it does very readily. With these we constructed a flat boat capable of carrying two or three tons. The way we got this across the stream was by stretching a large rope across, fixing it to a tree on either side, and then fastening a rope to each end of the boat, with a guiding rope fixed to a beam in the boat. By this means we towed the craft backwards and forwards with ease.

In crossing very wide rivers, where it was impossible to get a rope across, we constructed a large raft, and, starting from some convenient spot, drifted across as well as we could, with the assistance of long sleepers or oars cut from young pine trees.

Sometimes it took us quite a fortnight to get across a river, a method of travelling somewhat different from the present.

When we arrived at the Green River, the largest we had as yet met with, we built a house and established a ferry-boat. In view of those who were to come after us we left here five men, with instructions to charge ten dollars for every waggon they brought across. This ferry afterwards proved a very considerable source of revenue to the Mormons, as a way of transport, not only for their own people, but for emigrants bound for California.

We pushed on to Bear River, and across to a district of alkali beds. Here we had the misfortune to lose several head of cattle, through the herders allowing them to drink of the poisonous water.

Traversing this inhospitable waste without delay we again struck the verdant pasturage of the plains, and made our way through the hilly country into the valley beyond. In the far distance the inaccessible and snow-clad peaks of the Rocky Mountains glistened with all the hues of the rainbow.

The trials and troubles of pioneers opening up a new country seem never to have been appreciated at their full value. Crossing the plains with Brigham Young in 1847, and crossing in 1887, are totally different matters. At that time there were no comfortable ranches where one could take a rest or get a package of smoking tobacco or a bottle of " Minnie-wah-kah," or liquid-fire whiskey—no waggon-roads passing through cañons where all obstacles had been removed—nothing but an unbroken vista of solitude where the foot of man had never before fallen. I have gone up on a mountain peak, and, looking down on an endless plain, realised the meaning of "I am monarch of all I survey." There has been no one in the great stretch of country before me to dispute my passage, unless it was a grizzly bear, or one of his neighbours, a mountain lion.

Here and there on the plains we passed through, we saw a small band of Indians disappearing in the distance, as frightened almost at the sight of us as the birds of the air and the wild animals.

We travelled with an advance and a rear guard, and preserved as well as we could a military formation throughout the whole journey. Although at times we exchanged shots with the Indians, we never came to close quarters with them, and we never killed one.

Still plodding on, and encountering difficulties day after day, and surmounting them as they arose, we arrived early in July at the Wahsatch range. There our further progress was effectually impeded by the impenetrable barrier which rose before us. There then we pitched our camp for the night, before we sent out scouting parties to find a cañon through which we could pass.

Of the vastness and magnitude of these mountains no one who has not visited them has any conception. They are appalling in their weirdness. None of us had ever seen anything like this before, and we speculated as to what fate had in store for us on the other side, when the earthly paradise of the Promised Land should be opened up to our fevered imaginations. By this time I had caught the infection, and was as anxious as any of them to see what would be the result of our protracted wanderings. As I stretched out on my blanket that night I could not help chuckling to myself when I thought what a sell it would be if the other side proved to be an arid waste similar to the one we had recently traversed. I reflected upon my stupidity in having left my Indians, and over and over again wished myself back with them in the snug cotton-wood bottoms of the Republican River.

I was up betimes the following morning, and just as day was breaking started with a party of ten men in a northerly direction. The old Mexican took a similar number and started south. After riding about ten miles we found a small cañon, through which we penetrated some distance. Finding it held out prospects of carrying us right through, we returned to camp and reported the good news.

The other party were not so successful in their search. They reported a large cañon some miles to the south, which they had not had time to examine. This proved afterwards to be the celebrated Echo Cañon, twenty-three miles in length.

We pulled up stakes and continued our journey, arriving at the mouth of the cañon that night. Here we again rested, and pursued our route on the following day. Our progress was now necessarily slow, for we had to work for hours at a time clearing boulders of rock out of the way that the waggons might pass. Sometimes we went up hill, sometimes down, and the varied scenery through this superb pass was something beyond description.

Finally, we reached an eminence on the other side, and looked down. I shall never forget the impression made upon me. At first sight there seemed to be nothing but a vast mass of timber as far as the eye could see; yet looming up in the atmosphere, for the sun had not then cleared off the haze, was something in the distance like a black cloud. We sat down and watched this strange spectacle for fully half an hour. Then the sun coming out cleared the air, and we saw that the cloud was the summit of a perpendicular mass of rock rising from a gigantic lake that lay before us.

As we descended, and the sun became warmer and the atmosphere clearer, we were astonished to notice all round the extreme edge of the water, and stretching as far as the eye could reach, what appeared to us to be snow. It was glistening in the sun and reflecting rays we could not account for. We speculated as to what this phenomenon could be, and little thought that it was pure salt which the ebbing and flowing tide had cast up on the banks, there to crystallise in the sun.

Our entry was made a few miles north of what afterwards became Ogden City. Brigham Young not fancying the locality, we made a move forty miles due south, to a spot at the extreme end of the lake, where we corralled.

Brigham asked my opinion of the site he had selected, and I told him it was what I should call a swamp or frog pond. But he was more far-seeing than I gave him credit for, and pronounced it a fertile country, and the one the Saints had been promised.

It was very low ground all round, and there was an uninterrupted view for miles. One most remarkable thing was that a copious supply of fresh water could be obtained from many fresh-water springs, clear as crystal, which emptied themselves into the salt lake.

We corralled at 11 A.M. on July 24, and immediately proceeded to hold a religious function that lasted over a couple of hours. The old Mexican and I wanted to take our guns and go out and pot some of the birds

CHOOSING THE SITE

tantalising us by hovering within easy range. But we were forced to remain and take part in the ceremony, much against our inclination.

Most of this day was passed intermittently in prayer and feasting, and the following morning Brigham and Rockwell staked out a ten-acre plot, of which the corral formed the centre. Round this a mud wall was subsequently built, and the tabernacle erected upon the identical spot where we were encamped. A fort was also constructed as a protection against Indians or other enemies.

Scouring parties were sent out every day to report on the country, and follow the banks of the lake, which Brigham fondly hoped led to the sea, as it appeared to be tidal. But his hopes and ambitions in this respect were blighted, when after many days we returned with the report that the water all disappeared at the extreme end in a hole in the ground from which it ebbed and flowed.

Had there been an outlet to the Pacific Ocean there is little doubt in my mind that Brigham would have proclaimed himself King of Utah, for I had over and over again heard him discuss the project with some of his ministering angels.

We built a boat and made our way over to the islands. Of these we found three. On the one in the middle of the lake we found all kinds of eggs of birds buried in the sand, and left there for the sun to hatch. On the rocky island at one end were innumerable springs of ice-cold water, clear as crystal and as free from salt as if there had not been a grain within a thousand miles.

This island was immediately dedicated by Brigham to the service of the church, and utilised for the purpose of raising stock, or what was called the church herd. The few horses we had with us were taken over there. A very good place it was for them, for they were thief-proof, a circumstance which stood them in good stead some years later.

This island, in my opinion, was one of the safest places in the world, and I often thought, if circumstances ever necessitated my making myself scarce, I should fly to this spot and hide there amongst the rocks of Paradise.

We had a quantity of seeds with us, and the first thing done after the fort was completed was to till up the land around our settlement, and plant potatoes, buckwheat, turnips, and other vegetables.

Then the land was laid out in lots and preparations made for the incoming followers of Brigham, who were expected over in a few months.

These arrived sooner than was anticipated.

It appears that a body of five hundred had left the States to proceed to the Mexican war, and upon arrival down South only one hundred and forty of them were found fit to continue the journey. Consequently the three hundred and sixty returned ; but, instead of pursuing their route to the States, they struck out to

Laramie, with the intention of joining the pioneers in quest of the Promised Land.

Arrived at Laramie, they found that the party had left there a month before. So they followed our trail, and, much to our surprise, on August 29 they arrived in camp.

This was the signal for a round of rejoicings, kept up for a whole week.

Things were just quieting down a little when a further surprise came in the sudden advent of the

remaining one hundred and forty, who, ten days after leaving the main body in Mexico, found the war over, and followed in the footsteps of their companions, tracking them over the plains to where we were.

We now mustered six hundred and forty-seven beings, exclusive of the old Mexican and myself, and the camp presented an animated appearance, auguring well for the future welfare of the young colony.

Now Brigham Young decided to send a party back to Nebraska, in order to make arrangements for bringing out a large body of the chosen people. Ninety-two were selected for the purpose, and the old Mexican and I accompanied them. Brigham asked me to remain, but I was rather tired of the Latter Day Saints by this time, and anxious to get back to my squaws and the old life I could live without any feeling of restraint.

We had a pathetic leave-taking, which was again the occasion of a lengthy religious ceremony, and I galloped out of camp with a light heart and a full pocket, only too glad to think I had got safely away from this crowd of peculiar people.

CHAPTER IX.

FAREWELL TO THE MORMONS—TRAPPING WITH CANADIANS ON THE PLATTE RIVER—FIRST SCALPING EXPERIENCES—A BEAR STORY—ARRIVAL AT ST. VERAIN'S FORT—HOMEWARD BOUND—TWO BUCK ELK'S GREETING—EXIT ZINT-CALLA-WEE-AH—NEW MATRIMONIAL EXPERIENCES—CONG-HE-SAPA-WEE-AH.

E made our way back by the same route we had come, without any incident of importance until we arrived at the Green River. Here we found the party of five men left to work the ferry augmented by eight Canadian trappers in the employment of the Hudson's Bay Company. They had got out of their usual hunting grounds in pursuit of the buffalo, which they had followed down into this district.

Personally I was very glad to meet them, and, telling them my experiences of the Mormons, they asked me to join them. I was always partial to "fur snatching"—a very paying game. Besides, I thought that by accompanying this party I stood a better chance of dropping across the Sioux than by going with the Mormons to Fort Laramie, where I might possibly have to wait many months before meeting with any trace of

H 2

my band. As the Indians were always on the move my argument was that I could not do better than follow their tactics if I wished to find them. Accordingly, I put the Mormons in the right direction, and, wishing them good luck and a speedy journey, started off with my new friends, who were bound to the head of the Platte River.

A curious circumstance, that only came to my knowledge forty years after this parting, was communicated to me by Mr. Arthur Robottom. After I had left my Mormon companions they came, ten miles on the plains, across the large body of their people whom they were bound to the States to fetch out. This party consisted of 666 waggons, and over 2,000 men, women, and children. It appears that they were too eager to await the return of the pioneers, and worked themselves up into such a pitch of excitement about the Promised Land that they blindly followed the footsteps of Brigham, not knowing whither they would lead or what would happen.

The rejoicings were great at the meeting, and a grand dance and orgies took place, which were kept up all night. Even after all these years I feel mad to think I was only about twenty miles distant when all this occurred, and did not participate in the revels. I am sure the Canadians and myself would have enjoyed it, and we might have been of some assistance in scaring off a band of Ute Indians, who got in amongst the stock whilst the orgies were in full swing, and cut loose ninety-five horses. These Utes were followed two hundred miles into the Black Hills before they were made to relinquish their prey.

In about three weeks we arrived upon our trapping grounds and set to work after otter as well as beaver. We were very successful in our catches, but the pleasure of the sport, such as it was, was completely marred by the fact of our having perpetually to be on the lookout for hostile Indians generally, and particularly Utes, who seemed to have appropriated this part of the country as their own. We had several skirmishes with these latter, who, in addition to worrying us in other respects, were always trying to steal our horses. In all our little misunderstandings we managed to come off best, inasmuch as we were armed with rifles, whilst the Indians only had bows and arrows.

I killed and scalped my first Ute in one of these scrimmages. I had frequently grassed Indians before, but my fancy had never taken the form of scalp-lifting. These Canadians, however, made a practice of it, and their twitting me with being a squaw rather got my dander up. I resolved, therefore, that the first Ute I shot I would treat in the orthodox manner.

I am not particularly squeamish, but I must confess it was with no feelings of pleasure that I set about the task. The result was as may be expected.

I made a fearful mess of my initial subject. The great knack is to get the scalp-lock away from the skull, and this is only to be done artistically by making a deep incision with a sharp knife round the base of the lock, twisting the latter round the wrist, then giving it a strong sharp jerk, when it comes away readily enough. The incision must be made right down to the skull, or it is no use. Cutting through

the skin of the head is like cutting through the toughest leather.

After my companions had considerately shown me how to perform the feat, I found I could do it with the utmost facility.

I had seen the Sioux lift scalps over and over again; but I had never had the curiosity to watch them sufficiently closely to acquire the artistic touch necessary for the purpose. The way the Indians grow the hair, and plait it from the centre of the head from a circular parting, tends to the removal of their adornment with far greater ease than they themselves experience in taking the hair of a white man. The Indian grows his hair for the express purpose of forming a scalp-lock.

We on the prairies grow ours long because, as a rule, there is nothing to cut it with.

I used to sit and listen at nights to the stories of my companions about their fights with Indians. I thought I knew something about it, but my experiences up to then seemed child's play to what they had gone through, if all they said was true. I have since then had no reason to question their veracity.

We moved about from place to place along the river, always working up the stream, until at length we reached a well-timbered district, with thick brush all along the river's bank and extending some distance from the bank. At this point we could command a good stretch of water; and, seeing several weeks' work before us, we built a snug little shanty, and made ourselves as comfortable as circumstances would permit.

One night we were seated round our fire talking and smoking, when suddenly we heard the brush crack close to us.

One of our party, a one-eyed man, jumped up, clutched his rifle, and walked outside. It was pitch dark, no moon, and not a star to be seen. Within a few seconds of his leaving the place the report of his rifle was heard, followed by a movement in the brush. Then all was still.

Returning to us, he said:

"Pards, I have shot one of the biggest grizzlies that ever made tracks this side of the Snowy Range, right between the eyes."

We laughed at him, and said he couldn't have hit a tépee at ten yards' range a night like that; although we gave him credit for having scared away the animal, whatever it was, which had paid us a visit.

We went out at daybreak the following morning to look at our traps and bring in the captured otter. I was in advance of the party, and walked a few yards ahead of them in the brush. We had only started a few paces from the hut when I saw something black right before me which there was no mistaking. So I darted back, shouting "Bear! bear!"

We all dived into the hut and got our guns.

"Now, Pards," said the one-eyed man, "I want to bet you my share of this outfit that I shot him right square between the eyes. I know where to take aim through the sights of my old Kill Devil, which never misses a mark."

"All right, old Cyclops," we said, "we don't want to rob you; so no bet." Whereupon we all marched out, expecting to have a fight with Mr. Bruin.

I said, "Look here, boys, I'll heave a stone in, and when he comes out, take good aim and do him up in shape."

The one-eyed man jerked his head on one side, cocked his blind eye at an angle, and replied, "Trot him out this way, then. I want to fix him up the same as I did the one last night."

The word "Ready" being given, all triggers were

cocked, and I sent the stone crashing into the brush. But no bear came out.

A second and third stone followed, but with no better success.

Suddenly there was a rustling in the bushes, and out rushed one of our party, a Frenchman, whom we had not missed in the hurry and excitement of the moment.

He did not know what we were up to, but, suddenly catching sight of the same object I had seen, shouted "Bear!" and made a bolt for the cabin.

The one-eyed man's rifle here went off accidentally, and, by the merest miracle, missed sending Mr. Froggy to glory.

The latter, hearing the shot, naturally thought it was being fired at the animal pursuing him, and the way in which he bounded out of the brush convulsed us all with laughter.

Getting his rifle, he came back and joined the party, which now numbered six. A consultation ensued, and we resolved to go into the brush; three to fire simultaneously at the animal, and the remainder to fire a subsequent volley should the first not have proved efficacious.

At the word of command, the first volley was fired at the object, which, however, never moved; and then the voice of the one-eyed man was heard in a roar of laughter.

"Hold, boys!" he shouted. "I told you I had killed

him last night, and here you are making holes through a dead bear's carcass and spoiling his skin."

Upon this we went right in, and there sure enough was a large grizzly, stiff and cold. Upon examination we found, in addition to the three holes made by our

volley, that he had another right in the centre of the head between the eyes.

The one-eyed man, after all, was right. But the most remarkable thing was that he positively declared that he had only been humbugging us, for when he had fired in the dark he could not see a foot before him. He had not seen the animal, and had merely shot at random for the purpose of frightening the creeping thing, whatever it was, away. We voted old Cyclops the champion marksman of the outfit, and presented him with the skin as a memento of his exploit. The flesh of the animal, I need hardly say, was highly relished by us, and we feasted on it until nothing but the bones was left.

We had no more adventures of interest ; and trapped along until the spring, when we made our way down to St.Verain's Fort, then in the occupation of the American Fur Company. There we disposed of our skins.

My pals then bought whiskey for the purpose of trading with the Indians for ponies, and decided to try their luck down in Wyoming Territory, where, at that season of the year, they expected to find the Indians.

It was a long journey, and we were all the summer and the following winter in getting there. We took things very easily, and hunted during the fine weather, trapping when the cold season set in. Our brushes with wandering bands of Indians were pretty frequent, but we never had any stand-up fights of importance. We were on a sort of picnic this time, and went in for enjoying ourselves thoroughly.

At any particular spot we fancied we pitched our camp, and stayed there until we got tired of it. Then we moved on to another locality. In one place we stayed over three months, hunting round the entire district. We had got a few horses at St. Verain's, and upon these we packed our camp equipage. Each man also had a spare mount in case of accident.

I was not interested in the whiskey speculation I knew what harm it did to the Indians, and if by any means I could at this time have managed to spill the filthy stuff I would willingly have done so. About forty gallons of it the party had with them, and it was carried in small kegs containing one and two gallons each

The money I had obtained for my share of the sale

of our furs I had spent in presents for Zint-calla-wee-ah and her sisters. I bought them each a cotton dress, a lot of beads, brass finger-rings, brass wire for making bracelets, vermilion for painting their faces, shells for earrings, sugar, and—luxury of luxuries!—some coffee, of which they were passionately fond. I had some butchers knives for several of the young bucks, and a gallon of whiskey for my old friend Two Buck Elk. I flatter myself I did not forget any of them. In fact, I laid out all the money I possessed, including that I had received from the Mormons. For the tribe generally I had a supply of powder and lead, and a few old muskets. My purchases were so many that I had to buy two horses to carry them all.

During all those long months often I sat over the camp fire thinking how pleased my squaws would be to see me again, and what pleasure and enjoyment I should give them when I displayed all the presents I had bought.

The difficulty I experienced in looking after my treasures was a constant source of anxiety to me, and I fully determined that, come what might in the way of dangers, I would die fighting to prevent them from falling into other hands. Whenever I have made a promise I have always kept it, and this particularly with the Indians. When I parted with Zint-calla-wee-ah and her sisters I said I would bring them presents; and I was keeping that promise by bringing them earthly treasures such as their eyes had never feasted on before.

The first Sioux Indians we struck were a band under Old Whistler and Walk-under-the-Ground, who were both friends of mine. They had heard of my trip with the Mormons, and were very glad to see me back again. Spotted Tail, they told me, was with the Ogallala band, about sixty miles distant, at a place called Stinking-water Stream ; whilst my old friend Two Buck Elk with my squaws was down on the Republican River some ninety miles beyond that.

I was so anxious to get back to my squaws that I started off with my two horses alone. This was rather a risky thing to do ; but I was flying on the wings of love, and did not care what dangers I ran so long as I could speedily obtain the welcome which I felt was awaiting me. As I pursued that long and solitary journey across the plains, I built castles in the air of the excitement my advent would create, and the joy I should bring to those of my home who had been so long separated from me.

Arrived at length on the banks of the Republican River, I journeyed down for a distance of about twenty miles, until at length I struck the Brûlé encampment. There were the old familiar tépees, looking almost the same as when I had left them. The same horses were apparently tethered in the compound, and little or no change seemed to have come over the fortunes of my old friends.

Whipping up my two pack horses I rode gaily into camp, with my spirits almost at fever heat at the thought of once more being home again.

A few of the young men who were standing about came out to meet me, and gave me a cordial welcome. I inquired where my tépee was pitched, and was told that it was about half a mile down the camp and close to that of the chief Two Buck Elk.

I trotted down the line and made straight for the chief's tent, to report myself before going to my own domicile. Dismounting upon arrival, I tethered my horses outside the tépee, lifted the flap, and walked in.

My old friend was seated by the fire smoking his pipe, and his women were adorning with beads a buckskin jacket. Two Buck Elk started at seeing me, and, asking me to be seated beside him, said:

"Brother, I have bad news for you."

"Bad news, friend! What can that be?"

"Your squaws have gone; a buck has taken them."

This, indeed, almost took my breath away; but, quickly recovering my composure, I answered, "One buck taken them all?"

"Yes."

"Well, he has his hands full, any way. If he can live with them, I can live without them. When did this happen?"

"Some five moons since."

"Who has taken them?"

"Long Man."

"Where is he?"

"Here in camp. But never mind; I will give you some more squaws, just as good, if not better. I have your horses, also your tépee. I would not allow them to take anything away that belonged to you."

I at once saw the futility of saying anything or making a fuss. If my squaws had gone there was an end of them. As for Zint-calla-wee-ah, I felt too disgusted at the thought that she preferred Long Man—a tall thin Indian over six feet in height—to me; and as for her sisters, I inwardly anathematised and dismissed them from my mind.

I said, " Friend, when I entered this camp after my weary wanderings and long absence, my heart was filled with joy. Now, there is nothing there but grief. But never mind. I am grateful to you for looking after my interests. I did not forget you, and have brought you a small present." I rose, went outside, and brought in the keg of whiskey, which I handed to him, saying, " Here is something which you like, but do not drink any of it now."

I then left him and went down to the tépee of Black Bear, one of the tribe with whom I was intimate, and slept that night with him.

The following morning I returned to Two Buck Elk, and, finding him asleep, awoke him.

He said, " Brother, your fire-water was too much for me last night, and I do not feel much better to-day. Where did you go?"

" To Black Bear's. I have no home now, and he took me in."

" That is good. Come back to me in a short time, I want to talk to you."

Accordingly I went out and returned in about an hour, when I found the chief and his squaws eating. There was also another squaw, whose head was enveloped in a blanket.

"Here, brother," said the chief, "is a woman we will give you. You shall not be without a squaw."

Pulling the blanket from off her head, and observing she was a good-looking girl, I said:

"That is all right. You go out, my dear, and fix things comfortably in my tépee."

After she had retired with the other women I said to Two Buck Elk:

"Who is she?"

"Cong-he-sapa-wee-ah. She is eighteen years old. I have given a horse to her mother for her. She has been married before, and cost her late husband five head; but it is the best I can do for you at present. She has six head of horses of her own, so she brings you something."

I said, "You are very good to me, friend, and I am much obliged to you."

"You need not go through any ceremony of courting," he replied. "I have waived all that. She is yours. Now go and take her."

So I went into my tépee, where I found things pretty straight. Cong-he-sapa-wee-ah was seated on a buffalo robe, and I squatted beside her.

She did not say anything to me, nor I to her.

I thought, Well, I will make her speak in a moment. So I got up and began untying my presents. After having undone them all I turned to her and said:

"These are all for you. Do what you please with them."

She was simply thunderstruck, and, opening her eyes as wide as saucers, said:

"For me? What shall I do with them?"

"Anything you please," I repeated. "They are all yours. I like you as much as those presents represent. I can say no more."

Then I left her and went round the camp to see some of the Indians, and give them the few knives I had brought.

When I returned in about two hours I found my squaw had taken me literally at my word, and given everything away. Not one of the articles I had brought was left.

I thought to myself, this is a good beginning. Whatever your other failings may be, my dear, no one can accuse you of want of generosity.

She turned out a very good squaw. Although she was not what might be termed a beauty, she was sensible, and looked after my comforts well. Her only failing was her temper, and when that got the better of her I had to look out, for she would go for me with a knife. I christened her "Molly," and by that name she was always known in the tribe.

CHAPTER X.

CAMPING ON THE REPUBLICAN RIVER—DRUNKENNESS AMONGST THE BRÛLÉS—A DEATH IN THE FAMILY—INDIAN GRIEF—CONG-HE-SAPA-WEE-AH FILLETS HERSELF—TWO BUCK ELK'S COMMISERATION—A TRIP TO THE WAJAJAS—MEETING WITH A PARTY OF EMIGRANTS—NEWS OF THOMAS ATKINSON—A TRAGIC OCCURRENCE.

IN the spring we encamped on the Republican River, about sixty miles south of what afterwards became Fort Kearney. There was capital sport there, as the district was full of game of every description. Our tribe had sixty-five lodges, each containing seven Indians. Two Buck Elk was in command, and Black Crow second chief. I was looked upon as a sort of counsellor or friend of both, to advise and assist them in their dealings with the whites.

About this time (1849) the route to California was well opened up, and, in addition to frequent caravans passing through, mails were running every month over the route across which I had recently piloted Brigham Young. These mail-coaches were drawn by six-mule teams, and accompanied by an outrider. The journey was a pretty risky one, and very few undertook it.

We heard of these mails and their occasional running, from the caravans which we frequently came across. I noticed that the more caravans we met the more demoralised my tribe of Brûlés became. Whiskey grew to be a commodity they would sell their souls for; the more the settlers came out the

more they seemed to bring with them. Scenes of drunkenness became frequent in our once-happy home, and I saw that the time was not far distant when I should have to make tracks and either join some more sober band whose country did not lie on the route of temptation, or make a strike out on my own account in some direction I had not then settled upon.

My squaw Cong-he-sapa-wee-ah and I had got along pretty well up to this point, barring her periodical violent outbreaks of temper. She was a bit frightened of me however, and, although she made a terrible fuss, I don't think she would have proceeded to extremes, for fear of getting the worst of it. In other respects she was a good squaw, and attended to me better than any of her predecessors had.

Things, however, came to a crisis in rather an unexpected manner with her. A brother of Two Buck Elk, an uncle of hers, not in our camp, died, and news of his death was brought to us. Of course there was a terrible hullabaloo amongst the family, and Cong-he-sapa-wee-ah showed her grief as much as any of them. I got a bit tired of this after a couple of nights, and went out into the prairie, where I could be at peace and away from the infernal howling and moaning.

I had a good night's rest, and came into camp on the following morning, feeling quite fresh and ready to bear up against any amount of woe.

When I got to my tépee I saw a crowd around it, and found Cong-he-sapa-wee-ah's grief had taken an acute turn. She was giving away everything I possessed. My horses had all gone, my clothes, beaver traps, saddle and bridle, powder horn, and even my gun. I could not stand the latter going, and, seeing it in an old squaw's hand, I grabbed at and secured it. Even the tépee had been given to some brute who ought to have known better than accept it.

I could do nothing. The custom of the Indians is to give things away when they have a mourning fit on, and for what my squaw did I was responsible. Apart from this there was no way of getting the things back after they had once been given.

I went into the tépee, sat down, and looked at my squaw. If I hadn't felt so mad with her, I should have laughed outright. I never saw such an object as she

looked. With a butcher's knife she had hacked all her hair off, except a rough-looking fringe which hung in irregular lengths over her face. Her frock she had cut away up to the top of her thighs, and bound the remnant round her waist with buffalo thongs. And the sleeves she had cut off at the shoulders, displaying her bare arms.

I thought, Well, you're a pretty-looking object to be

any respectable man's squaw! Still I said nothing, but merely looked on. Her next performance was to cut gashes in her legs. These started at the top of the thigh, and followed one after the other down to the ankle. This she did down each leg, and, as some of them were half an inch deep, the blood poured pretty freely from them. Then she did the same to each arm, and finally she started out of the tépee, and marched round the camp, a distance of three miles, howling, and followed by a parcel of old hags, whom she had picked up *en route*, also howling.

I said to myself, Ta, ta, Cong-he-sapa-wee-ah; never again for this child. You were no great beauty before, but I'm darned if you ever sleep with me again with those fillets on your legs and arms. So I picked up my gun, went out of my now desolate tépee, and sat down on a hill about a quarter of a mile from camp.

I had been there about an hour musing, when a little daughter of Two Buck Elk came up to me, and said her father wanted to see me in his tent.

I accompanied the child back to camp, lifted the flap, and entered the chief's tent.

"Be seated, brother," said he; after which he lighted his pipe, and I lit mine.

"Brother," said he, "you seem to be looking downhearted. Cheer up. The sun will shine by-and-by. There are times when we all feel unhappy, but the Great Spirit above sees us, and will take care of us. He feeds the birds and the animals on the prairie, and he will look out for you."

I thought to myself, Yes, but if I wait for the Great Spirit to give me horses and something to eat, I shall have to wait a long time. Still I said nothing, and he continued:

"Your squaw has given away all your horses and everything, but never mind, you will have more. I give you my dun-coloured buffalo horse out of the herd; go and take him, and ride him, and if you want any more take them out of my herd; take any you like but the children's horses."

I thanked him, and said the one he had given me would be enough for the present. Then I went on, "I am going to Laramie. First, because my heart is sad, and the change will do me good. Second, because I am desirous of seeing the Wajaja band of Sioux, whom I have not met for some long time, and amongst whom I have many friends."

He said, "All right, brother, go, but come back soon. I shall miss you."

The fact was, I had made up my mind to get clear of the Brûlés for the reasons already stated, and the act of my squaw gave me a good opportunity. I put on a face of woe as long as a fiddle, and the next morning flung my rifle over my shoulder, and, getting on Two Buck Elk's dun-coloured buffalo hunter, rode solemnly out of camp. It was sixty-five miles to the Platte River, and I made my way straight to it, arriving by sundown. There, much to my delight, I found a party of emigrants encamped, numbering forty-five waggons.

They didn't much like the look of me when I rode into their camp. I had an old buckskin coat and leggings on, and was altogether one of the wildest objects imaginable. They took me for a cut-throat or horse-thief—anything their fancy chose. A white man

alive out that distance on the prairie was sufficient to create alarm in the minds of any peaceful body of emigrants. I sat on my horse in their midst for quite a while before any of them asked me to get down.

Then one old fellow said to me, " Won't you get down and have a rest ? "

I said, " I don't mind. I have ridden a long distance to-day and feel a bit tired." We got talking, and he told me the party came from Missouri. I asked if he knew Thomas Atkinson.

He said he knew him by name well. " He was my uncle," said I. I explained how it was I was out there alone. He was delighted to see me, and introduced me straight away to most of those in the outfit. His wife made me some coffee, and I presented her with a side of antelope I had shot on the prairie coming along. There was no fresh meat in the camp, and this was a luxury for them.

I found the party was bound for California, and I asked if I might accompany them to Laramie.

They said, " With pleasure."

I said, " Well, then, you shall have fresh meat every day," and I kept my word. Every morning I went out hunting, and kept the larder well supplied with game of all kinds. During the whole 300 miles we traversed not one day passed without their having fresh meat.

An incident occurred a few days after I was with this party of emigrants which made rather an impression on me. A man very well to do, down in Missouri, died, leaving two children, a boy and a girl. As the mother was already dead, he trusted them to the care of his brother. This man, with his two charges, was with the caravan. The girl was about seventeen, and the boy a year or so younger.

One morning the news went round the camp that this girl was very ill, and this was followed shortly afterwards by the statement that another stranger, this time a diminutive one, had joined the outfit in a most unexpected manner. At length the news leaked out that the guardian uncle was the cause of all the commotion, and a nice little scandal was sprung upon us quite unawares. The men got together and discussed it amongst themselves, and the women held private meetings in groups and had their say.

At noon we camped for dinner, and in the stillness of the prairie a rifle shot denoted that something was going on. I jumped up to see what it was, and soon saw the cause. The brother of the girl had taken his gun, walked up to his uncle, and shot him through the heart. That afternoon we dug a grave by the beaten trail, and laid the body in it just as it was; we had no wood to make a coffin, but we stuck a cross over the head of the grave.

Many is the time I have passed that mound and thought of the uncle and nephew. The boy gave himself up, and told the outfit to hang him if they thought proper, but, by universal acclamation, he was acquitted. He seemed quite broken down. All he said was that he had to do it.

CHAPTER XI.

ARRIVAL AT LARAMIE—VALAUNDRIE AND JOE JEWITT—CROSSING THE NORTH PLATTE RIVER—TARANTULA JUICE—THE RAW HIDE BUTES—CRAZY WOMAN'S FORK—TRADING WITH THE WAJAJAS—DISAGREEMENT WITH THE CANADIANS—WEE-AH-PEE-TA-CHA-LA—FIRST GOLD-FIND IN THE BLACK HILLS—REJOINING THE OGALLALAS—RETURN TO THE BRÛLÉS ON THE REPUBLICAN—EXIT CONG-HE-SAPA-WEE-AH—GATHERING CLOUDS—A GOVERNMENT COMMISSION TO LARAMIE—OFFICIAL PECULATION—DISSATISFACTION OF THE INDIANS—AN IMPENDING CALAMITY.

ARRIVED at Laramie I bade adieu to my emigrant friends. They, after a few days' rest, resumed their journey to the Far West.

At the Fort I met a party of Canadians who had been trading up the Missouri River. They had come down to the American Fur Company's depôt, just established here. Their object was to sell skins and purchase goods for barter with the Indians up in North Dakota.

The two chief men of the party were Valaundrie and Joe Jewitt. With them I engaged at a salary of seventy-five dollars a month to act as interpreter. This just suited me, for the Indians they proposed trading with were the Wajaja band of the Sioux, whom I wanted to meet.

Our outfit consisted of from twenty-five to thirty head of ponies. Upon them our stores were packed. There were no waggons in those ~~~~ for expeditions of this description. Each man had ~~ook after so many of the ponies, and was responsible for them and the packages they carried.

We set out from the Fort in October, and soon arrived at the North Platte River, when our troubles began. The North Platte is the worst river to cross

in America. At this point it is quicksand—dangerous to man and beast. A horse walking along the solid sand in a moment would sink down up to his belly, and if he was not at once got out, would in a few minutes be sucked under. I have seen many horses and their riders disappear in this way without being able to help. My usual plan was to throw a lariat over the rider and pull him out of his saddle, and save him first. Then if the horse had not sunk too deeply, we repeated the operation on it. Many is the life I have saved this way, and upon more than one occasion I have been rescued myself.

An Indian pony knows the dangers of quicksands, and instinctively avoids them. But an American horse will flounder on.

Once I saw a company of soldiers go into one of these sands, and those who got out saw their companions and their horses disappear one by one before their eyes. We selected a spot where the river was a little over a mile wide. There we built a raft, and, packing our goods upon this, drove the ponies into the water and swam them across. It took us a day to make the passage, and we arrived on the opposite side without accident to man or beast. I recollect that the water upon this occasion was very cold, and the quantity of "Tarantula juice" we had to drink to keep our circulation going was surprising.

"Tarantula juice" is two quarts of alcohol, a few burnt peaches, a plug of black tobacco, put in a keg and filled up to five gallons of water. This concoction was a great favourite with both trappers and Indians. It is the most intoxicating compound drinkable. Its effects last, and a man once drunk on it remains drunk for a week.

We continued our journey north to the foot of the Black Hills—to the Raw Hide Butes. This name is derived from the fact that one of a party of emigrants

who had sworn to kill the first Indian he met, here came across a squaw and her child. He made his words good by despatching them both, but atoned for his deed in an unexpected manner. The main body of Indians, discovering the murder, followed the caravan and insisted upon
the man
being

handed over to them, as against the alternative of the massacre of the entire party of emigrants. The position was accepted, and the Indians revenged themselves by skinning the murderer alive at this point.

We followed the stream here for some days, and then

crossed the Cheyenne River, ultimately reaching, in December, a place called "Crazy Woman's Fork." The Wajajas were permanently encamped here for the winter. We pitched our tents alongside theirs and remained with them until the following spring.

My old friends were very pleased to see me, and as I was popular with them I was of great assistance in the trading operations. These ultimately turned out the most profitable the Canadians had ever been engaged in. I made a fool of myself over this engagement; but although the experience was dearly bought, I was not caught in the same way again.

As I have said, my pay was seventy-five dollars a month, but for anything I wanted in the way of luxuries from the store I had to pay.

Upon meeting my Indian friends, in order to facilitate the trading operations in the interests of the Canadians, I gave one or two little feasts to the chiefs of the band. These feasts were very modest, merely a cup of coffee and a cup of sugar, a couple of cups of flour and a cup of dried apples mixed with water and baked. These were unheard-of luxuries in these days with the Indians, and worth in point of value more than their weight in gold. In fact, I afterwards saw more than two ounces of gold given for one ounce of either of these luxuries. The price given by the traders for these at the Forts was, comparatively speaking, high, but nothing in proportion to the value at which they retailed them to the Indians.

When I totted up accounts with the Canadians I found they had charged me their trading price for everything I had from them. Instead of having any pay to receive I was their debtor in the sum of thirty dollars.

This so disgusted me that I refused to return to Laramie with them. They said they would make me. I said they would have to fight the Wajajas to get me. I told the chiefs what had occurred, and they said that if the Canadians did not make tracks pretty quickly, and leave me to do as I pleased, they would know the reason why.

The next morning the party went off with their ill-gotten gains, and at a pretty quick pace, for some of the young bucks who went out to have a look for them reported that they could find no trace of them within fifty miles of camp.

A few words on the method of trading with the Indians may not be uninteresting. This was carried on in the following manner. A tariff of prices was arranged by the boss or the bosses of the outfit by aid of a cup as it was called, which was in reality a tin pannikin holding about two-thirds of a pint. This was the standard measure, and everything was calculated by it. So many cups of coffee or other stores were given for so many buffalo robes or other skins.

A few days after the Canadians had taken their departure, the Wajajas struck their camp and went about sixty-five miles up into the Black Hills. I accom-

K

panied them. They fixed me up very comfortably, and Iron Bull, the chief of the band, presented me with one of his daughters for a squaw. Her name was Wee-ah-Pee-ta-cha-la, or the Short Woman. She was fourteen years of age, and reminded me very much of my former love, Wom-bel-ee-zee-zee.

After we had been in the hills a few days, an Indian came to me with a piece of quartz that had a solid chunk of gold weighing about six ounces attached to it. He asked me what the yellow-looking stuff was. I asked him where he got it. He had found it in a little creek. He had lain down to take a drink, and seeing something shine in the water, picked it out with his knife. I asked him to give it to me, but he refused, saying he would keep it until he went to Laramie. He had a suspicion it was gold, of which he had heard, and nothing would induce him to part with his treasure, or take me to the place where he had found it. The thought that gold was there worried me to such an extent I could not sleep at night. I got up and walked about for hours, arguing to myself where the Indian could have found it. Often I sneaked out of the camp in the early morning and prospected around until I was fairly tired out, but not so much as a grain of alluvial dust did I find. And yet it must have been there, or the Indian could not have become possessed of it. Over and over again I tried all my wiles and fascinations to persuade the Indian to part with his piece of yellow clay, as I called it; but he said No, it was a charm, and he would keep it. Every time I went out hunting I separated from the other members of the party, and examined all the creeks, but I could find nothing. I was convinced that there was gold somewhere thereabouts and I determined, if ever I had a chance, to return some day and have a good look round for it. That I did return will be seen later on.

In the month of September the band went down to Laramie, and there I left them and struck down to the Republican River again, where I joined the Ogallala band, into which I had been originally adopted, and which was under the command of Whistler. My squaw, Wee-ah-Pee-ta-cha-la, wanted very much to accompany me, but I told her she had better stay with her people, as I was only going on a visit, and would return very shortly. The fact was that I had become utterly tired of her. She was lethargic, and apparently indifferent whether I cared for her or did not.

Three of the young bucks of the Wajajas accompanied me on the trip, and we stayed with Whistler on a visit during the whole of the ensuing winter.

Nothing of particular interest occurred during that season. We hunted and trapped as before, and managed to kill time in the humdrum way peculiar to life amongst the Indians. Whistler wanted to present me with a squaw, but I declined, having already had enough of matrimonial experiences.

After about six months' stay I left the Ogallalas

and went down the Republican River, a distance of about sixty miles, to the camp of the Brûlés.

When I left them I made up my mind not to return. Yet I had a strong attachment for Two Buck Elk, and felt that I would like to see him again. There never was an Indian on earth with a larger heart or more generous disposition than this chief, and I believe he cared for me perhaps more than for anything or anybody in the world.

His liking for whiskey was not altogether his fault. Had temptation not been put in his way he would never have sought it. The demoralisation of the Indians has been brought about by the whites.

I have witnessed the commencement and end of that demoralisation, and I say here solemnly, and wish to have it placed on record, that when I first joined this band I found them a set of innocent, harmless children. When I left them they were, as I have said, completely demoralised, and the result was brought about by that arch-fiend drink. For this they have to thank the white traders, who cheated them out of all their hard-earned savings in the way of skins and other products for this vile compound, the ruin of their homes, the cause of all their subsequent strife.

The most unfortunate thing that ever happened to the Brûlés was the route to California passing through their country. The more this was opened up, the more whiskey they obtained. I tried hard to get them away into another district, but failed. They were like moths fluttering round a candle. Nothing would move them.

When I arrived on this occasion, I found them well set up for meat, but they had hardly a buffalo robe amongst them.

Two Buck Elk was delighted to see me, and shortly after my arrival struck his camp and went off after the buffalo.

The hunting of this animal was now carried on, not, as formerly, for the meat, but for the skins alone. These were the charms that secured the drink, and the way in which every member of the tribe devoted himself to the slaying of these animals was worthy of a nobler cause.

I inquired after my late squaw Cong-he-sapa-wee-ah, and found that a few weeks after my departure she had paired off with a young buck. So whatever qualms of conscience I might have possessed with regard to my union with the daughter of the Wajaja were quickly dispelled.

I must say I had often wondered how she was getting on, and I must confess that when I heard of her perfidy I was delighted beyond measure. I only hoped that her new husband was having as lively a time of it as I had undergone.

I told Two Buck Elk that I had become a woman-hater, and he laughed and said, "Brother, you will get over that in time. When you do, come and tell me, and you shall have the finest young girl in my band." I must say it was not the absence of offers that prevented my embracing matrimony again, for most of the fathers of marriageable daughters invited me to become their son-in-law. But I was obdurate.

After hunting in the district of the Big Solomon River we worked back to the Republican, and from there on to the South Platte, to dispose of our skins with the traders and emigrants.

About this time events occurred which, in a great measure, were the means of an alteration in my future mode of life. Up to now the entire country round had belonged to the Indians, but as the whites came pouring through it troops were sent by the Government for their protection, and forts established from Laramie right down to Santa Fé in New Mexico. These forts were protection as much for the traders as for the caravans. They were havens of refuge along the entire caravan route to California.

The Indians foresaw their doom by the increased traffic through their country, and protested. A commission was sent out by the Government to negotiate, with a view to their guaranteeing the safety of the caravans upon receiving an annual subsidy. This was fixed at some thousands of dollars, and it was agreed that it should be paid in goods, such as blankets, cloth, cotton stuff, powder, muskets, beads, kettles, and in fact whatever articles were required. These were sent to Fort Laramie, the general rendezvous, where the various tribes would come for their share of the tribute. Government agents were appointed, and everything fixed to the satisfaction of both the contracting parties.

This was the bright side of the arrangement, but dark was the way in which it was carried into effect.

The Government agents, finding themselves in possession of such valuable commodities, hit upon the expedient of meting out only a small portion of the subsidy, and trading off the remainder, the produce of which they would put into their own pockets.

The Indians could do nothing. When they did complain their remonstrance was never forwarded to headquarters at Washington. The whole of the officials were in the swindle from the Chief Commissioner downwards, and the poor Indians were the sufferers.

This state of things was not likely to last long, as events proved.

At first it caused a considerable amount of ill-feeling against the whites amongst the tribes. After the manner of their race this was borne in silence; but it smouldered on, and eventually burst forth in an unexpected manner.

Coming events cast their shadows before them, and isolated collisions between the whites and the various tribes began. Little love was now lost between them, and it only required the application of a lighted fuse to the train of powder for an explosion to take place.

CHAPTER XII.

ESTABLISHMENT OF FORT KEARNEY—THE SPARK THAT FIRED THE TRAIN—MASSACRE OF TWENTY-NINE SOLDIERS—SPOTTED TAIL ON THE WAR PATH—GENERAL HARNEY TO THE RESCUE—THE BATTLE OF ASH HOLLOW—ENGAGEMENT AS INTERPRETER AT KEARNEY—SPOTTED TAIL SENT TO FORT LEAVENWORTH—BUILDING THE NEW FORT—AN INDIAN SURPRISE—A FLIGHT FOR LIFE—A TARANTULA INCIDENT—TRAPPING WITH HAL GAY.

WE have now arrived at the year 1853. In the fall of that year Government established Fort Kearney, about 300 miles east of Fort Laramie.

About this time a party of Mormons were passing through to Salt Lake City. Some thirty miles below Laramie they left one of their cows, which had become footsore, on the banks of the Platte River. Leaving the cow there for a day's rest, a party returned on the following day to drive it on into camp.

In the meantime a band of Indians had come along. As they were in want of meat they killed and ate the cow. The Mormons upon arriving found nothing but the skeleton left. At this they were naturally very irate, whilst the Indians were proportionately penitent, offering to pay for the damage they had done. The Mormons, however, would listen to no explanations or apologies. They started off to the fort in a state of high dudgeon, and reported the circumstance to the commanding officer with many embellishments and untruthful details, magnifying the incident into a brutal attack by the Indians upon a quiet and peaceable party of emigrants.

The result was that a lieutenant and twenty-eight men and an interpreter were sent down to the Indian encampment, about twelve miles on the south side of the North Platte River. This village consisted of some 2,000 Indians, none of whom had been implicated in the cow incident, and consequently knew nothing about it. The name of the officer was Lieutenant Gratton; that of the interpreter, a half-breed, Wyuse. The party was armed with two pieces of artillery—a 10-lb. and a 6-lb. brass gun—and officer, interpreter, and men were all drunk when they arrived on the scene of operations.

Taking up a position on a hill overlooking the village, the interpreter was sent in with a message ordering the chief to come up immediately.

No attention was paid to this command, the Indians not understanding what it meant—or for what the soldiers had come.

In a short time the interpreter again returned, to say that if the chief did not put in an appearance within five minutes the village would be fired upon.

This riled them, and the chief sent a message to the

effect that they must all be drunk, and had better go back to the fort. If the white chief there wished to talk to him he had better send sober men whom he could understand.

The result of this was that firing instantly commenced from the artillery; the shots were directed through the tépee

poles. The first cut down several, and the second passed through the chiefs' lodge, killing an old bed-ridden chief and wounding several of the women.

These two shots were all they fired. The blood of the Sioux was up. They made one charge upon the party and killed every one of them.

The interpreter started off on his horse towards the fort, but was overtaken by one of the Indians—his own brother-in-law. Wyuse threw up his hands. But the

Indian said, "Brother-in-law, you have made my heart sad. You have come down here with these drunken soldiers and attacked us while we were at peace. We have killed all of them. Now I am going to kill you with one of your own shots." So, with the revolver which he had taken from the lieutenant, he blew his brains out.

The Indians broke up the gun carriages, and tried to make holes in the guns by firing bullets at them. I saw these guns, with the shot marks on them, when they were ultimately recaptured.

When this incident occurred I was with Two Buck Elk on the Republican River, about 100 miles southeast of Cottonwood Springs.

News was brought down to us of the massacre of the troops, and instructions from Spotted Tail to go on the war-path at once; that soldiers were coming down to fight us; and that all bands were to concentrate in his part of the country without delay.

Mot-to-a-wa-yu, or "The Bear that lay amongst the Rocks," was then chief of the Sioux Nation, and Little Thunder and Spotted Tail were the two chiefs in command of all the Indians in the neighbourhood.

I had a consultation with Two Buck Elk as to what was to be done. He said he did not want to fight the whites, and was quite content to remain where he was, hunting and trading in peace.

Ultimately it was decided that I should go to Fort Kearney and ascertain if the reports we had heard were true. If they were I was to remain there, as I could not fight against the soldiers. If they were untrue I was to return as speedily as possible. Two Buck Elk's last words to me were, "Remember, brother, I don't want to fight, and I wish you to tell the soldiers that."

When I arrived at Kearney I heard the whole story, and that the soldiers were on the point of marching to the relief of Fort Laramie, which it was feared would be attacked and taken by the Indians.

After the massacre Spotted Tail and six of his chiefs had waylaid the mail, robbed it, scattered the letters all over the prairie, shot the driver and the passengers, and stolen the mules.

This brought General Harney out with reinforcements, and he marched right on to Laramie in search of the Indians.

On his way thither he came across Spotted Tail at a place called Ash Hollow, midway between the forts. Following him by a forced march, Harney made him fight before he could amalgamate with another band. The result was that nearly the whole of the Indians were killed, and two of Spotted Tail's squaws and three of his children were captured.

If the Indians at this time, instead of being scattered all over the country, had only concentrated their forces, they would have killed every white man in the country, soldiers and all, for they numbered over twenty to one.

This battle put an end to the outbreak for the time being, but it was only the foreshadower of subsequent events, such as have had, perhaps, no equal in the world's history.

The captured squaws, children, and other prisoners were sent down to Fort Kearney, and brought in a few days after my arrival. I recognised them at once, and going up to the squaws, said I was sorry to see them there.

As I was the only white man in the fort who could speak the Sioux language, I

was appointed interpreter. There were about twenty-five prisoners in all, and many of them were badly wounded.

Spotted Tail's squaws asked me to write to him and say where they were. This I did by sending a letter to Fort Laramie, where it was translated to some of the Sioux, and the message sent to him somehow.

General Harney was still at Laramie. Much to his surprise, some ten days after Spotted Tail had received my message, he turned up at the fort, and, with two of his chiefs, gave himself up as a prisoner.

Spotted Tail immediately asked for the General, and walking up to him held out his hand, saying:

"Brave man with the three stars, you have captured my wives and children. I want to die with them. I fought you, and I fought you hard, but against odds. I surrender to you, not because I am whipped, but because you have captured my wives and children. Do as you like to me, hang or shoot me if you will, but let me see them first."

The General replied:

"Spotted Tail, I like you because you are a brave man, and I will see that you are treated as a brave should be. I will send you to where your wives and children are."

So he was sent to Fort Kearney, where I received him.

He cried like a child when he saw one of his little children shot through the leg.

After the meeting with his wives I had a long talk with him. He wanted to know where he was to be sent. I told him to Fort Leavenworth in Kansas, there to be kept a prisoner.

He was put in a six-mule waggon with his squaws and sent off. I wished him good-bye and told him to cheer up, and that we should meet again. As a matter of fact he was kept a prisoner for two years. It was the first time I had seen him since the memorable day when I left him to guide the Mormons to Salt Lake. I told him he made a great mistake in fighting the soldiers. He said he had no idea there were so many as he found out. He thought that those who had met and beaten him were all the whites in the world.

I was offered a billet by the Government agent to help in the construction of a larger and stronger fort at Kearney, and was engaged to drive a team to haul in the wood for that purpose, and also for the winter's supply of fuel.

The soldiers had to cut down the trees, load the waggons, and unload them at the fort. All I had to do was to deliver my loads safely.

The place we were working at was only three miles from the fort; but it was pretty dangerous work, as we were frequently attacked by Indians. One day they jumped us and sent us flying in all directions; it was a case of "every one for himself." I never saw soldiers run so fast. I hadn't a chance to get away, so I crawled in amongst a heap of loose logs that I was loading up with. The Indians cut my team away from the waggon and went off with them.

When they had gone I crawled out, swam the Platte River, and made tracks to the fort as quickly as I could, where I reported three men dead and several wounded.

Tarantulas were our most dangerous enemies.

Whilst we were wood-cutting, they would get in the bark, and, before they could be detected, they would have stung or crawled over some part of the body. Even in crawling over the hand they leave a red inflammatory streak behind, which subsequently turns black, and the flesh rots off, while mortification and blood-poisoning supervene. I remember one day one of the soldiers threw a log over his shoulder, and, not noticing one of these reptiles on it, got stung in the neck.

He threw the log down at once, and, turning to a man standing near, said, "Take this knife quickly, and cut a big lump of the flesh out of my neck," he putting his finger on the spot.

The man was frightened, and refused. Whereupon the soldier pointed his revolver, and said, "If you don't I'll shoot you." This quickened the man up a bit, and he took out a thick piece about as big round as a ten-dollar piece. Strange to say this soldier lived. A tarantula bite is always fatal, whereas a rattlesnake's is not. There is one antidote for a rattlesnake's bite, and I have saved many lives with it. On the prairie grows a sort of creeper with a pod something like a pea, only the seeds are no bigger than mustard seeds. These pounded up, and put into a slit made over the bite, will immediately stop any ill effects; that is if the remedy is applied soon after the bite has taken place.

I stayed working at the fort until it was finished, and left there in the fall of 1855, starting out trapping with a man named Hal Gay.

CHAPTER XIII.

DOG TOWN—THE ROBBERS' ROOST—A ROVING SALOON—CAPTURE AND BURNING OF THE SHANTY—RETURN TO DOG TOWN—"SKINNED OUT"—TRADING FOR ALEC CONSTANCE—A TRIP TO FORT LEAVENWORTH—GENERAL ALBERT SIDNEY JOHNSON—A FEW WORDS ABOUT THE MORMONS—THE GOVERNMENT EXPEDITION TO SALT LAKE—ENGAGEMENT AS SCOUT AND GUIDE.

HAL GAY was a smart devil-may-care sort of fellow, and one that I felt I could work with. So we pooled our wealth together, and bought spring traps, a tépee, a few head of horses, and started off to try our luck with the beaver. I knew all the streams round about, and the only spots where the animals were to be found. It took us a couple of months to get to the ground. Then we set seriously to work, first going down both the Beaver Rivers, the Short Nose, and Little and Big Solomon. Then we worked north towards the Platte River, and from there to the Republican, down

L

on to the Stinking Water and Red Willow, and so back to Fort Kearney, where we sold our furs for quite a decent sum.

A small town named Dog Town had sprung up in our absence, about three miles from the fort. It consisted of two stores, a few dwelling-houses, and four whiskey saloons. Hal Gay and I went down there, and, putting our capital together, started a whiskey bar. This brought the number up to five.

Our shanty was the best of the lot, and, as we were both popular men, it was not long before we were doing the best trade in the place. All the soldiers from the fort used to patronise us, and we hit upon the expedient of starting a private room for the use of the officers, with a gambling saloon leading from it. Every one, far and near, came to our place, which we called "The Robbers' Roost." The opposition shanties melted away one by one, and we had the monopoly of the trade.

We were on the direct route to the West, and a provost marshal was sent down from the fort to see that no caravan started out beyond Dog Town unless it mustered over a hundred men. This was on account of the Indians, of whom a few wandering bands were always on the look-out to attack any small party.

This all just dovetailed in with our ideas, for the provost marshal stood in with us, and would detain the caravans as long as he could in order that we might skin the emigrants out of their money either by gambling or by drinking.

I never had so much cash in my life—it just came pouring in. As business increased we provided for the demand by establishing monte, poker, faro, dice, roulette, and every game calculated to take the fancy.

In fact so popular did our place become that we built quite a big gambling saloon, in which many a poor fellow lost not only his money but his life.

The shootings subsequently became so frequent that

we had to establish a grave-yard at the back of our place a hundred yards or so out on the prairie.

There are tricks, they say, in every trade, and ours was no exception to the rule. Our game was to get the emigrants in to drink and gamble. Once they were there we could look after them, but they were a bit shy, and wanted coaxing in. This we used to work in the following manner.

Hal would disguise himself, rubbing a lot of dirt in his hair, over his face and hands, and putting on some dirty ragged clothes. Then he went down to the caravan corral, talking to some of the men, and brought them up to the town. He then strolled along to the Robbers' Roost, and invited them in to have a drink. Once in, it was not long before he got them into the gambling saloon, where he began to play, and invariably won by an arrangement he had with the banker, who was in our employment.

Having won a pile he stood more drinks, and as a result some of the strangers soon started in. He left off then, for the banker invariably gave him a dollar to go and have a drink, saying his luck was far too good, and if he kept on winning all the money, there would be none left for his pals to take away.

I don't say there was any cheating done, but the bank invariably came off the winner.

I attended to the bar whilst all this was going on. That was my department, and pretty busy I was too, for the more they gambled the more drinks I sold.

Finally things became so warm and the shootings so frequent, I had a consultation with my partner, and suggested our clearing out before we got into trouble. He was quite of my opinion, and we cast round for a purchaser, and, finding one, sold our interest in the concern for seven hundred dollars. This was for the goodwill of the business and stock; the house we only rented.

There was an emigrant in the town who had come along with a caravan, and had remained behind his party to gamble. He had a house on wheels—it was twenty-two feet long, and quite a nice-looking little shanty, well painted, and as comfortable a house as one could wish for. He got cleaned out at our place, and had nothing but this left. He sold it to us, and we fixed it up as a bar, and started up and down the road between Dog Town and the old California crossing on the Platte River, afterwards better known as Julesburg.

This was about one hundred and sixty miles farther west. We would attach ourselves to any caravan going along—the larger the better— and afterwards return with any party

coming back. Finally we became so brave that we used to start out alone and wait for the caravans on the road. One day, as we were jogging along merrily on our homeward trip for a fresh supply of whiskey, a party of Indians swooped down on us. We saw them coming, and didn't wait to see who they were; a glance was sufficient to tell us they were on no peaceable mission. We just cut a horse loose apiece from the traces, jumped on, and rode off as fast as we could.

We had too good a start for them to follow us. They took all the whiskey we had, and then set fire to our house. Looking back we saw it in flames, and a crowd of drunken redskins dancing round it.

Fortunately we got clear away, and, after doing a twenty-five mile spin, arrived in Dog Town thankful that we had escaped with whole skins.

We put up in one of the shanties that had been started as a boarding-house, and lived like gentlemen on our means.

The Robbers' Roost was then about fifty times as warm as it had been under our management. Hal and I were both frequent visitors there, especially in the private gambling saloon, where, finally, we met the fate of our previous customers, and both got skinned out. We managed to stay on until the spring, and then had a serious talk about our next move.

Things by then had settled down a little with the Indians round about Fort Kearney. They didn't like the soldiers at all, and had come to the conclusion they had better give the district in which they were to be found a wide berth.

Hence an old Frenchman named Alec Constance,

who had for years been in the employment of the American Fur Company on the Missouri River, had the courage to start a ranche about forty miles west of the fort, at the mouth of a creek called Plum Creek.

As we were stone-broke, we engaged with him at seventy dollars a month apiece to help him in his business. He started us each in an outfit and sent us in different directions. Hal was sent to the Ogallala camp, and I to the Brûlés. We neither of us did very well, for the old man's tariff was too high, and the Indians refused to trade with us. When we got back, I said to Hal, "We shall never do any good as long as we stay with this old skinflint." Hal thought the same. Fortunately, a party of

seven men came along bound east, towards Fort Leavenworth, and I joined them. Hal said he didn't want to go that way, so I left him.

Upon arriving at Leavenworth I bade adieu to the party, and fell in with Majors and Russell, who were freighting to all the forts on the California route for the Government.

They introduced me to General Albert Sidney Johnson. He was then organising a large expedition to proceed to Salt Lake to punish the Mormons, who had become very strong during the last ten years.

Brigham Young and his saints had outgrown their discretion, and suddenly took to murdering emigrants who did not belong to their denomination, to robbing trains, and to killing people who were bound for California.

Some few words with reference to these people may be interesting here, as they will explain the position at this time that necessitated the Government sending out the expedition in question.

In 1848, after the finding of the Promised Land was known, the tide of Mormon emigration set in, and flowed west without intermission up to the time of which I now write. Many is the caravan of poor deluded creatures I have seen wending their weary way across the great desert, with a courage and perseverance which, if they had only drifted into a proper channel, would have been worthy of the highest commendation.

They were hard-working, persevering people of all ages; old men and women trudging along trundling hand-carts, whilst others were carrying loads on their backs calculated to make a mule grunt. Half of them were bare-footed and with their feet bleeding, but still they tramped on.

The elders preached to the people—on Sundays

especially—and pretended to heal their wounds. They buoyed them up by telling them that Christ suffered and died for them, and that they must suffer if they wished to reach the Promised Land.

The buxom young girls were taken more care of, and made to ride in the waggons, that they might be of use when the journey's end was reached. Their lot was to be divided amongst the elders of the party and those who had preceded them.

The class of people who made up these Mormon caravans were generally very poor and ignorant. Some, however, amongst them belonged to a better class, and I always fancied these had joined to save their necks from the gallows of the district from which they had migrated.

The secret of polygamy amongst the Mormons was this. They thought that if each man had ten wives, and each wife had from three to five children, in twenty years' time they would be strong enough to protect themselves from the Gentiles.

Unfortunately they had miscalculated their chances of success in this laudable project. Brigham Young, as the increased influx of emigration poured in, saw this, and hit upon the expedient of drawing the attention of the United States Government upon him by perpetrating the outrages I have mentioned in order that troops might be sent out. This would put money into circulation, and provide his people with a home market for their grain, hay, and other produce.

Whatever wild scheme he had at first of securing to himself the reins of government over that portion of

America—and it was his intention at one time to form a monarchy, with himself as king—were dissipated when he openly cast down the gauntlet to the United States Government.

His people were getting too strong for him, and he saw no way out of the difficulty but the Jesuitical " doing evil that good might come." Becoming desperate, the Mormons were clamouring for groceries, tobacco, and provisions generally, and the only way to avert difficulties was the method he adopted.

That he never intended to fight the troops I am convinced. I knew him too well, and told the general so when I was introduced to him.

As I was the man who had taken Brigham Young across in 1847, and presumably the best guide for the expedition, my sudden advent at Leavenworth was looked upon as a great stroke of luck by General Johnson. He begged me as a personal favour to accept a post in connexion with the expedition.

I did not care where I went or what I did. I was getting pretty well accustomed to the ups and downs of life by this time. And I wanted to see Salt Lake City again and what progress my quondam friends had made during the ten years they had been left to their own resources. Consequently I jumped at the General's offer of one hundred and fifty dollars a month, and walked out of his office duly fixed up in my new capacity as scout for the United States Army, with fifty dollars on account in my pocket and a big cigar in my mouth.

CHAPTER XIV

BREAKING IN MULES—EN ROUTE FOR UTAH—A STARTLING INCIDENT—WINTER AT HAMS FORK—STARVED OUT—PASSAGE OF THE ROCKIES—ARRIVAL AT SALT LAKE—CAMP FLOYD.

N June 14, 1857, the order was given for those who were to form part of the expedition to clear out of Leavenworth, and go under canvas at Salt Creek. This was a general camping-ground for emigrants bound west—about six miles due west from the fort. Abundance of grass, wood, and water was to be found here, and no more favourable spot could have been chosen for the purpose.

We found thousands of Mexicans on the ground freighting to Mexico and other points on that route, and altogether the scene was the most lively I had ever witnessed.

Our expedition consisted of some two thousand soldiers and over two hundred waggons, each waggon drawn by six mules. It took some two or three weeks to get the teams all loaded and the soldiers ready for the start. This interval was employed by the noncombatants in breaking in the mules, more than one-half of which had never before been in harness. This was done by the waggon masters—each of whom was responsible for thirty teams—taking them on to the prairie, there filling the waggons with sand, starting off for fifteen or twenty miles full gallop, pulling up short, forming a corral, getting out their dinner, eating, jumping up, and starting off home again. In this way the mules, after a few lessons, became quite tractable and gentle.

My principal amusement was to go out with these parties and see the fun. I took great delight in tearing over the prairies in this harum-scarum manner, and never saw a team yet that could go too fast for me. At times there was more sport than we wanted, for a whole train of teams would stampede and tear off madly, upsetting and smashing waggons, and killing mules, whilst some of the leaders would break away from the harness and run for miles before they could be recovered.

At length everything was in readiness, and we 'broke" camp and started on our long journey. It had been an exceedingly wet season; the prairies were deluged with water, and as the ground was very soft we made but slow progress. For the first three days we only succeeded in getting about half the waggons a distance of four miles, the others remaining in camp. By degrees we moved them up through mud and slush knee-deep, and, finally reaching more solid ground, made our weary way through Kansas into Nebraska, crossing *en route* several streams greatly swollen by the rain. At some of the larger streams we had to give in, and sit down and wait until the waters subsided.

We went on in this way until we arrived at the South Platte River by the old Californian crossing. Here our real troubles commenced. What with the melted snow from the mountains and the swollen river, it was impossible to get across in the usual way. We waited several days, but instead of receding the flood rose higher. Our ammunition was packed in zinc waggon-boxes made expressly for the purpose, and these were ferried across on rafts. The waggon-boxes we caulked to prevent leakage, then propped them up on blocks to keep them from floating off the running gear, put twenty-four mules to each waggon, and swam them over. In this way we got over the South Platte River, after drowning several mules and two men.

At Fort Kearney we passed through Dog Town. The provost had nothing to say this time. The poor old Robbers' Roost had again changed hands, and become quite respectable. The gambling saloon had disappeared; the fort had turned its guns on it, with the intimation that if it did not close in a few hours, it and its occupants would be blown into a better land. In its stead a comfortable hotel had sprung up, and, cruellest of blows to me, had changed its name.

Twenty-two miles from the South Platte we struck the North Platte at Ash Hollow, and had to lower the waggons down the mountain side, which is there nearly perpendicular, for a quarter of a mile. This was more easy than crossing the river.

Everything after this went on well, until the whole command received a shock which nearly scared it out of its wits. One of the zinc ammunition boxes, presumably by the jolting, exploded one of the cartridges. The case contained over a thousand, and these went popping off, one after the other, until all were expended. There was some consternation whilst this was going on. The shots were flying out in all directions, amidst

yells, shrieks, and execrations. The waggon-master had the presence of mind to gallop his team out into the prairie, whilst the entire outfit made for the best cover it could find. The officers tried hard to get some one to go into the waggon and drag out the case, but no one would. The driver, who was wonderfully plucky, kept his team well in hand and never moved, knowing all the time he was sitting on a magazine which might blow him to pieces at any moment. When it was all over we went out to him, but the strain had been so great on the poor fellow's nerves that he was mad. He was called the Lightning Torpedo Man after that; but although he subsequently recovered he was always more or less silly.

Nothing farther of special interest occurred until we arrived at a long valley, at the extremity of which Hams Fork is situated. There, to our dismay, we found the Mormons had entrenched themselves on the side of the mountains. Not only had they built breast-works of rock, but in the cañons they had constructed dams in which an immense quantity of water was stored, so that on once lifting the sluice gates sufficient water would pour down to drown every man of the expedition and wash us clean out of the hills.

General Johnson, however, was too wary to run headlong into the trap that had been prepared for him. He ordered the command to effect a flank movement and drove the Mormons over the hills into the city of Salt Lake.

On sending out scouting parties it was discovered that the enemy had fortified every coign of vantage so strongly that it was impossible for us to attempt to get into the valley without reinforcements. We had to settle down, pitch our camp for the winter, and wait until they came out from the States in the following spring.

We selected a fertile little valley, well wooded and intersected by a mountain stream, out of the way of danger. Then, pitching our tents, we made ourselves as comfortable as circumstances would permit. The cold weather soon came on apace, and with it the snow, which, at first settling on the mountains, rapidly moved down to the valleys and enveloped us.

After a while our supply of provisions began to run low, and an expected train of commissariat waggons was looked for eagerly. These were much overdue, and great anxiety was manifested at their non-appearance. No one thought that any harm could possibly happen to them. There were ninety waggons of provisions expected, each drawn by six yoke of oxen.

At length, one day our scouts returned with the dreadful news that all had been lost. The Mormons had been too clever for us. Crossing the mountains to the south-east of us, they worked round to our rear, and, intercepting the convoy on the way, captured and destroyed everything, burning the waggons and stores, and driving off the stock.

This was a terrible blow, for there was nothing but starvation before us. Mr. Lot Smith was the gentleman who was the hero of this episode, and we vowed a vengeance upon him which he would not have forgotten if he had fallen into our clutches.

How we managed to exist during those cold and long winter months is a matter of American history. Our rations were again and again reduced until there was absolutely nothing left to cut down. Over and over again I have seen the men steal the small ration of corn for their horses and greedily eat it, and when the poor starved beasts in their turn would succumb, their riders feasted off their bones, picking them as clean as would a mountain wolf.

An end, however, to our troubles came at last, in the shape of the long-expected reinforcements, and in the spring of 1858 we boldly pushed through the cañon I had returned by on the occasion of my previous visit and marched upon the city.

No opposition was offered to our approach, and luckily for us, for had there been we should never have got in. The cañon in parts is only wide enough to permit a single mule team to pass at a time, and the Mormons, if they had wished, could have crushed us by throwing pieces of rock down, as well as drowning us out by their sluices. The Rocky Mountains at this point present one of the best natural-fortified positions in the world, and I firmly believe the Mormons could, if they had chosen, have held it against all the troops the United States Government could have brought against them.

The few of the enemy we did see fled from us like wild turkey.

Arrived at the city, looking very different from what it had when I saw it last, we were, by a divine inspiration on the part of the General, not permitted to enter. Well it was, for we afterwards learned that the Latter

Day Saints had laid mines in each house, connecting them in such a way that at a given signal we should all have been blown to pieces. This was lucky escape number two. Our instructions were to move on to Rush Valley, forty miles south-east of Salt Lake, where we established Camp Floyd.

All the Mormons by this time had disappeared. We drew the country far and wide, but could not find one. As soon, however, as they saw that we meant permanently settling in our camp, by building a fort and houses, they came back to the city, and an understanding was come to between the chiefs and the General, with the result that peace was proclaimed. Following this was an official announcement for grain and hay to be sent in for the horses. We used to take from fifty to one hundred teams, and go to the small towns round about to procure grain in the form of barley, oats, wheat, or anything we could get hold of. This was precisely what the Mormons wanted, for, in addition to finding a market for their produce, this put money into circulation.

After we had been established a few weeks, hundreds of the saints, who had apostatised, came flocking to our standard, begging us to get them out of the country. This the Government of protection did, sending thousands away, providing transportation and protection for them to California. Without this protection they never would have been able to leave Utah, for a vendetta was sworn against all apostates, and any that were caught were made away with by the Destroying Angels and their followers.

CHAPTER XV.

THE MOUNTAIN MEADOW MASSACRE—ARRIVAL ON THE SCENE.—
DISCOVERY OF THE SOLE SURVIVOR—RETURN TO CAMP FLOYD—
LIFE IN DOBIE TOWN—A DISAGREEABLE ADVENTURE—A FIRST
WHITE LIFE—TRACKS FOR PROVO CITY.

THESE were exciting times for many of us. I succeeded in becoming duly installed as a Government waggon-master, with a large number of the teams under my command. Besides other duties I was called upon to perform, one was to go to the scene of the Mountain Meadow Massacre with a party of troops and bury the bodies of the victims.

The scene of this butchery was about eighty miles south of Camp Floyd, on the Californian route, and the massacre was one of the greatest blots upon the Mormon persuasion.

The circumstances were briefly as follows.

A party of wealthy emigrants left California for the States, and returned with their wives and friends. The caravan was a particularly rich one, and carried luxuries and delicacies that only the rich could afford. The Mormons allowed them to proceed through Salt Lake City unmolested, but, desirous of possessing themselves of their chattels, and also of paying off a score with the emigrants, who had scoffed at them whilst in the city, they sent down word to John D. Lee, who was the bishop of the district through which they had to pass, to slaughter them all, men, women, and children, and not to spare a single life.

This was done by Lee's followers disguising themselves as Indians, and attacking the caravan at the spot indicated. There was a small stream here, about sixty yards from the place where the emigrants had corralled at the first signal of alarm.

The sham Indians rushed upon them, but were driven off. They, however, took up a position guarding the approach to the stream, and cut off all communication

with it. In this way, as days went on, and the emigrants became in want of water and went out singly for it, they were shot down by the Mormons.

Girls, and even children, were sent out with pitchers,

but they all met the same fate; the Mormons, secreted behind the rocks, shot all who approached. In this way they killed every one, and eventually became the possessors of the caravan.

Our mission was, in addition to burying the bodies, to chastise the Mormons for their cruelty, and the troops required no inducement to do this. They had not forgotten the capture of our provision trains, and many were the deep anathemas hurled at the unrelenting scoundrels as we made for the scene of action.

Arrived there, the most horrible spectacle imaginable met our gaze. There were skeletons all over the place shining in the sun, picked as clean as ivory by the vultures and wolves. Many were lying in the few yards' space that separated the ashes of the corral from the water-course. Beside them were their pails and other articles for carrying water, showing how they had fallen. Here and there, hanging on the sage brush, were tresses of women's hair, and bones were scattered about wherever the wolves had gnawed them.

The soldiers were much overcome at the sight, and many brave men shed tears as they stooped to pick up all that remained of their fellow creatures. Every trace of a human being that we could find we reverently buried, and then retraced our steps homeward, making a slight détour of between seven and eight miles to call at a Mormon settlement which we had been told was in the vicinity.

There we went to the principal house in the place

The village was deserted by the men, who had all fled, not caring to settle scores with us. Indeed, from the time we left Salt Lake we had not come across a male Mormon of any description.

In the stables of this house we found several fine carriages and horses, quite out of keeping with the surroundings. These at once excited our suspicions. The women that we saw were also dressed in silks and satins, and wearing these garments as ordinary day clothing. The house we ascertained belonged to John D. Lee, the bishop of the district.

No one would give any information; the women knew nothing, and flatly refused to answer any of our queries. We determined not to be done, and orders were given that every house in the place should be thoroughly searched. Whilst doing this we found a child in one of them, a pretty fair-haired little thing of about three years of age. Her hair hung in ringlets down her back, and she was both bright and intelligent, of a breed not to be expected amongst the class of people who inhabited the place.

She was brought to me, and I took her to the officer commanding the expedition. He put her on his knee and began playing with her. We thought as we could get nothing out of the women we would try the child.

After a time she became very talkative, and we romped about with her, crawling over the floor and amusing her to the best of our ability. When her confidence was thoroughly obtained we led her on with questions, so that when one of the elegantly dressed women was brought in, she pointed at her and said, "That my mamma's frock," pointing to the dress that the woman was then wearing. Then she said, "Naughty Indians come and kill mamma, papa, and aunty." This was conclusive proof that we had found the perpetrators of the outrage, and it was as much as the officers could do to prevent the men from lynching every woman in the village.

We camped there for the night, hoping to get hold of some of the men, and the following day scoured the country round in search of them, but unsuccessfully. Then we reluctantly resumed our journey, taking some of the women with us and the child.

The child was the only one saved out of the hundred or more constituting the caravan. If she is alive now, she will doubtless remember me should she ever read this book, for she was placed under my charge, and I brought her into Salt Lake City and handed her over to the General.

John D. Lee was caught some five years later, and executed for this and other murders.

Returning to Camp Floyd I resumed my duties as a teamster, until one day a paymaster came out with a lot of specie and gave us all eighteen months' arrears of pay. The sensation of having so much money all at once was too much for me, and I suddenly developed a great distaste for my occupation.

Just outside the camp there had sprung up a small

town called Dobie Town, from the dobies or sun-dried bricks of which the houses were built.

A young teamster named Louis and myself decided to try our luck there. We sent in our resignations, and started, bought a shanty, and opened it as a whiskey-saloon. I was always very partial to making as much money as I could with a minimum of labour, and with the experience of the Robbers' Roost fresh in my mind, I knew this was an easy way to set about it.

There were plenty of cut-throats, gamblers, and thieves there who supported us, and as the troops also favoured us with their patronage, we saw before long that we were in for a very good thing. I believe we should have made a fortune if we had only stayed, but my unlucky star was always in the ascendant, and something invariably happened which snatched the prize from me just as it was within my grasp. This time it occurred very unexpectedly. One night, as I was taking a stroll down the street for a little fresh air, I passed an opposition gambling hell of very bad reputation.

I just peeped in through the window to see how they were getting on. There I saw two men with their bowie knives drawn, standing over a man who was stretched on the floor. I thought to myself, "Hallo, here's a murder. I am better out of this," and I walked away quickly. I was only a few yards past the door when one of the men came running after me, and inquired what business I had to look in at his window. I apologised, and said I was only looking for a friend.

He then called me all the names he could think of, and said he would teach me better manners, winding up by making straight at me with his knife, and expressing a determination to have my heart's blood.

I didn't want any row with him, and started off running as fast as I could. He, however, was the quicker of the two, and finding him gaining on me rapidly, I drew my six-shooter, and called back to him to stop, or I would shoot him. At the same time I stopped and tried to dodge him.

He would not listen, and made a dart forward, but I slipped out of his way, and fired a shot in the air to let him know that I was capable of defending myself.

This seemed to enrage him the more, for he now came at me with his knife like a bull at a gate.

I thought, " Well, you'll soon make mincemeat of me if I don't stop you." So

taking aim I planted him one in the " bread basket," which caused him to pull up very quickly.

He threw up his hands and fell backwards with a groan.

I told him I was not to blame; that he would have killed me if I had not protected myself; and as I saw some people coming who had heard the shots, I bolted off to my place as quickly as I could.

There I told my partner in a few words what had occurred, and cleared out without a moment's delay.

In those days the settlement of these matters was usually decided by the majority. I did not know what friends he had, but a glance told me that the one or two in my place at the time would be no assistance to me. I therefore thought discretion the better part of valour, and the sooner I " got " the better.

Starting out in the dark, I tramped off and made tracks for Provo City, a Mormon town up the Jordan River, and arrived there in a couple of days, footsore and weary.

In a few days I received a message to say that the man was dead, and that his demise was not regretted. I was also informed that I was thoroughly exonerated, and a universal desire expressed that I should return. This invitation, however, I declined, on the ground that if I returned I should probably have to kill some of his friends, who would try to avenge his death, or should get killed myself. The law of six-shooters was the only one then in existence, and revolvers were called into requisition to settle all matters in dispute.

CHAPTER XVI.

MEETING WITH DANIEL SPENCER—BULL-WHACKING TO CALIFORNIA—DISAGREEMENTS IN THE OUTFIT—SEVERANCE FROM THE PARTY—FIVE HUNDRED MILES ON FOOT—SCARING A CARAVAN—FALLEN AMONGST THE UTES—A PAINTED MORMON RENEGADE—STARTED AGAIN—ARRIVAL AT BEAL RIVER.

THE Government supply trains that had been coming into the country in abundance had for some time past been drawn by cattle, as the supply of mules was exhausted. These cattle were not worth sending back to the States, and were therefore offered for sale in Utah.

The spring of 1859 had now set in, and the prospect of fine warm weather opening up, made a Californian named Daniel Spencer, whom I got to know in Provo City, hit upon the expedient of purchasing a large number of these beasts for transport to San Francisco as beef.

The Government preferred to sell them in large batches, and he purchased 3,000. Having done this his next move was to search round for bull-whackers to drive them over.

Besides others he asked me to join him. I was willing enough to go, but did not feel disposed to leave my young partner Louis in charge of the whiskey store at Dobie. So I wrote to Louis telling him my intention, asking him to sell the place for the best price he could, and to join me as soon as possible.

I knew this trip would just fit in with his ideas, for he had an uncle in Frisco, whom for some time past he had been very anxious to join.

Accordingly he sold up everything that belonged to us, and came over and joined me. I took him to Spencer, who engaged him in the same capacity as myself, at a salary of twenty-five dollars per month, and everything found.

Twenty-five men were engaged. All of them had been in the Government service as teamsters, and all received the same pay, with the exception of the foreman, a young man, and a perfect gentleman in every respect. I do not know what he got, but my impression always was that he had some interest in the speculation.

We started from Provo Cañon, where the cattle were herded, and proceeded comfortably on our journey for some few days. We were twenty-seven all told, and my first impression was that we should have a pleasant time, indeed a sort of picnic, for all the men were good fellows, and I knew many of them.

As we got further from Utah, however, and well on the Californian trail, Daniel Spencer began to show himself in his true colours. He was the meanest man I think I ever met. Even the old Frenchman Hal and I had traded for at Laramie was not to be compared with him.

We could hardly get sufficient stores served out to us, and we lived almost as badly as during the famine on Hams Fork.

We complained over and over again, but were only met with overbearing observations and abuse. Spencer also developed another unexpected trait, thrashing such of the men as answered him back. The result of this was that some of the outfit left him, and returned with parties we met on the road bound from California to Utah.

Up to this time he had never said a word to me, for I had not given him cause; besides, I worked very hard, and was a bit of a favourite with the young foreman.

Rows were frequent, and the men kept returning, until, by the time we arrived at the gravelly ford of the Humboldt River, there were only eight whackers left, and they were obliged to work day and night to keep the stock together.

We had now covered about 500 miles of our journey, and I was wondering what the next stretch would be like, when, as my luck would have it again, Spencer fell foul of me. I never knew why.

I had stood guard two nights in succession, and worked during the day as well. Coming into camp soon after daylight, hoping to get a little sleep, I met him, and he ordered me to return to the herd until breakfast time.

I said I could not. I was tired out, and should be able to do no more work until I had a couple of hours' rest. I could scarcely keep my eyes open.

He said if I did not go he would make me, and came towards me with his whip.

I drew my pistol, and levelled it at his head. I should have blown his brains out at the first lash.

Just then the foreman rushed between us and said, "Mr. Spencer, your conduct towards your men has been disgraceful. This man has done his duty like a man, and now you are endeavouring to impose on him as you have upon the others. Now I want this stopped. You have only eight men left, and if you don't mend your ways you'll die with your boots on, for the men won't stand your abuse any longer."

Spencer had also drawn his six-shooter by this time, and I was watching his every movement, so as to be ready to get in the first shot.

The foreman made him put up his pistol, and I turned round and saw Louis with his rifle fully cocked, resting on a waggon wheel. Said he, "Go in, Pard, I'm here!"

Then I went down to the waggon, got out my rifle, returned to Spencer, and told him I wished for a settlement, requesting him to pay me for the time I had worked.

He said he would not pay me a cent.

"Very well," I replied, "I shall have to pay myself, and I give you notice of my intention. I shall follow you, and stampede your stock, and see if I can recover what is due to me in that way."

He flew into a violent rage, that necessitated the foreman again stepping in between us. The latter said it was only right I should be paid for my services, that I had worked honestly and well, and because we chose to quarrel that was no reason I should not receive what was my due up to the moment of the disagreement.

With a bad grace Spencer fished out some thirty dollars. These I put in my belt, tied my hair bridle round my neck, fixed up my shot pouch, slung my rifle over my shoulder, and prepared to start back.

I first went over to the boys, shook hands with them all, and told them I was going back to Salt Lake City. Louis said he did not want to return to Utah, and would submit to anything so long as he could join his uncle in California.

"That's all right," I replied. "You go on, my boy; I have no uncle waiting for me, and it matters little where I go as long as I get away from that man."

Spencer here came over to the crowd, and said to me—

"What are you going to do, Nelson? You are surely not fool enough to think of returning alone, and on foot?"

"Yes, I am," I replied.

"But," he continued, "the Pi-Ute Indians are very numerous between here and Salt Lake City, and you have a good 550 miles to cover. It is madness; besides, we are half way on our journey. Come, be reasonable, put down your gun, and go back to your work."

"Mr. Spencer," I said, "if you have completed your sermon, allow me to have the floor for a moment. I consider you the most unreasonable man I have ever met. You do not know what it is to have good men about you until you lose them. I am going to prove to you that I am one of those good men, and, mark my words, you will miss me before I have been gone many hours. It is far better for us to part now. Your temper is a little too hasty for me, and I know what mine is." This I said cocking my eye down the barrel of my rifle.

"Very well," he answered. "I shall have nothing more to say to you beyond this. I shall give you no food to take on your journey."

"Oh, that won't hurt me," I said; "what the eye doesn't see the stomach doesn't miss. Good-bye, boys," I shouted, as I waved my hat, and stepped out with a terrible craving for breakfast which his last words had suddenly awakened.

After covering about five miles I could stand it no longer, so I shot a jack rabbit which came skipping across my path. Then I made a fire out of the sage brush, skinned and roasted him. Refreshed with a drink of water from a stream I again continued my journey, buoyed up with the reflection that I was at least independent and monarch of all I surveyed.

In this way I travelled for three days, living on rabbits, birds, and anything that came within easy range of my gun. My progress had been pretty lively, as I had been making the best time I could by running and walking, or rather sprinting, the whole time.

Suddenly, as I was urging on my wild career, and rounding a huge boulder of rock, I came upon a party of emigrants corralled.

They were running in all directions, women and children screaming, dogs barking, some of the men on the top of the waggons, some underneath, and two in front of the corral with their rifles cocked and pointed at me.

"Good morning, strangers," I said, taking off my hat, and making them a polite bow. "You seem in a rather excited state. What's up?"

"Just you stop where you are," was the reply, "or we'll blow your blessed brains out."

"Thank you," I rejoined, "your kind offer is quite unnecessary, although I appreciate it all the same. Will you oblige me by telling your captain that a gentleman would like to speak to him?"

In a few minutes a good-looking squatter came out with his rifle at the present, and made straight up to me.

I stood where I was, leaning on my gun, and posing in as artistic a manner as the circumstance of the two fellows with their rifles still levelled at me would permit, apart from the fact that those on and below the waggons had now armed themselves, and were covering me at all points.

"Stranger," I shouted, "I am a friend. Tell your pards to put up their guns; surely it does not require fifty of you to shoot at one poor devil lost on the prairie."

"Who are you, and what do you want?" he inquired.

I told him in a few words, and he invited me into the corral. "If you'll give me something to eat," I said, "I shall be eternally grateful to you."

"You have come at the wrong time to get any food," they replied, "for we have just been attacked by the Utes, and expect them again every moment."

"I think you must be mistaken," I said. "I know the Indians you mean. We camped here six days ago, and they did not interfere with us. What have you been doing to them?"

"Nothing," they replied. "Two of our men went down to the stream to get water, and had a lot of arrows shot at them."

"Oh, that's nothing," I said; "that's only their playfulness. But since you are all a bit scared I woud advise you to get along on your journey as quickly as you can. Any way, Utes are nasty vermin and very treacherous, and the sooner you put a few miles between yourselves and them the better it will be for your stock. You are right on their camping ground here, and perhaps they don't like it. They are not likely to follow you. I'll go down and talk to them, and that'll give you an opportunity of getting a good start."

They tried hard to dissuade me from my project, and offered to take me through to California free of charge if I would stay with them.

I thanked them for their offer, but said I had business in Salt Lake City, and must get on there.

I was again told I was a fool and would be killed. They gave me a drink of whiskey and a biscuit, and I wished them good-day and went on, whilst they whipped up their teams and started off as if the devil himself was after them.

I made my way straight down to the stream. When the Indians saw me coming all alone, they came out of the high cane-like rushes, which

were very tall there, and stood right in my path. I still went unconcernedly on until I got up to them, when one of them, a tremendously tall fellow, asked me in broken English where I was going, and if I was a Mormon.

"Yes, I am a Mormon," I replied, "and I am going home to Salt Lake City."

"What ward do you live in?"

"No. 15, just below the Court-house."

I saw at a glance that he was a white man, although he was painted, and guessed he was one of the fanatical renegade-destroying angels, whose mission was to kill every white man not belonging to the sect, and particularly those who were apostates.

He motioned me to follow him, and I followed. He led the way through the thick cane into a clearing where they had cut the cane down and made it into tépees resembling huge sheaves of corn piled up. On the outside of these, the children had dug holes in the ground. In these holes they were crouched like prairie dogs.

We entered one of the tépees and sat down on a bear-skin. A squaw came in with some boiled venison, and cake made out of grasshoppers, a favourite food of the Indians, made by pounding the insects up and mixing with deer fat; the mixture is made into rolls and dried, when it is ready for use.

The Ute squaws I observed were very primitive in their costume, wearing nothing but a girdle round the loins, made of the skin of ground moles. These were very pretty in colour, some being black, some yellow, and some white.

After finishing my repast, I was put through my facings, and had to answer innumerable questions, all of which I did apparently to my interlocutor's satisfaction. He did not let out much himself, and I took good care not to let him suppose I could see through him. It was as much as I could do not to laugh at his attempts to keep up the conversation in broken English and by signs. No Indian that I ever saw, be he Pawnee, Cheyenne, Sioux, or Ute, had a "mug" like he had; and as for his nose, it was raised in Kentucky, or my name is not Nelson. My opinion was that he had been driven out of the Mormon community for some crime, and had found refuge with these Utes, who numbered from fifty to sixty all told. I explained how I had quarrelled with the cattle party, and was on my way back. He said I had better stay with him until a party came along the other way, as I had a long journey before me and it was not safe to go alone.

I replied that I preferred to get along, and that I was anxious to get back to my wives. It might be months before I could strike a party coming from California, and whilst I was waiting I was earning no money for the support of those I loved so dearly. In fact, I pitched such a yarn, that, desperado as he was, it had a visible effect upon him.

Finally, he said that he admired me for my good qualities, and would not detain me. So, calling one of his squaws, he made her pack me up some food to take by the way, and wished me good-bye. I started once more on my journey.

I sauntered leisurely along until I was well clear of the cane brake, and then I started off at a run, which I kept up until I had placed a good twenty miles between Mr. White Chief of the Utes and his band of murdering rascals. I was not quite satisfied in my mind whether he might not repent of his leniency, and suddenly develop a craving for my gun, pistols, and ammunition. As to his followers, my hair, which was long and wavy, offered an attraction which made all their mouths water whilst I was in the camp.

Whether they ever started after me or not, I do not know. I kept on my erratic course for six days and nights, and eventually reached a small Mormon settlement of some ten or fifteen houses on the Bear River. I put up at a ranche, and stayed there a week, as my legs were so stiff and swollen, I could hardly move. In fact, the morning after my arrival I tried to get up, but could not. I had covered the distance in pretty good time, considering the country I had passed through, and, reckoning it over three hundred miles, had done on an average about sixty miles a day.

CHAPTER XVII.

MEETING WITH BILLY CAMERON—RETURN TO SALT LAKE CITY—INTRODUCTION TO JOSHUA ALPIN—HUNTING FOR WORK—PONY EXPRESS TO WINTY VALLEY—"A NARROW SQUEAK"—CONVERSION TO MORMONISM—BRIGHAM YOUNG AGAIN—BROTHER NATHANIEL JONES—APPOINTMENT AS MAJOR DOMO.

HILST I was resting at the ranche I made the acquaintance of a man named Billy Cameron, who had married the daughter of Joshua Alpin, a Mormon priest.

I got along very well with Cameron. He would come into the ranche and sit and talk to me whilst I was lying on my back.

When I told him I was going to Salt Lake City, he said his father-in-law lived there. If I liked he would give me a letter of introduction to him, and I could stay there a week whilst I had a look round to find something to do.

I said I was much obliged to him, and he gave me the letter as soon as I was able to move. I started off with it to see what luck had in store for me this time in the modern Jerusalem.

The distance to Salt Lake City from Bear River was some sixty miles, and this I tramped in easy stages. I had had quite enough of trying to break records against time, and I hobbled along as comfortably as circumstances would permit. It took me three days to do this journey, and when I did arrive I was as fit as a fiddle.

I easily found old Josh Alpin, presented my letter, and was well received. The old man and his wife appeared good kind people, and asked me to stay and make myself comfortable until I got fixed up. They had emigrated from Texas some years previously. He was a very staunch Mormon, and a very prominent member of the church.

I did not wish to be a burden upon these people, so I offered to pay for my board, but they would not allow this. Then I said I would avail myself of their hospitality for a week.

I found my quarters very comfortable, and determined to stay there; but as they would not allow me to pay anything, I hit upon a plan to get even with them.

The old man was very fond of tobacco, so I kept him well supplied with this. Beef was a luxury they could not afford; I would go to the butcher's and order some. With this and other things, although I was not a paying boarder, I squared the old people in a roundabout way.

It was a much more difficult matter to obtain work than I anticipated. There were so many men in the city like myself, discharged from the Government service, that directly anything offered there were twenty ready to jump into it. I fooled around for several weeks waiting for something to turn up, but somehow it never did.

During this time old Joshua was always preaching to me, and trying to convert me to Mormonisn. He said I could never expect to get along in the world and prosper so long as I lived in darkness and unbelief.

I told him what Two Buck Elk said about the Great Spirit feeding the birds and the buffaloes, and said I guessed, no matter what I believed in, I should always get enough to eat.

He seemed to take the same view that I did when I first heard Two Buck Elk say this, and pointed out that a man did not live to eat alone, that he had another mission to fulfil—to become prosperous, till the soil, fructify the earth, and a whole lot of other things, which, boiled down, were reduced to my becoming a Mormon straight away. He told me that if I did he would ensure me more work than I could do, in a light, easy way, and that my life would be one of perpetual happiness and bliss.

"Well, Joshua," I said, "I will think it over and let you know when I have fully made up my mind one way or the other." I resolved inwardly that as long as I had a dollar left I would be independent of the Mormon crew, whom I heartily despised.

There seemed a prospect of luck turning with me at last. One day I fell across A. B. Miller, the superintendent of the Pony Express Agency, then running to California. He told me that the Pi-Ute Indians had broken out along the route, and had scared his two riders, who were the half-breed sons of a Captain Egan, by telling them that if they came through their country again they would be killed. So there was no one to take the mail. Miller was under a penalty of one thousand dollars fine every time it was not carried through to the next station in Winty Valley, 115 miles distant. Every one he asked to go laughed at him, and suggested his carrying it himself. At length he offered me 250 dollars to take it and bring the mail waiting at Winty back.

I asked him what use the money would be to me if I was killed.

He said he did not think the Indians really meant killing, and that probably they would not molest me, as their difference was merely with the half-breeds.

Finally I consented to have one try, if only to show the other boys that I had more pluck than they.

Every one said I should never come back, but I laughed at them and said I should probably never be missed if I did not.

Miller fixed me up on a good horse, and I started off, and in due course arrived at the station. This I found in ruins and still smouldering. The Indians had killed the postmaster, burnt him and the house, stolen all the stock, and cleared out.

I didn't wait there long after making this discovery but just took the trail back, not allowing any grass to grow under my feet *en route*.

As I was passing through some small cedars on the side of a mountain, I

came across an Indian standing in some bushes by the side of the road, waiting for whoever should pass with the mail.

When I was opposite to him my horse smelt him, and jumped on one side. It was very dark at the time, and all I saw was the flash of his rifle as he fired. It was a narrow squeak for me, as the bullet cut off a lock of my hair and passed clean through my hat.

I made through the bush and down towards a stream not more than thirty-five feet wide, but very deep, and with very steep banks.

A bridge had been built across this, but a party of

the Indians were guarding it, and fired at me. So I turned sharp to the left and went up the stream. When I reached the bank I plunged my spurs into the horse and he jumped half-way across. Down we went into deep water, where I stuck on and reached the opposite bank in safety. Here I jumped off, and taking the bridle tried to get the horse up the bank. He understood exactly the position we were in, and made a desperate effort to get up, and succeeded.

I remounted, and away we went. We had covered about three hundred yards when, all at once, the faithful animal reeled and fell dead. Whether he had been shot or had broken a blood-vessel I did not wait to see. I seized the saddle-pockets, threw them across my shoulders, and made straight into the bush.

How I got through that night I do not know. I heard the Indians yelling after me, and it was twenty miles to Salt Lake City. I reached it at last as completely done up as I had ever been in my life.

The following day a party of fifty men went out to rebuild the station, but it was no good. The Pony Express business had to be stopped, and I was the last man that made an effort to run it up in that district.

When I showed Miller my hat and where my missing curl had been, he laughed and said, "A close call for you, old boy."

This was all I received for risking my life to Winty Valley. As I had not succeeded in bringing back the other mail I was not entitled to my two hundred and fifty dollars.

The days and weeks rolled on, and still nothing turned up. The winter was setting in, and I knew it was no use going east until the spring. At last old Joshua Alpin said that if I would let him baptize me he would ensure me a steady job for three years.

One Nathaniel Jones was about to be sent on a special mission to England, and my duty would be to take charge of his establishment during his absence.

I knew Jones by reputation as a very well-to-do man, with a nice house. He was a sort of high priest in the emigration department of the Mormon Government.

I thought I might just as well have the billet as be kicking up my heels all the winter doing nothing, and if my getting it depended upon my being baptized, I might just as well go through that tomfoolery as not.

Accordingly I went to old Joshua and told him I had at last seen the error of my ways, and was quite prepared to join the Army of the Lord.

The old man and his wife were delighted, and it was decided that I should be received into the Church the following morning.

At sunrise he and I started off alone down to a tanyard a short distance from the house. No one else was present. The ceremony was a very brief one.

We found, let into the ground, a tank containing about one hundred gallons of water. Into this we jumped hand-in-hand, with our clothes on. I remember that jump. The water was bitterly cold, and came up to our chests. Then he said some prayers over me, dipped my head under the water, and christened me Brother Nelson. In five minutes it was all over, and I came out a full-blown, shivering Mormon. We made our way up to the house, wrung out our clothes, dried them at the fire, and sat down to breakfast. My name was duly entered in a book and sent to the bishop of the ward, who in turn sent it on to head-quarters.

I went to the tabernacle two or three times a week and twice on Sundays. I was introduced to Nathaniel Jones, and put on the devout accordingly, playing up to my new position as a sober, steady, God-fearing young man. Personally I did not care a rap about Mormonism, but I was cute enough not to do anything that would jeopardise my getting the billet I had almost caught my death of cold for.

I must candidly confess I saw nothing repulsive or bad in the Mormon religion. The only thing I objected to was polygamy—and I was not particularly squeamish about that, considering my experience with my own squaws. But what can be tolerated in an Indian cannot in a white woman—at least, that was the view I took of it.

I found the Mormons, as a rule, a hard-working class of people, who thought they were doing right. They had been gulled by a few smart men like Brigham Young, Joseph Smith, Heber C. Kimball, Joseph Young and his brother, Daniel Wells, and a number of others, who feathered their nests by fattening on their poor deluded followers.

Brigham Young was certainly the smartest man I ever saw. If he had been President of the United States instead of Utah, his name would have been handed down for generations; but, like a good many others, he fell short of what he aimed it.

I have heard him preach more than fifty times, and I must do him the justice to say he did not go in for hell and damnation, as many of the other priests did. His creed was simply—Be kind, good, and just to all mankind; take plenty of wives, multiply and replenish the earth. Teach this to your children, who will be the only children of God. We are the Latter Day Saints. Our salvation is ensured.

Out of the tabernacle Brigham was a very sociable and convivial fellow. He was very pleased to see me again and to hear that I had at last entered the Church. He reminded me that ten years of my life had been wasted, and that if I had taken his advice and done so when at Laramie I might have occupied by this time a high position under him, like many of the early pioneers.

He next inquired what had brought me to Salt Lake City again, and I told him I had come with the troops, and that immediately upon my arrival I had seen the error of my ways, and hastened to receive absolution upon the first opportunity. I further said that during the ten long years we had been separated I had wished over and over again to be received into

the Church, and that now it had happened I was just as happy as I had before been miserable.

He was pleased to see that my eyes had at length been opened, and he knew when he first met me on the Platte that sooner or later I should be received into the fold. The Great Book said they were to increase and multiply and replenish the earth, and he hoped I would settle down and take many wives, and so carry out its precepts.

I said that was just what I intended, directly I had decided what I was going to do.

He replied that he would recommend me highly to Brother Nathaniel Jones, and that I might consider myself already appointed. Then he introduced me to his daughter Luna, and invited me to come to his house as frequently as I chose. This I did, and all the ensuing winter was there pretty often. I became a great favourite with his wives, and by them was introduced to all the best families in the place. Luna and I were great friends, and in all the dances that were given I was either her partner or dancing in the same set with her and her father.

Old priest Alpin set to work and fixed up the agreement with Brother Nathaniel Jones. I was to act as his major-domo, having full charge of his establishment, his cattle, his wives, and everything that was his, for which my pay was to be forty dollars a month and everything found. This agreement was to extend over three years. Directly this was signed by Brother Nathaniel and myself, he packed up his traps and started off on his mission, whilst I was duly installed in my new position as the friend of the husbandless and the protector of rank and beauty.

The night Brother Jones departed, I was initiated into my duties by old Joshua's wife who pointed out to me that as long as I made myself popular and preserved harmony, my life would be one gigantic holiday. I knew, or was getting to know, all the best people, amongst whom Brother Jones's wives moved, and all that was requisite to land me into the high road to fortune was to be active, industrious, and attentive to Brother Nathaniel's interests. Then I would be looked after by those in high office, who would see that my next position was one that would bring me better fortune.

I promised to be good and do everything I could for the welfare and comfort of my fair charges, and was accordingly taken round and introduced to them, with some amount of pomp and solemnity.

CHAPTER XVIII.

LIFE IN A MORMON HOME—SISTER ANNIE—REBECCA'S JEALOUSY—A SISTERLY "MILL"—BROTHER WILLIAM GODBY TO THE RESCUE—PEACE AGAIN—TREACHEROUS INDICATIONS—A DÉNOUEMENT—A REFUGE WITH GODBY—AN UNLUCKY INCIDENT—PETE DOTSON—FAREWELL TO SALT LAKE CITY.

BROTHER JONES' house stood in a two-acre square block. It was a substantial-looking building, two floors in height, and built very much in the shape of the letter L. The stables adjoined the house, and in front was a garden, and a large paddock at the rear. Brother Nathaniel had three wives. No. 1, the eldest, was named Rebecca; she was a woman of about forty-five to fifty, and had two daughters aged sixteen and fourteen years respectively. Sister Rebecca was not what I should call an unamiable woman. She appeared to me to be jolly enough, but with a sad weariness about her; whether it arose from her connection with Brother Jones or from Mormonism generally I never ascertained. She had her quarters at what might be termed the top part of the letter L.

Her daughters, who were fine-built, strong, healthy girls, were relegated to the second floor of the house, and had the whole run of it. One of Brigham Young's wives was teacher to these girls.

Wife No. 2 was named Sister Mary; she was a tall, thin woman, about twenty-four, with brown hair, blue eyes, and a pale complexion. She had one child about a year old. Her apartments were situated mid-way along the downstroke of the letter.

The third, Sister Annie, was a young English girl of eighteen, who had only just come out to Salt Lake, and was married to Brother Nathaniel but five weeks before his departure. She lived at the apex of the angle.

My quarters were at the extreme end of the letter, and consisted of several rooms. Beyond my part of the building the stables and outhouses were situated.

Each wife, it will be seen, had her separate apartments, but all were connected by a passage running right through the house.

The domestic arrangements were worked on the following principle.

Each wife would run the establishment for a week.

We had no servants, and had to do everything for ourselves.

The wife who was in office for the week would give me the list of things she required, which I would order in. No matter what she wanted, she could have it by applying to me.

At the end of the week I collected all the bills, and took them to Brother William Godby, priest and druggist, who acted as Brother Jones's banker. He gave me the money to pay the accounts, and I handed him the receipts.

I commenced with the old lady, and we got along capitally. Everything she wanted she had, and the old girl seemed to quite cheer up. I took the head of the table, in accordance with Brother Jones's parting instructions; for we all grubbed in the rooms of the wife who was in power for the week; and I kept her in a good temper by telling her lots of stories she had never heard before. I felt before the first week was over that I was going to be pretty popular with the ladies.

My work for the first few weeks was getting in wood for the winter supply. There was a mule team, a waggon, and a buggy in the stable, and I had to look after and feed the mules. Taking my team in the morning, I started off and cut down a load of wood, brought it home about one o'clock, had dinner, and then was ready with the mules to drive the ladies out in the buggy. This was quite a neat turn-out, and the way in which I whipped the mules up and made them spin through the streets was the envy and admiration of all the Mormons in the city.

Every day we started out and paid visits, usually winding up with a dance, of which my ladies were passionately fond, and came home by midnight. Frequently the dances were given at our place.

"Brother Nelson" was quite an institution at these gatherings. I dressed myself up well, and played my part admirably. I was always very sanctimonious when in company.

I got on very well with all three wives, who loved me like a brother. I laid myself out for having a high old time—and I had it.

Sister Annie was my favourite. My quarters were close to hers, and I suppose that is how it was I saw more of her than the others. This girl was, as I have said, only eighteen years old. She was of medium height, an alabaster complexion, jet black curly hair, and black eyes. I had never seen anything like it before, nor have I since. Perhaps her beauty had a greater effect on me then than it would have now. Any way, I fell desperately in love with her, and she had a strong attachment for me.

This was not to be wondered at. I was a young man in the prime of life, and I flatter myself not unpleasing in appearance. My spirits were always buoyant, and so were Sister Annie's, whilst Rebecca wandered about as if she had lost a dollar and was hunting for it. Sister Mary was soured and cross, and rarely, if ever, smiled, and she had her baby to attend to.

I was pretty full of fun, and kept the whole household in a state of high spirits as well as I could. In fact, I think I honestly earned my pay in this respect.

I was in the height of my enjoyment, and hoping that Brother Jones would get drowned on his trip back from England when the time came for him to return, or that something would happen to prevent his coming back and claiming Annie. One day, whilst Sister Mary was running the house, old Rebecca flew

into a rage, and said something to Annie at dinner-time which, whatever truth there might have been in it, I felt pretty certain she could not prove

I said, "Sister Rebecca, you should not make any such remark about your sister Annie; I think it very unkind of you, and I am sure if Brother Jones were here he would be very angry." Putting on my most sanctimonious air, I continued, "And I consider these reflections upon your dear sister most unjustifiable and exceedingly improper." Whatever my peroration might have been, it was suddenly interrupted by Annie, who, giving me a look brimful of affection, jumped up and flew at Sister Rebecca with both hands.

I sat watching the progress of events for a few moments. Then, thinking that Brother Jones intended me to be lord and master during his absence, I grabbed at them both, calling upon Sister Mary to help me to part them. After a long struggle we succeeded in doing this, but not before Sister Rebecca had lost a portion of her curls and two or three of her front teeth.

I was apparently most virtuously indignant at all this, but chuckling inwardly at Rebecca's discomfiture. I saw that the only thing to be done was to put on a bold front and brazen things out. I went off immediately to our guide, philosopher, friend, and spiritual adviser, Brother William Godby, and giving him a moral, well-varnished description of the occurrence, protested my inability to live with my charges peaceably in the Lord until the devil, which suddenly had seized Sister Rebecca, had been cast out from her. Sister Annie, I explained, was as innocent and harmless as a dove, in no way to blame, and what she had done was only in self-defence. Finally, I begged the old druggist to come over with me and prescribe for Sister Rebecca, and see what could be done to cure her.

Rebecca had about four hours praying with him right off, and had to swallow about a dozen bottles of nasty-smelling, green-looking medicine, which the old man told me in confidence would quiet her nerves.

Whether it was the preaching or medicine that did it, I do not know, but things were apparently set right, and we went on for a few weeks as harmoniously as before. But I was always on my guard, and took good care not to be caught napping. At length I discovered that Sisters Rebecca and Mary had formed an alliance, and were both on the watch to catch Sister Annie and myself together. This was not good enough for me. I didn't mind having one woman to fight against, but the two of them, assisted, for all I knew, by the two daughters of Rebecca, were more than I could stand. I knew that probably I should be hanged, have my throat cut, or be made away with in some way or another if I was caught, so I went straight to Sister Rebecca and said to her:

"Sister, you are very silly to act in this way. Here you are, an old woman with two grown-up daughters, and you are jealous of me because I have joked and played about with your sister Annie, who is, after all, only a girl, two years older than your eldest daughter. You ought to know better. I am surprised at you. I have tried my best to make all your lives happy since I have been here, and you only repay me by trying to do me the greatest injury in your power. I have determined to punish you for it, and I shall do so by leaving you; and when I have gone you will see what a mistake you have made. I cannot afford to lose my reputation by allowing myself to be watched as you and Sister Mary are watching me. If you had left me alone all would have been well, and nobody any the wiser. Now I shall have to tell everybody it is on account of your bad temper that I am obliged to leave. You will find that my successor, whoever he may be, will not take the interest in you I have done."

She was very much upset when she saw I meant business, and cried a good deal, swearing she loved me and I must not go.

I said, "Yes, I have loved you like a brother should, and Sister Mary also."

With the latter I had a similar scene, but she went into hysterics and kicked about so that I had to call in Sister Rebecca, who threw a pitcher of water over her and brought her round.

But the worst parting of all was with Sister Annie; she, poor girl, cried her eyes out, and I thought her heart would break. She got into a corner and sobbed for hours. I tried to console her all I could, and told her it was better for us both that we should part.

Finally I packed up my things, and absolutely had to tear myself away from the house, thankful I had got out of it with a whole skin.

If the explanations I had heard had only been made to me before, I should have known how to act. But even then it would have been most difficult to have favoured one without giving offence to the others. No man was ever placed in a more embarrassing position than I was with these three women, and I am sure the most sensible thing I could do was to clear out.

I went straight over to old Godby and told him that it was impossible for me to remain any longer with Sister Rebecca in the house. She was little or no better, and grumbled and quarrelled at everything I did. She made her other sisters miserable; I could succeed in pleasing them, but felt that if I were to remain there a hundred years I should never do anything to satisfy her. So I had come to the conclusion that life was far too short for me to waste it in the effort. In conclusion I considered myself a grossly ill-used personage, and rather than give Sister Rebecca the opportunity of saying that I paid more attention to her sisters and her daughters than I did to her, I had left the house and come over to report myself.

Brother Godby expressed his sorrow at my determination, and said he had the greatest faith in my integrity; I was not to worry myself on that score. Indeed, he thought so much of me that he would like me to come and run his house for him in the same way that I had been doing Brother Jones's. Godby was so busily occupied in building some houses, he had not time to attend to his home as he liked until his building operations were completed. I said I had no objection, and was accordingly installed as a sort of steward.

The old man had five wives, and they were all young, the eldest being only twenty-six, and the youngest sixteen. This establishment was run in precisely the same way as Brother Jones's, each wife taking her week as it came round, when we all boarded with her.

I must say I never saw any one get along with five women so well as old Godby. I never heard a cross word between any of them during the whole four months I was there. I set about my work and never paid any attention to any of them. Brother William always had his eye upon me, and was watching me all over the place. It was out of the frying-pan into the fire so far as the watching was concerned, and this worried me. At times when I thought the old fellow was looking after his building, he would turn up in the most out-of-the-way places about the house, where I believe he had been hiding for hours on purpose to catch me. I was, however, always on the alert, and no one could have steered a more honourable and straightforward course than I did. Once bit, I thought, twice shy. Things were going on so comfortably at old Papa Godby's, as I called him, that I believe I should have lived there for years, or until the old man died, and then perhaps have married all his wives myself, had not my unlucky star again shone out just when it was not wanted.

A Gentile hotel had been started in the city, and one of the waitresses was a good-looking English girl to whom I was very partial; we used to go out together and compare notes about the Mormons. I never told her that I was one—in fact, I swore I hated them as heartily as she herself did; but one Sunday night we had been out walking, and wandered into a man's garden, where we got larking about. He sneaked out and caught us, and, recognising me, reported me to Brother Godby.

This was a fine thing for my reputation. Here was I, a psalm-singing goody-goody young Mormon, bowled out at one go. Away went my good character, and I stood revealed in all my bare iniquity. I thought to myself, John, my boy, you had better seek some more congenial atmosphere before anything more is found out about you. Accordingly I cast round to find somebody who was going anywhere, or doing anything, whom I might accompany and so get away from the city.

This I knew was no easy matter, for apostates were well looked after by the destroying angels, and few who signified their intention of leaving got away safely, unless under a Government escort. Many men, women, and children have been butchered trying to escape from the Mormon Hell, and yet the murders could never be traced to any individuals. I knew, though, who were the moving spirits, and these were Porter Rockwell, who knew me well, Bill Hickman and his son, All Huntington, Lot Huntington, J. C. Luice, and others. I was therefore not anxious for it to get wind that I intended making tracks.

At length I fell across a man named Pete Dotson, an old freighter, who was loading thirty-three waggons with flour to take to Denver. This it appeared was the very first consignment of flour that had ever left Salt Lake City, and as it was the pioneer trip of what afterwards became a great trade, it occasioned some little interest at the time.

I engaged with this man as assistant waggon-master, and agreed to join his outfit when it was one day out from the city. He was to keep dark and not tell any one that he had engaged me.

I looked unconcernedly on when the train took its departure, and with a lot more Mormons wished it good luck and a safe journey across the mountains.

Then I returned to Brother Godby's, and spent an anxious day and night. I was not by any means in favour now, and where all before had been smiles, I met with nothing but frowns. Even the nice little wives turned up their noses at me.

Long before daybreak the following morning I was up, and, bidding a mental adieu to everything around me, I started off as hard as I could go after the caravan. I met one or two people I knew in the city, who asked me where I was going in such a hurry, and I told them I was carrying some medicine from Brother Godby's to some one sick.

Arrived at the mouth of Echo Cañon, I stopped for a moment to take breath, and there, as solemnly as I had taken it up, I laid Mormonism down for ever. I had

had quite enough of that to last me my lifetime. Turning round and taking a final look at the city where I had had as much fun as most men, I put on the steam and doubled through the cañon as fast as my legs would carry me.

CHAPTER XIX.

NEMESIS, OR THE DESTROYING ANGELS—ENEMIES IN THE CAMP—A DISCOVERY—A SURPRISE—THE PRISONERS AND THEIR SENTENCE—ANOTHER BEAR STORY—ST. VERAIN'S FORT—A BIG DRUNK—ARRIVAL AT DENVER—A GOOD RESOLUTION—TRACKS FOR CIVILISATION—A PASSENGER FOR OMAHA—TEAMSTERING AGAIN—ILL-LUCK ONCE MORE—A RAVING MANIAC—DEATH OF THE MULE—UNDER ARREST—ESCAPE—THE "WAGGON BOSS" SHOT—SWIMMING THE PLATTE RIVER—ARRIVAL AT JOHN YOUNG'S RANCH.

ABOUT half way through the cañon, that is about twelve miles from its mouth, I overtook my friends. They had corralled for the night, and were just getting under way when I reached them. I was quite ready for breakfast after my long run, and a bit tired, so I crept into a waggon and remained there for the greater part of the day.

This I thought was discretion. For two whole days I was scared out of my wits for fear some of the destroying angels should get wind of my departure, and follow and kill me in order to save my soul—that was their way of putting it when any one apostatized and left the valley. However, I was on the look-out, and determined to sell my life dearly.

Our party numbered thirty-three, all of whom we thought were Gentiles anxious to get away from Utah. Actually there were three Mormons amongst them, cattle thieves, who had joined for the purpose of stealing our stock. I did not know them, nor did they know me. They were working in connection with some confederates who were following us at a safe distance. We had hard work getting over the mountains, and were pretty tired out when night came. Whilst stretched out under the waggons resting, the second night we were out, I overheard a conversation between these three men, that put me on the alert and disclosed the whole conspiracy.

The arrangement was that whilst they were on guard at night their companions were to come and take the cattle off in small bands, so that we should imagine they had strayed. A signal, given during the day, was to communicate when the three would be on guard, so that the plan could be carried out.

I told five of my best men what I had discovered, and we decided to send a runner on to Salt Lake City to hurry up Pete Dotson. He had stayed behind to bring on more cattle which were not quite ready when the train started.

We went on for two more days, as I was anxious to put as much distance as possible between the city and ourselves before I did anything. Then I gave instructions that the three men were to go on guard that night. We turned in as if we expected nothing, but I put on a double guard over the waggons, so that they could not rob the train.

About one o'clock in the morning I and my five men loaded our rifles and double-shot guns, and crept out to where the Mormon guard were, and watched them. They had evidently signalled their companions, for we saw four men ride down to the cattle, select eight or nine, and drive them off.

I said, "Ready! fire!" and all six guns went off at once. Owing to the darkness and the distance we did not kill any of the men, but we shot one of their horses and wounded one of themselves. This man we captured and he let out the whole secret.

Our three men we put under arrest until Dotson arrived the following morning. Then we tried them, and sentenced them to work for nothing all the way to Denver. They were to be deprived of all arms, and either of them touching a weapon, or attempting to escape, was to be instantly shot.

The man we had wounded we thought would die. We managed to keep him alive for two or three days, and then sent him back by a party we met bound to Salt Lake City.

It was the 15th of October when we left Salt Lake City, and in the mountains the winter had fairly set in; the snow was so heavy in places that we had to work for hours to shovel it away in order to find the trail.

We at length arrived on the banks of the North Platte River, and camped there. The stock were feeding on the mountain-side, and two Danes of our outfit were herding them. One of the Danes had a small shot gun for killing sage hens for supper.

Whilst he was wandering around with one eye on the stock and the other on the birds he came suddenly upon a grizzly bear, and in his fright fired at him. The small shot only stung the bear, who made for him.

I looked up, hearing the report, and saw what was happening. The Dane stood perfectly still; the bear walked up, hugged him lightly, and then laid him down and covered him with leaves and sticks. After this he went down to a pool of water and had a drink, preparatory to feeding off our Dane.

I got my rifle, and with two or three of the men went after Mr. Bruin. We could not help our man in any way; it had all happened so quickly. We knew we could do him no good, and all we wanted now was to kill the bear.

We found him enjoying himself by the pool, and promptly put a few bullets into him, which settled his hugging for ever.

Then we dug up the man, who, strange to say, was alive. We carried him into camp, gave him some whiskey internally, and rubbed him all over with it externally. On the following day he was able to sit up, and in a week he was well and able to go about his work again. I thought every rib in his body must have been broken, but whether he was of a particularly wiry build or not I can't say. Anyhow we looked upon him as a perfect marvel, for if any man ought to have died he ought.

Game was very plentiful in this part of the country, and we had a good time generally whenever it came within range.

Some twenty-five miles before Denver is St. Verain's Fort. This we reached in safety, and encamped for the night.

Here some of the teamsters stole a couple of sides of bacon and some sugar and coffee from the store, and traded them for whisky with a French Canadian living there. A great drunk ensued as a natural consequence, and a corresponding row in the camp when it was discovered. Pistols were going off all over the place, but when we swept up the pieces in the morning nobody was found killed.

It was early in December that we arrived in Denver, which then only consisted of about 100 log shanties of the worst possible description. The place had only just sprung into existence, and was the head-quarters of the miners who were coming out to the Rocky Mountains prospecting. They were a pretty hard lot there. I thought I had seen a few rough customers, but these beat anything I had yet come across.

Putting up at the best-looking hut in the place—the Denver Hotel—I lit my pipe and sat down to consider what my next move would be. I had some 1,500 dollars with me, about the largest sum I had as yet possessed that I could call all my own. As I was perfectly indifferent what became of it, I turned several schemes over in my mind, and finally hit upon one. I would go down to Charleston and see my parents, if they were still alive. From the day I had left my uncle's to the present moment I had heard nothing of any of my family.

This project I thought a most laudable one, and I lost no time in putting it into execution.

First I went to a Jew ready-made clothes store, and bought two complete suits of modern cloth garments, boots, and so forth. My costume hitherto had consisted of buckskins and moccasins. Next I laid out some money in buffalo robes for my mother, a buckskin suit, beaded, for my father, and other presents for such of my relatives as I could remember. For myself I purchased a fine gold watch, which subsequently turned out to be brass. I gave 75 dollars for it.

My hair, which was hanging in long ringlets down my back, I had well brushed and oiled, and my beard trimmed. Putting on my new rig, out I sauntered down the street in tight boots, which were most uncomfortable at first, fancying myself as neat-looking a chap as any of them. I hunted round to find the most expeditious means of striking the Missouri River.

This I did by falling across a man named Bill Martin, who had come up with a train load of provisions. He had disposed of them, and was starting back to Omaha for a fresh supply. His empty waggons he was filling up with a load of passengers, each of whom he charged 25 dollars, board included.

There was just room for one more when I appeared on the scene; so I promptly paid my fare, went back to the hotel, secured my treasures, put them on board the waggon, and the caravan started.

There were thirty waggons in all, and we made very good progress as far as the South Platte River, at the junction, close to the military crossing. Here one of the teamsters was discharged for drunkenness, and Bill Martin tried hard to replace him from amongst the passengers. The weather, however, was so frightfully cold that none would volunteer. At last, as it was a question of the waggon going on or remaining behind, I took the job, upon the understanding that the 25 dollars I had paid should be refunded me, and I should receive 25 more when we arrived in Omaha.

Accordingly I took the ribbons, and we frisked along swimmingly.

There were lots of ranches springing up by the road, and whenever we could get into one to sleep we did. The settlers charged us a quarter of a dollar a head. We brought our own blankets, and slept on the floor, or wherever we could find room, as long as we could get under a roof and protected from the cold and snow.

AN IMMERSION

Two of us slept in each waggon—very poor shelter when in the open—and we always tried our best to corrall for the night close to any shanty, however humble, that we might come across.

One day I felt very unwell; the cold had affected me internally, and I could not drive my team. I got my "bunkey," or travelling companion, to drive for me, and went on myself in another waggon in which was a small portable stove. We were about half a mile ahead of my waggon, when some one came on to us with the news that my "bunkey" had stopped at a small dobbie house, and left the team at the door whilst he went in to take a drink. The mules, thinking they might as well do the same, strayed down to the river close by, dragged the waggon on to the ice, and the whole outfit fell in.

Ill as I was, I scrambled out and went back. I found the mules and waggon in about four feet of water, and apparently firmly wedged in the ice.

Setting to work with all the assistance available, I got them out at last, but got wet through myself. Nothing would then do but that I must take a drink.

I said I did not wish for anything, but the men said I must, and should drink with them, and they got larking about and trying to pour the whiskey down my throat.

At length I said, "If you'll stop this fooling I will drink with you." One of them handed me a tin mug full of liquid, and I drank it at a draught.

Whether it was the weak state I was in or not, I do not know, but that one drink did it. I went as mad as any lunatic on the face of the earth. I knew perfectly well what I was doing, but could not restrain myself from doing it.

We stayed at this dobbie house for about three hours, by which time it was quite dark, and then had to put on the steam to overtake the rest of the caravan. The men who were with me were all drunk.

I tried hard to get the team along, but the more I tried, the slower they seemed to go. Whether it was the standing in water so long had affected them, or standing about afterwards, I do not know. I remember, after we had been quite a long time on the road, coming to a hill. We were half-way up this when the waggon came to a halt. I coaxed and whipped and swore at the team, but could not move them. My companions in the waggon were all sound asleep, oblivious of everything that was going on. Finally I thought, as the mules would not go for the whip, I would prod them with my knife. So I crawled down on to the back of one, and reached over to give her a dig. Whether I slipped or struck too hard I do not know. I remember the knife slipping in right up to the hilt, and the mule fell dead on the spot, the blood spurting up like a fountain. I put my hands on it and tried to stop it, till I got smothered with it.

I thought, "Here's a pretty go. It is useless attempting to go on." I could not drag the dead animal away from the traces, and as to my companions all I could get from them was a drunken grunt when I tried to rouse them.

Leaving the waggon standing in the road, I made my way to where the outfit had corralled, and was questioned as to what had become of my team. I said I had killed them, and, as my appearance denoted something had happened, parties were sent back along the road to see what it was. I was grabbed: my pistols were taken away from me; I was thrown into an outhouse and safely locked up, and a guard with a loaded rifle stationed outside the door.

I don't know how I passed the night. I have a dim recollection of swearing that I would kill everybody in the outfit, and as I was generally looked upon as a man of my word they knew better than to come too near me.

The following morning, when I had sobered down a little, I was let out, after promising to be good and not injure any one, but at the same time I was given to understand that I should be handed over to the authorities, for killing the mule, when we arrived at Kearney.

This preyed upon my mind, and I took another drink to drown my sorrow. I had not really recovered from the effects of the previous day's libations, and this additional stimulant started me off again.

I first went to Miller and asked him what he valued his mule at, and said I would pay for it. He said that he would take no payment, that the "boys" had offered him 200 dollars, which he had refused, and he was determined to hand me over to justice for the wanton cruelty of which I had been guilty.

I said I was mad and did not know what I was doing.

He replied that I should be put somewhere where I

would not have a chance of getting mad again for some time to come.

I made up my mind I would not be taken alive, and I accordingly went to some of the boys and told them I meant stepping it. My "bunkey" got my pistols, and, handing them to me, promised he would look after my belongings and deliver them to me in Omaha, where I arranged to meet him.

Wishing good-bye to the few of my friends who happened to be there, I started off down the road, determined to hide anywhere out of the way until the caravan had passed on.

I had not gone far when the waggon boss came running after me, and said, "No, you don't! You're my prisoner, and I mean to keep you and hand you over to justice, as I told you."

"All right," I replied; "if I'm your prisoner you'd better make me so. Here I am; take me if you can."

He pulled out a Smith and Weston pistol and said he would shoot me if I moved a step.

I looked at the tiny weapon, laughed, and told him to go on shooting. That popgun wouldn't hurt me.

At this he commenced firing. He emptied all his barrels at me, but never hit me.

Just then a big Jew Dutchman, one of the passengers, came running towards us with a pitchfork in his hand. This gave the "boss" a little more courage, and he said, "Now if you don't surrender at once I'll kill you."

I laughed at him again, and said, " If you don't get out of this I'll kill *you*."

He made a grab at me, and I pulled out one of my pistols, shot him through the shoulder, and he fell.

The Jew dropped his pitchfork and bolted back to the camp as hard as he could run. I knew it was no use staying there, as I should have the whole outfit after me, so I started off running down to the river, intending to get across on the ice. When I got on to it, however, I found it would not bear me, and in I went.

The river here is about a mile wide, with only deep water here and there. Breaking the ice as I went, and swimming and wading as necessity arose, I at length reached the opposite side, thoroughly exhausted. After a few minutes' rest I again started off to run. It was bitterly cold and blowing terribly. My clothes were soon frozen upon me, but still I kept on; how I lived through it I cannot understand.

At length, after covering forty miles, I arrived at a ranch, just opposite Fort Kearney, kept by a man named John Young, and he took me in. I told him everything, and he promised to secrete me until I had a chance of getting away. I promised to pay him well for it, and as an earnest of my intentions gave him a twenty-dollar gold piece and my buckskin vest. He lent me some dry clothes, and fixed me up as comfortably as he could.

CHAPTER XX.

A LUCKY MEETING—EN ROUTE FOR OMAHA—TRACKED BY THE DUTCHMAN—A SCENE WITH THE COACH—OMAHA AT LAST—OLD FARMER KEATS—ARRIVAL OF THE CARAVAN—MEETING WITH THE "WAGGON BOSS"—ROBBED BY A "BUNKEY"—LIFE AT KEATS'S RANCH—CORD-WOOD CHOPPING AT FLORANCE—TEAMSTERING TO FORT DESMOINES—LOADING WITH FLOUR FOR DENVER—FROM TEAMSTERING TO HUNTING—BUCKSKIN JO'S GULCH—A HUNT FOR A JOB—CONTRACTING FOR VENISON—"HOLD! ENOUGH!"—GAMBLING FORSAKEN—RETURN TO THE "GLORY HOLE."

N the third day I was with John Young a small waggon came along with three men in it and stopped at the ranch. I slipped into a cupboard to make myself scarce until they had gone, as I always did when anybody hove in sight. Whilst in hiding I thought I recognized the voice of one of the men, and the more I listened the more I was convinced that it belonged to some one I knew, although I could not put a name to him. At length my curiosity got the better of my discretion, and I kicked at the door until they let me out. Then I discovered the two men were teamsters I had known in Salt Lake City.

They were surprised to see me locked up in this way, and asked what was up. I gave them an account of my woes, and they said they would take me along with them (they had come from Salt Lake,  and were bound through to Iowa), and would drop me at Omaha if I liked. I said I would like it very much; that was just what I wanted; so bidding good-bye to John Young, I got into their waggon, which with its stove was very comfortable, and away we went.

My friends told me they had crossed the river at Kearney. The river there was only knee-deep. They had heard of my escapade at the Fort, and that my late outfit was lying up there for a few days until the snow was over.

The third day we were out, the coach from Kearney to Omaha overtook us, and seated on it was the Jew

Dutchman who had come after me with the pitchfork. He could not see me, as I was lying inside the waggon and peeping through a hole in the canvas. The coach drove up alongside our team, and the Jew shouted to my friend who was driving—

"Say! Have you seen anything of a man going down the road on foot?" and he added a description of myself. My friend replied, "Yes, we saw him."

By this time I had buckled on a pair of pistols, and, getting up, I crept to the front of the waggon and answered him myself. The coach was full of passengers, amongst whom were several women.

I said, "Here I am, Mr. Jew Dutchy. What do you want with me?"

"I have been deputed to follow you and arrest you."

"I am sorry to hear it, but I suppose you'll have to do your duty." Saying this I got out of the waggon and into the road, pulling out both my six-shooters and cocking them. Then I said, "Come down and take me."

He made a move to get off the coach. To do this he had to turn his back upon me. I let him get down on to the front wheel, and I said, "My friend, I think you've gone far enough; you'd better stop where you are."

The driver shouted to him, "Look out!"

He turned his head over his shoulder and looked down the barrels of both my pistols, which I presented at him.

In the twinkling of an eye he was on the top of the coach again.

The women inside began screaming.

"Ladies," I said, "don't be alarmed. I shan't hurt you. My reckoning is with the lanky Dutch Jew on the roof."

"I shall catch you in Omaha," he said, "and settle with you there."

"All right," I replied. "If you catch me in Omaha you'll never want to catch me again. I give you this advice, as I don't want to hurt you."

The coach drove on, and that was the last I ever saw of this amiable gentleman.

About a week afterwards we arrived at our destination, and put up at an hotel, where we stayed two days and had a "high old time." At the end of it my friends continued their journey and I stayed behind.

All my good resolutions about going home were now thoroughly dissipated, and I determined to wait on the quiet until the caravan arrived, when I could see my "bunkey" and get back my things.

Whilst in the hotel I had made friends with an old farmer named Keats, whose ranch was about six miles from Omaha, on the plains, and he asked me out to stay with him. The house was on the highroad, and all vehicles coming from Kearney had to pass it.

About the tenth day they came along. We let them pass, and then hitched up a spring waggon and drove into town after them, taking good care not to overtake them on the road.

I was walking down the main street with the farmer, when who should we meet coming towards us but the "waggon boss" I had shot. I walked straight up to him, and, to my surprise, he smiled and said—

"Well, John, how are you?"

I had my eye upon him, expecting he wanted to take a shot at me in return.

I said, "You shouldn't have shot at me, and I wouldn't have done that," pointing to his arm, which he had in a sling.

He replied, "I expect a good deal of it was my own fault. I never intended to shoot you, only to frighten you, and I didn't know you had a pistol; you only did what I myself should probably have done. I have heard all about the cause of the trouble, and you were not to blame so much as I thought. The men told me how the one drink maddened you. Your shot nearly settled me, however, and I have been suffering great pain. The doctor tells me I shall be all right before long. I don't bear you any malice. Come in and have a drink, which I hope will do neither of us any harm."

This behaviour almost took my breath away, and he, I, and the old farmer went in and had a long chat. I enquired after my " bunkey," and heard he had gone off with my things directly the caravan arrived, ostensibly to find me and hand them over to me. When I left the " waggon boss" I left him as a friend. We never quarrelled afterwards, and whenever we met always had a drink together and chatted over the little affair. I tried all I could to find my " bunkey," but failed. He had skipped across the river into Iowa with about 500 dollars of my money, all my new clothes, and other property. I never heard anything more of him from that day to this.

I stayed a month with old farmer Keats and his family of grown-up sons and six daughters, of whom the youngest was 15. We amused ourselves pretty well at the ranch, and gave three dances a week, to which all the people living around were invited, and I paid the bills.

My money soon gave out at this; and then I went up to Florance, a few miles above Omaha, whence the Mormons had first started. There I started chopping cord-wood at $2\frac{1}{2}$ dollars a cord. A cord consists of pieces of timber cut and split into 4-feet lengths, piled in a heap 4 feet high and 4 feet long. The most I could do was a cord and a half a day. This occupation was a great come-down from my late millionaire method of living, and after six weeks of it I gave it up as too hard work.

One day down in Omaha I met a man with five or six bull teams who wanted to hire some teamsters. He was going into Iowa, to Fort Desmoines, some 160 miles distant, to buy flour to take to Denver and sell to the miners who were working on Pike's Peak, Buckskin Jo's Gulch, &c. He offered me 20 dollars a month and my board, and I settled with him. There were four teamsters besides myself, who were paid; and about a dozen other men, who had been chopping wood as I had, and wanted to get up to the mines. These men received no pay, but simply rations for their services.

We went to Fort Desmoines, filled up with the flour, and returned to Omaha, where we picked up the helpers and the "boss's" wife and started off on our journey.

Everything went along very satisfactorily this journey We crossed the Platte River by a ferry at Platte Mouth, and getting on to the plains, found game very plentiful.

I said to the "boss" one day, "Lend me your rifle" (my late bunkey had stolen mine), "and I'll go out and shoot an antelope."

He said, " I don't believe you've ever seen an antelope, much less killed one."

"Well," I replied, "I guess I can kill one if I can only see him."

He laughed, and said it was a waste of powder and shot, but as I was a good teamster he would humour me by lending me the gun and a few rounds of ammunition if it pleased me and I promised not to hurt myself.

I thought this a good joke, but I did not say anything. Anyway I went out, and, much to their surprise came staggering back to camp with an antelope on my back.

· After that I did no more team-driving, but was appointed huntsman to the outfit, whom I kept supplied with meat for the rest of the journey. The "boss" lent

me a horse, and I had a fine time out on the plains, enjoying my old life, of which no one knew anything, for I kept my own counsel and never said a word as to who I was or what I had been.

Denver was reached at last, and no sale for the flour being found there, as was expected, we took the outfit up to Buckskin Jo's Gulch, about six days' journey and right up in the mountains. Here the "boss" built a house, which he turned into a store and boarding-house. I stayed until everything was snug and comfortable, and then started up the gulch to try my luck at gold-hunting.

The place was pretty full of all the blackguards in creation, there on the same racket. I expected to find gold hanging on trees from what I had heard of it and from what I had seen in the gambling saloons at night, where the miners came in with bags full of nuggets, which they gambled away as if they were so many lumps of stone. In my sweet innocence I thought all I had to do was to go and pick it up. When I got right into the gulch, however, I was wofully undeceived.

I just marched up to a place where they were working in a mine. Probably sixty-five men were there. I enquired for the " boss," and asked if he wanted any hands.

He said no, he didn't.

I went to several others, but all were full up.

At length I walked up to the head of the gulch, where I found a man sitting on a rock, watching some fellows hauling quartz down a mountain by means of bullock-hide boxes slung on a rope. I said to the man—

" Are you the 'boss' of this digging?"

" I guess I am."

" Do you want a man?"

" I don't know. What can you do?"

" A little of everything."

" Well, I want a couple of men.'

"What to do?"

Pointing up the hill, he said, "To pull down the quartz."

I looked up the hill at the fellows working, and noticed that they took one step up and fell back two when pulling up the empty hide boxes. The hill was about the steepest I had ever seen and almost perpendicular, with footholds cut in it that seemed as upright as a ladder.

"How much do you pay a day for that kind of work?"

"Two and a half dollars."

"Thank you. Good day. That's not good enough for me," and I retraced my steps to my friend the storekeeper's.

He enquired if I had found any work, and I said, "None that suited me." Then I made him a proposal that I would supply his boarding-house with wild meat of any kind at 10 cents per lb., provided he sold me his old rifle for 4 dollars. The stock had been broken off and patched on again with raw hide, but I had shot with it and knew how to use it.

He agreed, and the following day I started off on my first trip as a trader huntsman. I was on foot, and had gone about a mile, when a black-tail deer jumped up, and I killed him. He weighed 140 lbs., and I carried him in on my back.

Every day I went out, and I killed more than I could carry. My friend lent me a mule to transport the carcasses. In this way I used to bring in from three to six deer a day, until at length the supply was greater than the demand.

My friend then went to the only butcher in the place, and arranged with him that he should take as many as could be supplied at a price of five cents in excess of my contract price.

This was good news for me, and in a week I had them both crying out, " Hold! Enough!"

Venison became quite a glut in the place and every one was feasting on it.

I was making on an average over 20 dollars a day, and found my occupation more congenial than pulling hide boxes up the hill.

At night I went and gambled all my earnings away. Sometimes I won, but very rarely. When there was too much meat in stock I took a rest for a few days, as I did not want to make either of my customers take more than they could get rid of.

Finally they said they could not take more than 130 lbs. a day. That was all they could sell, and I was not to bring in any more.

I determined to give up gambling and save my money until I had enough to go down to Denver and embark in something else. This I religiously adhered to, and when I had saved 300 dollars I gave up hunting, bade my friends adieu, and slinging my rifle over my shoulder tramped down to the Glory Hole.

CHAPTER XXI.

DESPERADOES IN DENVER—"THE ROCKY MOUNTAIN NEWS"—A SCENE AT THE DENVER HALL—A RESOLUTION TO QUIT—ACKLEY'S RANCH—ENGAGEMENT AS BAR-TENDER AND FACTOTUM—PINING FOR FREEDOM—COTTON-WOOD SPRINGS AGAIN—AT BILLY HILL'S—FIRST MEETING WITH DAN SLADE—THE STORY OF JULE BERG—A CLOSE SHAVE—A BRAVE BRITISHER—DEATH OF BILLY HILL—TRACKS FROM THE RANCH.

ENVER at this time was "red hot." It was full of gambling hells and grog shops, and a lively place for murders. There was no law there but that of the sixshooter, and the man who had killed the most of his fellows was counted the best among them.

I went to a boarding-house and lived on my means. As I could find no work likely to suit me, I passed the time in hanging around, at Pike's Peak principally, where I saw a lot of fellows hanged and shot. It was a common thing to find four or five swinging of a morning. At Denver this was particularly the case, especially on Cherry Bridge, which crosses the creek of that name. The marauders were made to mount the hand rail, to which a rope had been fixed, and the noose being slipped over their necks they jumped or were pushed into eternity.

The Vigilance Committee were answerable for this. They were a body of peaceful miners who took the law into their own hands to

protect themselves. All the store-keepers were in this organisation, formed to put down the lawlessness of the desperadoes, who were getting the upper hand and doing as they pleased.

During the time I was knocking round I saw over 150 of these gentry despatched. The others took warning and left. It is impossible to conceive a greater set of scoundrels and villains congregated together in one place than were here at this time. They were, however, taught a lesson in the end which brought them to their senses.

A newspaper, the first that had appeared, "The Rocky Mountain News," was started whilst I was in Denver. The first number was full of scathing articles against the gamblers and blacklegs generally: in fact, the paper was run in the interest of the Vigilance Committee and law and order. The composing offices were in a log shanty, and the printers had to set the type with their six-shooters and double-barrelled guns lying on the benches beside them. I saw three of these men killed whilst they were peacefully carrying on their work.

The editor's name was Byers, and I knew him well. He never showed outside his door whilst these articles were appearing. The rowdies were always on the lookout for him, and directly he made any movement to leave his house half a dozen bullets would bury themselves in the woodwork. He stood this state of siege until the Vigilance Committee succeeded in clearing out the gang, when he became a great man in the town, very wealthy, and a State senator.

A row I got into there will show the state of lawlessness that then prevailed.

I happened one night to go into the Denver Hall, the largest gambling saloon in the place. It was pretty full at the time, and most of those present were drunk. I was not gambling myself, and just walked round to have a look at the various games. Suddenly a disturbance occurred about the centre table in the room. A pistol was fired, and a man fell off his chair dead. This resulted in a free fight. The doors were locked, lights blown out, and general shooting commenced. Bottles and tumblers were flying in all directions. I got into a corner, thinking I would not take any part in the fight, but I got a glass tumbler in my eye, which knocked me senseless for about five minutes.

When I regained consciousness the bullets were whizzing about me in all directions. Thinking it about time to have a look in, I yelled out, "Deal me a hand, boys!"

It was pitch dark, and whenever any one spoke or made any movement the others would shoot in the direction from which the sound proceeded. Directly I spoke six or seven pistols went off at once, the bullets striking the wall just over my head and on each side of my body.

I laid down under a large bench near, and every time I heard a shot, I fired in the direction whence it came.

We kept this up for over a quarter of an hour, when the people outside burst in the door. Immediately there was a stampede for the street. Some did not even try to go out by the door, but smashed the windows with chairs and got through them.

I lay where I was till the crowd had cleared off a little. Then I groped my way out as well as I could and as the blood pouring from my face would permit me. I lost no time in making my way to a drug store, where my wound was dressed; then I got some people to lead me home to my boarding-house. During the night I made up my mind that Denver was no place for me, and I determined to clear out of it at the first opportunity that offered.

In this fight seventeen men were killed, and thirty-five were wounded. The row commenced over a game of monte. One man lost his money, and began shooting the oil lamps out, in doing which he killed a man opposite him, and then the fight commenced.

It was more than a week before I could get the bandages taken from my eyes and move about. After three days' enquiry I fell in with a party who had brought up provisions from Omaha and were returning for a fresh supply. With these people I paid my way as a passenger to Omaha. Of the two places the latter was preferable. I was not very particular what I did or where I went, but I felt that any chance I might have was not to be found in Denver and its district.

We got as far as the Platte River, about nine miles above the old California crossing, and put up at a sort of hotel and store, kept by a man named Ackley and known as Ackley's Ranch. These places had sprung up all along the road, and were havens of refuge for caravans at night time, especially in the winter months.

I got chatting with Ackley the night we arrived, and he asked me if I would stay and help him run the establishment. I was willing enough, so he engaged me at forty dollars a month. The next morning the others continued their journey, and I started on my new duties.

The house was of sod, with wooden windows, and roofed with pine poles covered with turf and mud. There were three rooms: the bar, about 20 feet by 16, which contained the stores and the liquor; a sleeping-room, about 16 feet square; and the kitchen and dining-room, about the same size. We had stabling for 125 horses, and a corral behind the building which would hold sixty waggons and included

a hayrick and granary. On one side of the corral was a long shed, in which the emigrants slept, and cooked their meals at a stove fitted up for the purpose.

My business was to look after the emigrants, show them where their quarters were, and sell them whatever grain and hay they wanted. Any spare time I filled in behind the bar, mixing and dispensing the drinks for one and all who came along.

This was in 1862. The Indians at this time were very peaceably disposed, and always coming to the ranch to trade and buy stores and whiskey. Sometimes they camped close to us for weeks at a time. Many of my old friends used to come along, and we had "high old times" together. The Cheyennes were our chief visitors, and amongst them was an old chief named "Friday," who hunted for us and kept the ranch well supplied with antelope and buffalo meat. We used to make a lot of money for this old chief by selling his meat to the emigrants. The proceeds we always handed to him, but somehow it came back to us again in exchange for whiskey and stores sold at *our* price, not his.

I liked this sort of life immensely, and as I got along capitally with Ackley the time passed very pleasantly. After three months, however, I felt that I had to make a change. I used to look out over the prairie and wish myself upon it. Even old Friday I envied, who came and went as he liked, whilst I was tied up like a hobbled horse. At length I could stand it no longer, and I told Ackley I must leave him, as indoor life did not agree with me.

He offered me fifty dollars a month to stay, and said he liked me very much and could find no one to replace me.

This was all very complimentary and satisfactory. I told him I was sorry to go, but I should go mad if I stayed.

He still thought I wanted more pay, so he asked me

to fix my own terms, and anything I wanted I should have.

My reply was, "No, Ackley; you have treated me well. There is no man I ever met that I like better than you; but I must go because my life is out there," and I pointed to the prairie. "I thought when I came I could settle down; but the old feeling has come over me, and go I must."

We parted the best of friends. He had two other men with him, who were always engaged hauling wood, so he was not left alone; and I started off with a party that came along, and went with them down the Platte as far as Cotton Wood Springs.

About two and a half miles from the springs another ranch had sprung up, belonging to a man named Billy Hill. It was a similar place to that I had left, and when we arrived I found the "boss" wanted a man to help him as I had been helping Ackley.

I was now down in my old ground, a place that always had a great attraction for me. The Sioux were all round about the district, and I thought I might as well accept the engagement until I made up my mind what to do. At any rate, I knew that if I remained I was bound to meet with the Indians, who would be sure to come to the ranch to trade. Consequently I arranged with "old Billy" to enter his service at twenty-five dollars a month.

After I had been with him a month he took his teams and went off to Omaha for a fresh supply of goods, leaving me to run the ranch. As I was quite alone I hit upon the expedient of forming a body of Indian police for my protection. Some of the Brûlés, under the chiefs Iron Crow and Dogbelly, were up at the ranch at the time, and as they knew me I arranged with them, for a small present of coffee and sugar, to see that I was not molested.

One day a coach from Fort Kearney drove up with half a dozen men out on the " bust." Amongst them was a very remarkable man named Dan Slade. This man was one of the most notorious rowdies on the road, and had committed more murders than any one in that part of the country.

He was a division agent or superintendent of a hundred-mile stretch of the Overland Stage Company.

Birds of a feather flock together, and it was a well-known fact that Slade had under him a harder set of assistants and helpers generally than any one on the line.

He had an inconceivable hatred for Canadian Frenchmen, many of whom were along the road at the mail stations, and when he came on to his section he swore he would run every one of these men out of the country.

He commenced operations by shooting any one of them he came across, and making things simply unbearable for the others. Nothing could be done. He was in his own district, and as chief of it had matters generally his own way.

After amusing himself pretty well at the other end of the line he came up to the Old California crossing, its eastern extremity. Here the stage was kept by one of his *bêtes noires*, named Jules Berg.

This man was a very peaceable, steady old fellow. He had been there some time, and had accumulated about one hundred and fifty head of cattle. These he had just sold and delivered to a man on the North Platte, and returned to his ranch with the money tied in a buckskin sack which hung on the horn of his saddle.

Slade and his party of eight or nine ruffians, all drunk, as was their wont, were awaiting the old man's return. When he arrived they seized and tied him to a post in the corral in the rear of the ranch. Slade took out his knife, and cutting off one of his ears stuck it in his pocket, and then he and the rest of the gang returned to the ranch and took a drink.

After a while they again visited their victim, abusing him, spitting in his face, and so forth. Then Slade cut off the other ear, which he placed in his other pocket, and the party again returned to the ranch to take more drinks.

Jules begged them to let him loose and give him a chance, when he offered to fight them all; but this they refused.

After a while they returned and commenced torturing him by shooting him in the arms and legs and through the fleshy part of the body without hitting any vital part.

After amusing themselves in this way, and prolonging his agony until they were tired, they all drew their six-shooters and fired a volley into him. Then they took the sack containing his money, returned to the ranch, where they destroyed everything they could lay their hands upon, and decamped.

In commemoration of this event the town which sprang up at the California crossing was, and is to this day, called Julesburg.

In this way Slade and his party rode up and down his stretch of line, perpetrating outrages of every description, and in all killing some thirty people. All their murders were committed in the most cowardly manner, and only when the odds were about eight or nine of them to one.

I did not know them at first when they arrived at Billy Hill's ranch, but hearing the coach drive up, and knowing that drinks were requisite, I promptly put them forward on the bar counter

Slade, who was a tall, heavy-looking fellow, with small deep-set eyes and the look of a wolf, came in first, and stepping right up to the bar, leant his elbows on it, and staring me full in the face, said, in an overbearing and bullying tone:

"Do you know me?"

"No, I don't," I replied.

"Well," he said, "I am the man who killed the Saviour."

I held out my hand to him and said:

"How are you, Mr. Saviour-killer?"

As he and his companions were all half intoxicated the better plan was to humour them.

As he let go my hand, however, he picked up the decanter of whisky and aimed a blow at my head with it.

Fortunately I dodged my head, and, raising my left elbow, caught the blow there. At the same time I stooped down, and with my right hand clutched an old double-barrelled shot-gun, which had the butt-end of the stock sawn off, and was a sort of an elongated pistol.

This I cocked as I brought it up, and presenting it at his head, fired. Fortunately for him one of his companions knocked the barrel up, and the charge of twenty-four buckshot went through the roof of the shanty, making a hole the size of a plate and scattering the turf in all directions.

This sobered him for an instant, and he backed to the end of the cabin, where he stood and stared at me.

I kept my finger on the other trigger, ready to pull at an instant's notice.

His friends here interposed, and said: "Hold on, boy! This is all fun; don't let's have any fighting."

I said: "Well, if this is your fun, I don't want any of it."

Finally peace was made, and we all had a drink. I told Mr. Slade he had had a narrow squeak. It was not the only one he was destined to have that afternoon.

An English emigrant drove up to the shanty whilst they were there, and as he was getting down from his waggon, Slade stepped up to the counter, and snatching up a four-pound weight which stood by the scales, heaved it through the window at the emigrant's head, just missing it.

This was too much for the Britisher, who was as brave a chap as ever stepped. He turned round, and seeing there were about eight of them, he stretched out his arm, dragged his rifle out of the waggon, stepped into the shanty, cocked it, and presenting it at Slade's head, said:

"You heaved that weight at me. What did you do it for?"

Slade said it was only done in fun; and the others, trying to make peace, apologised for him, and begged the Englishman not to notice it.

He said that if Slade undertook not to bother him again it was all right. This was promised, and I took the opportunity of putting the Britisher in the kitchen with his wife, who was with him.

I got rid of Slade's lot after a while, and they went along the road, about two and a half miles, to the ranch of a Canadian named Toefield. They drove him out of it and then broke it up, leaving him with instructions that they would return in a week, and if they still found him there he would be shot.

Finally, Slade and his gang got so hot they had to be removed from our district. He was sent further west, where he perpetrated such outrages that the Road Company discharged him.

He, with about fourteen of his gang, then went up into Virginia City, Montana, and formed a band of sixty to seventy road agents, or highwaymen. The Vigilance Committee went after them, and catching Slade and twenty-seven of his men, swung them all up in one day.

Slade's wife, when she heard he had been captured, was forty miles away; but springing on her horse, she arrived where he was just five minutes after he had been strung up. Her intention was to shoot him, so that he should not be hanged. She was a braver woman than he was a man, and to my knowledge subsequently shot three of those who had assisted in hanging him. Finally she had to leave the country in order to save her own skin.

Old Billy had been away about twenty days, and everything was going on comfortably at his place, when word came that, in a dispute with a man on the ferry-boat crossing the Hoop Fork, close to Omaha, he had been shot dead.

Shortly afterwards his wife and her brother came on with the goods and to take charge of the ranch. I couldn't stand this chap at any price, so the second day after his arrival I put my things together in a small bundle and cleared out.

CHAPTER XXII.

WITH THE BRÛLÉS ON COTTONWOOD SPRINGS—A NEW SQUAW—RAGE—CONSOLATION—"HU-PA-SAP-PAH-WEE-AH"—AN IMPRACTICABLE MOTHER-IN-LAW—ENGAGEMENT WITH THE GILMAN BROTHERS—THE CALIFORNIAN TELEGRAPH LINE—EXIT "HU-PA-SAP-PAH-WEE-AH"—TRADING WITH SPOTTED TAIL AND TWO BUCK ELK—BUILDING FORT MACPHERSON—JOHN GILMAN MARRIES—AMONGST THE CHEYENNES—TRADING AT LARAMIE—A VISIT TO THE OGALLALAS—"OP-AN-GEE-WEE-AH"—MARRIED ONCE MORE—CHEYENNES ON THE WAR-PATH—RETURN TO GILMAN'S RANCH—ENGAGEMENT AS SCOUT, GUIDE, AND INTERPRETER AT FORT MACPHERSON—CARRYING DESPATCHES TO FORT HAYES—A LYNCHING EPISODE—TWO YEARS OF GUERILLA WARFARE.

THERE was not much speculation on my part as to where I should go. I made my way down to the encampment of my friends the Brûlés, who were glad to see me, and gave me a warm welcome.

After I had been with them a few days the chiefs, wishing to do me every honour in their power in return for many trifling things I had done for them whilst at the ranch, suggested my taking to myself a squaw.

I said I didn't mind, as I felt like settling down now. Accordingly, a young girl of about seventeen was found for me, and I gave her brother a double-barrelled shotgun for her and some beads, coffee, and bacon, representing a few dollars in value. I also sent to the ranch for some clothes, which Billy Hill's widow made up for her. In addition, I laid out seventy-five dollars in provisions and furniture for the tépee, which I made as snug and comfortable as any in the camp.

A marriage amongst the Indians, as I have already explained, was not legal unless a horse changed hands over the union. As in this case no such transfer had been made, this alliance was strictly one not contracted in accordance with the rules and regulations of the Sioux nation.

However, as the lady's brother made no objection, and he was the principal party concerned, as she had no mother or father, I said nothing.

We established ourselves very comfortably in our tépee, and everything went on satisfactorily for about a month, when one day I went up to Cold Springs, about twenty miles distant, to see a man I knew who had a ranch there. I was only absent for twenty-four hours, but when I returned I found my squaw had given away provisions, tépee, everything, and eloped with an Indian buck.

This made me feel hot under my jacket, and I went round all the tépees in search of the runaways, intending to make things lively for both of them. They were too cute for me, however, and had slipped out into the prairie. I never saw either of them again.

My friends the chiefs were sincere in their commiseration at my loss, and told me there were as good fish in the Platte River as ever came out of it, and that I had better look round for another squaw and not worry myself about trifles.

I took their advice, and by eight o'clock the following evening I had found another. Her name was Hu-pa-sappah-wee-ah, or the Black-ring woman. She was twenty-two years old, and had married a soldier at Fort Laramie, who died. By him she had a half-breed boy, then two years of age. I gave some blankets, blue cloth, and beads for her, and buying another tépee, took her home to it, starting in this time by reading over to her the rules and regulations of the establishment.

She promised to be good, and we began our housekeeping very satisfactorily. This, however, did not last long, for in a few weeks her old mother and the rest of her relations wanted me to take charge of them as well. I told them that when I married the girl I did not marry the whole Sioux nation, and flatly refused to feed and clothe the portion of that nation related to her.

Then trouble began in camp, so I broke up my establishment and sent my squaw back to her friends, saying I would go and find work elsewhere, but promising to return frequently to see her.

I was at first undecided where to go, but remembering I had heard that two brothers named Gilman had just started a ranch about fifteen miles along the road towards the east, I went up there to see if they wanted any hands.

These two men were twins, named respectively Jerry

C. and John K. Their age was about thirty years, and both were tall men. John was a big burly fellow, and Jerry as tall, but as thin as a lath. They had started one of the largest ranches along the road, and when I arrived were at work building the shanty, helped by six men, who were lumbering up the logs.

I made a trial engagement with them for one month. My duties were the same as at Billy Hill's, and my pay fifteen dollars per month. This was small, but I knew it would soon increase.

We had stabling for one hundred and seventy-five horses, and a large corral capable of holding any number of emigrants. Traffic was pretty brisk along the road just then. Waggons were nearly always in sight, and thousands of emigrants were making their way to California.

In a week or ten days we got shipshape, and business commenced in real earnest. At the end of the first month I received twenty-five dollars instead of fifteen, and before the end of the third my pay had increased to sixty-five dollars per month. My value was not only in my aptitude for looking after the business generally; the Gilmans discovered that my knowledge of the Indian language was of use to them, and they were consequently very anxious to keep me.

After I had been there about three months the telegraph line to California was commenced, and the Gilmans secured the contract to furnish the telegraph-poles. These were of cedar, which grew abundantly in the cañons about five miles from the ranch.

I had charge of eight men and some waggons. My duty was to lumber up these poles and pile them along the road in stacks. This job was usually finished about one o'clock, when my work commenced in the ranch, either attending to the emigrants or fixing up drinks for the travellers.

About twice a week, in my off time, I ran down to the Indian encampment to see my squaw and take her coffee, sugar, and other things. One day, when I came home with a larger parcel of delicacies than usual, I found she had disappeared with a buck. It was the same old tale over again. Once more a wifeless man, I had to face an unsympathetic and relentless world. Two or three drinks, however, straightened me, and I returned to my duties a greater woman-hater than ever.

During the winter I took a couple of waggons and two teamsters for the Gilmans, to trade with the Indians on Big Turkey Creek, about one hundred and fifty miles away. There I found the Ogallalas, Brûlés, and a few Cheyennes, and amongst them my old friends Spotted

Tail and Two Buck Elk. Spotted Tail had been released from prison and returned to his tribe. Both were very glad to see me again, and I passed a very pleasant three months with them, returning to the ranch with the whole of my stock sold out and laden with a good supply of furs.

I believe I had four hundred and seventy-five of the best buffalo robes alone, besides other skins, raw hide lariats, &c.

The robes cost about one and a quarter dollar each, and sold at five dollars; the lariats cost twenty-five cents, and sold at four dollars. In addition, I had two thousand dried buffalo tongues, for which I paid thirty-six cents a dozen, and resold to the emigrants at twenty-four dollars a dozen.

My first experiment in the trading line resulted in a very handsome profit to my employers. I shall never forget the looks of astonishment on their faces when I counted out my treasures. They would hardly believe that I had done so well, and they made me a present of a horse, saddle, and bridle, and raised my pay.

From that time I never did any more hard work, such as lumbering, &c., but I became a sort of foreman of the establishment.

In the spring of 1863 the Government decided to build a fort at Cottonwood Springs, which was named and known as Fort Macpherson from that time.

The Gilmans obtained the contract for building the fort. It was constructed of red cedar logs, of which I superintended the delivery. We had seventy men engaged in this work alone, besides several more who were chopping three hundred cords of wood for the use of the garrison, three companies of cavalry. We also secured the hay contract, which kept us busy all the summer.

Besides other things, we did a tremendous trade in cedar wood, which parties returning to the States with empty waggons bought from us, and sold at a handsome profit.

In the autumn, business had increased to such an extent that the firm built another ranch at the Fort, and John Gilman got married to an American girl and established himself there to look after it.

The following winter I was sent out trading again, and this time my pay was five dollars a day, or one hundred and fifty dollars a month. I had two waggons, each drawn by six yoke of oxen, and two men to assist me. We went on to the Republican River, and there found a band of Cheyennes.

We drove into their camp, not knowing who they were until we got right amongst them. They refused to let us leave, and soldiered us, *i.e.*, placed sentries all round the outfit. Their object was to force us to trade with them at their price, a fourth below ours. This I refused to do. Then they became very angry, and declined to trade at all or permit me to leave the camp.

After a week I succeeded in bringing them round to my view of things, and commenced to trade. When a few robes had changed hands they tried to do me again, and recommenced their old tactics. Finally I " squared "

MARRIAGE THE LAST

White Antelope, the chief, by giving him a feast of apples baked with rice and served with hot coffee. This had the desired effect, and we traded off pretty satisfactorily.

However, the business was not nearly so remunerative as my previous venture had been, and I determined not to trouble the Cheyennes again for their custom.

In the spring of 1864 the Indians all congregated as usual at Fort Laramie to receive their tribute from the Government for the right of way on the California route through their country. I took a waggon and a man with me, and went up there to trade with them for buckskins, returning in about two months, very successful.

Upon my return, finding things a little slack at the ranch, I determined to take a holiday, and accordingly I went down on a visit to the Ogallalas, who were then on Prairie Dog Creek, some one hundred and thirty miles from the ranch. There I stayed for about a couple of months.

It was here that I met my present wife. She was a daughter of Old Smoke, chief of the Bad Face band of the Ogallalas. She was twenty-three years of age and a widow. She had been previously married to a half-breed named Drapes, who had died from the bite of a tarantula. She had one child, a daughter five years of age.

I took a fancy to her, and made up my mind she would just suit me. Her name was Op-an-gee-wee-ah, or the Yellow Elk woman. She was good-looking, tidy, apparently good-natured, and always working. I thought, "This is just the woman for me," and I made up my mind she should be my squaw.

She was then living with her two brothers, Lone Wolf and Torn Blanket. I spoke with them on the subject, and they were agreeable. It was arranged that, as I intended coming back in the winter with a trading outfit, the marriage should stand over until then.

Returning to the ranch, I resumed my duties during the autumn, and when the winter set in I started with my waggons and two men down the Republican River to pick up the tribes. These I found without much difficulty, and lost no time in opening up the negotiations which would once more land me in matrimony.

There was a great deal of diplomacy requisite on my part this time. Op-an-gee-wee-ah being the daughter of a big chief, a considerable amount of bargaining was necessary, and as my friends thought I was very good game to be shot at, in view of the multitudinous treasures in my outfit, which they took for my personal property, I had to smoke many pipes in consultation before terms were finally settled.

At length I gave to Lone Wolf the "magic" horse, emblem of *bonâ fide* matrimony, and to her other relatives various presents. She had nine brothers; it may be imagined I had to "shell out" pretty freely. In all, I reckon it cost me more than 250 dollars.

My tépee was erected next to Lone Wolf's, and we were duly installed therein. I little thought then that the alliance I was entering into would be of lifelong duration.

We got along capitally all through the winter. My men and I traded with all the tribes that found their way up to our village, and we passed our spare time in as pleasant a manner as any one leading our life could possibly wish.

Op-an-gee-wee-ah, or Jennie, as I christened her, understood me perfectly. Association with her former husband had taken the rough edges off her, and she

had become familiar with the habits and customs of the whites. She prepared the food and looked after my two men, who had a tent next door to ours, and altogether during the time we were out we had a regular picnic.

This, however, was not to last for ever. Something always seemed to turn up just as I was settling down and becoming comfortable. This time it took a turn I least expected.

A party of Cheyennes, one day in February, came into the village laden with plunder of all descriptions I saw at once that they had fallen foul of the whites from the kind of property they had with them, and I ascertained that a rupture had occurred, with, as result, the entire nation going on the war-path.

Knowing the peculiarities of the Indian race and the facility with which one tribe could lead on another, I thought the best thing I could do was to clear out whilst I had a whole skin. This I did not feel safe in doing on my own account, for fear of meeting any Cheyennes on the way back. So I persuaded Lone Wolf to let me have an escort of Sioux to conduct me and my waggons back to the ranch. He assented, and leaving Jennie in charge of her brothers, my men and I whipped up our waggons and made all possible haste to the Gilmans.

I had my suspicions that this action of the Cheyennes would end in a terrible row, and they were well founded. I did not know, however, that two years would elapse before I saw my squaw again.

The Sioux escorted me safely, and then returned to their camp. The Gilmans already knew of the outbreak, and told me the Cheyennes were having a lively time, burning ranches and slaughtering their inmates wherever they could find them. The soldiers were after them, hunting them down in all directions.

This went on for some weeks, and we were kept pretty well posted from the Fort as to what was going on. At length, the soldiers, in their eagerness to hound down the enemy, chevied them into the Sioux country, and, unable to discriminate between one Indian and another, they killed a party of the Sioux, mistaking them for Cheyennes. The result of this was that the whole Sioux nation rose as one man to avenge the death of their comrades.

In our part of the country about thirty thousand Indians were on the war-path, and it was therefore unsafe for us to continue at the ranch. We accordingly carted the greater portion of the stock up to the Fort and moved into the branch establishment.

Taking things all round, we were in a pretty precarious state at this time. The War of the Rebellion was in full swing, and no troops could be spared by the Government to garrison the forts along the California route. The Indians, therefore, in a great measure held their own against the soldiers, who, although well armed and equipped, had generally to give way in face of the overwhelming numbers of the enemy.

Finding that my knowledge of the country round was of as much value as my acquaintance with the Sioux language, Major O'Brien, the commandant at Fort Macpherson, appointed me the Government scout, guide, and interpreter to his district. The result of this was that I became permanently attached to the Fort, and no expedition could go out without me.

The Indians at this time caused us great annoyance; they would cut the telegraph wires and attack the ranches along the road, and we could do little or nothing to prevent it. The mere handful of soldiers at the Fort, numbering in all only about three hundred, were fully occupied in keeping the route clear up to Fort Kearney on the east, about ninety-five miles distant, and Fort Sedgwick on the west, about sixty-five miles. At each of these forts there was only about one company in garrison, who could not assist us in any way, as they were required for the protection of the forts.

The emigrants were still coming along the road, and part of our duty was to escort them from Kearney down to Fort Macpherson. Parties were also coming up from Denver in large numbers, and between the two routes our work was pretty well cut out. At Fort Macpherson we used to rally them until they numbered at least one hundred waggons and two or three hundred men. Nothing under this number was allowed to proceed along the road on its own account.

In this way two years passed, little being done on the part of the troops beyond keeping the Indians, as well as they were able, off the route and as far away from the Fort as the means at command permitted. I varied the monotony by carrying despatches now and then to Fort Hayes, in Kansas, about three hundred miles distant.

On one of these trips I arrived at Hayes just in time to take part in the lynching of a youth who had been on the look-out for some little time to waylay and rob me. He was a regular young desperado, only about nineteen years of age, and had already killed several men. All he would have got out of me would have been my horse and despatches, neither of which were worth much. However, they tickled his fancy, and for some reason or another he desired to have them. Fortunately for me he had been captured the morning of my arrival, and was just being taken to a telegraph-pole as I galloped into the place. My advent lent an additional interest to the proceedings, and I was asked to take a last look at him before he

was sent to glory. This I did with great pleasure, and I gave my assistance in expediting him on his way.

A rope was fixed round his neck, and the other end thrown over the insulators. A ladder was then set against the pole, he was made to mount it, the ladder was kicked away, and several willing hands hoisted him up, made the rope fast, and let him swing.

It was rather a crude way of dispatch, but efficacious, although not so speedy as the method practised in jail.

Over and over again I have had to run for my life whilst carrying these despatches, which no one else would volunteer to carry. The Indians, as a rule, I could outdistance, and, at any rate, I was always prepared to meet ; but these murdering cut-throats, who were driven out of settlements, looked upon every white man as their natural enemy. They would pot at me for the mere devilment of the thing, and kill me if they could, just for the sake of killing.

CHAPTER XXIII.

THE TREATY OF 1866—THE FIRSTBORN HALFBREED—INDEPENDENT TRADING—FROZEN BUFFALO—WHITE ANTELOPE AGAIN—LONE WOLF TO THE RESCUE—OUT OF THE FRYING-PAN INTO THE FIRE—MASSACRE OF TWENTY SOLDIERS—CAPTAIN EGAN AND PARTY SAVED—BACK AGAIN AT MACPHERSON—"MORE WAR"—COLONEL BROWN'S EXPEDITION—DUTIES OF A GUIDE—CAMP ON THE REPUBLICAN—"A THOUSAND DOLLARS FOR A VILLAGE"—A RECONNOITRE WITH BELDON—THE KENTUCKY RACER—INTO A HORNETS' NEST—ESCAPE—SIX DAYS AND NIGHTS' FIGHTING—A DRIFTWOOD FIRE—LASSOING A CAVALRY HORSE—RETURN TO CAMP.

IN 1866 peace was made with the Sioux and Cheyennes at Fort Laramie, and trading operations with the Indians were again opened up. The Gilmans wanted me to go out with an outfit, but they did not care to undertake the risk on their own account. I therefore offered to embark in the speculation, provided they would give me something to go with on credit. This they did to the tune of 3,275 dollars, and for it I obtained a waggon, six yoke of oxen, and the stock I needed.

With this I went down south to meet the Indians

returning from Laramie, and struck them at Medicine Creek, about eighteen miles south of Fort Macpherson.

Here I met my squaw, and found that during my absence she had presented me with a daughter, who was then over twelve months old. We were very glad to meet again, and I took her and the child into my outfit. The Indians could not stay to trade, as they were bound for the Republican River to meet a larger band of the Sioux coming up from the South. It was arranged that we should follow on, and join them at the mouth of the Stinking Water River, about one hundred and fifty miles distant.

The winter at this time had fairly set in, the snow was over three feet deep, and we had great difficulty in making our way through it. Often I had to work hard all day shovelling the snow away, and at night I would not have made more than a mile progress.

My outfit consisted of six people—*i.e.* my squaw and the child, myself, two teamsters, and a young Indian boy, about ten years of age, whom I had adopted, and christened " Jo."

I shall always remember that winter, for it was the coldest I ever experienced. In a gulch that we passed, we came across more than three hundred buffalo that had been frozen to death. Some were standing, and others were leaning against each other. All were as hard and immovable as if carved out of rock. I killed many deer and elk whilst they were fixed in the snowdrifts, and thus kept our larder supplied.

In February the snow suddenly disappeared, but the streams were very high, and we had to wait a long time on the banks before we could cross them.

One day my Indian boy, who had been watching on a hill, came running into camp and reported that a war-party was in sight. We hardly had time to make preparation when they swooped down and surrounded us. There were seventy-five of them, and they were Cheyenne "dog soldiers," who had come from Southern Kansas, where they had been fighting the coloured troops sent out to protect that part of the country.

The party were on their way north to the Platte River to intercept the caravans coming along the Denver route to Julesburg. We were not anxious for a fight against such long odds, but we got our guns out and waited for them to open the ball.

Jennie went out to talk with them, as they all knew her, and ascertained that they knew nothing about the treaty of peace and were still on the war-path. As the chief, however, expressed a desire to see me, she bade him lay down his arms and come into our tépee to have an interview.

This he did, and came in with his blanket over his head, in the Indian fashion. I stood in the centre of the tépee with my rifle in my hand, and on my right stood the two teamsters with their guns, whilst the boy was behind us with a six-shooter in each hand.

When the chief took his blanket from off his head I at once recognised him as White Antelope, into whose camp I had inadvertently run some time previously.

As he was a brave of great influence with his tribe, I lit my pipe of peace and offered it to him, but he refused to smoke with me.

A DUBIOUS MEETING

I then reminded him of the time I had traded with his band. He said that he remembered it very well, and that I had traded very hardly with him.

Jennie then gave him some coffee and meat, after which he made signs that he would come back soon, and went out to join his party. He could

talk Sioux very poorly, and the conversation was carried on principally by signs.

We were still uncertain what turn affairs would take, and we set to work as hard as we could to load every weapon we had and get a supply of ammunition ready in case of emergency.

Looking out of the tent I found that some of the braves had gone down to the bend of the river where my oxen were, driven them up, and were going to have a feast. They had already killed two of the fattest and best, and were on the point of slaying the others, when White Antelope interfered.

Thinking that conciliatory measures were the best, I got Jennie to make a feast for them of dried apples stewed in sugar, with flour, some hot coffee and bread. I opened out three pairs of three-point blankets for the chiefs, and gave each man some tobacco and a butcher's knife.

After the feast I made a speech to them, inquiring why they wanted to rob and kill me, pointing out that, if they did do so, the whole Sioux nation would avenge us. I told them the Ogallalas were not far off, and that if we were molested in any way they would have to answer for it to them, and as my squaw's relations were very numerous they would have plenty to do to settle with all of them.

Whilst we were talking I heard a noise outside, and who should appear upon the scene but Lone Wolf, Jennie's brother, and twenty-five of his warriors! If they had fallen from Heaven they could not have arrived at a more opportune moment.

We were naturally very glad to see them, and our pluck went up at a bound. Lone Wolf said that he had become anxious about our non-appearance and had come out to look for us. He soon settled matters with White Antelope, and insisted upon his band paying double for the damage his braves had done us; the result was that I received in compensation for the two slain oxen and the things I had given them, two mules and some buffalo robes, which made the transaction anything but a bad deal for me.

The following day we moved on and travelled until we reached the camp of the Sioux; but, as luck would again have it, I was jumping out of the frying-pan into the fire.

It appears that the Cheyennes, after leaving us, continued their journey west towards Denver, and two days afterwards fell in with a party of cavalry, twenty in number, going to South Kansas with despatches from Colorado. A fight ensued, and every one of the soldiers was killed.

We knew nothing of this, and the first intimation I had was a party of cavalry overtaking us, who were following their comrades and had come upon their dead bodies. Following the Cheyennes' trail in the *wrong* direction, they tracked them to where they left us, and then got on to our trail in the firm belief that we had committed the massacre.

Lone Wolf sent out twenty of his braves to inquire what the soldiers wanted and why they were following him. At the same time he made Jennie, myself, my two men and the boy, prisoners, and put us under a guard. In about an hour I was put on a horse and brought into the village, and five Indians were left to guard my outfit.

The soldiers were then six miles from the village, and I was sent six miles the other side of it. They were determined to put plenty of distance between us. Whatever their intention, however, it did not answer, for they came out after me and brought me back to interpret for them.

In the meantime nearly all the Indians had gone out to meet the troops, and were lying in ambush for them.

When I learnt this, I mounted the first horse I could find, and rode for dear life to where the Indians were, and said to them:

"Let me speak to the white chief and explain the matter before he falls into your trap." They said, "You can go if you please; but remember, if the soldiers come down here we shall kill every one of them."

The troops were all drawn up in line ready to charge. They numbered eighty, had a fieldpiece with them, and were under the charge of Captain Egan.

The Indians mustered 1,500 warriors. I took a piece of rag, tied it to a stick, and galloped down between the opposing forces. The soldiers levelled their rifles at me, and I had a narrow squeak of being shot, but on I went. At length they recognised me, and I rode up to Egan and tried to explain the matter.

I told him that the Indians said he could not go any further through their country, and if he and his men did not return immediately they would kill every one of them. He asked me how many Indians there were.

I answered: "Enough to kill every one of you with clubs, without firing a shot."

"Well," he said, " I've a very good mind to turn the soldiers loose on these red devils, Nelson."

"Captain Egan," I said, " I've told you exactly the position of affairs. If you choose to wilfully sacrifice your own life and that of your men I have nothing further to say."

He considered for a few moments, and then asked

me to tell the Indians that his horses were tired, and that as soon as they were rested he would return.

I begged him, for God's sake, to go at once, or he would be a dead man. He took my advice, and ordering his men to the right-about galloped back.

I returned to the Indians and was taken back to the camp a prisoner, only to be taunted with the cowardice of my white brothers in not fighting.

As yet they had not taken my pistols from me, but now they asked for them. I told them plainly I would not give them up, and that if they took them they would have to kill me first. They were hesitating, when Two Buck Elk, happening to come along, stepped forward and said he would kill the first man who touched a hair of my head.

Jennie and my two men were brought into the camp, where we were given a tépee, and a guard was placed over it. Here we were kept for six long months, and not allowed to go outside the precincts of the camp.

One day, without any previous warning, they came to me and said I might go home.

I did not require to be told twice, so hitching in my bullocks to the waggon, putting Jennie and the baby inside it, and mounting my two men on the mules, we cleared out and started on our one hundred and forty mile journey to Fort Macpherson.

Arriving at the Fort, we found things in as unsatisfactory a state as they could be. Although peace had been made with the Indians generally, only those bands which had gone to Laramie seemed to understand that it was with the whole nation. Those who had not attended the gathering were still under the impression that they were at war with the whites.

The settlers on the road would not come out and open their ranches, as there was always the fear of their being attacked by some marauding band.

I cleared up my reckoning with the Gilmans, and found that, after returning my unsold stock to the store,

I had made a profit of several hundred dollars on the winter's trading. As there was nothing else for me to do, I resumed my position at the Fort as scout, guide, and interpreter, and was employed on the special duty of accompanying the men who, under a guard of soldiers, were re-erecting the telegraph-poles which the Indians had amused themselves by pulling down.

Suddenly, for no other reason, as far as I know, beyond that of general grievances, the whole Sioux nation again started on the war-path, and things became exceptionally lively around the Fort.

The few settlers that were left stood a very poor chance, and those that could came running into the Fort for protection, leaving their ranches with thousands of dollars' worth of stock in them. The whole country far and near was up. In Kansas and Nebraska the redskins swooped down on all the whites they could find, killed them, and stole their stock. They thought that, if they could run them out of the country, they would be left to live in peace and unmolested, as in the days of old.

Round Fort Macpherson we had quite a number of people living in tents, as there was not accommodation inside the stockade for them.

All traffic along the road was stopped, except for large trains numbering three hundred to four hundred waggons and not less than a thousand men.

A large number of troops came out and fortified the forts all along the route. At Macpherson alone we had about five hundred cavalry and two hundred and fifty infantry.

I held a post of considerable responsibility as chief scout and guide to the garrison, and had several men under me.

It was finally decided that an expedition should start out from the Fort, and additional troops were sent from the States for that purpose. These were mostly volunteers, of whom the greater portion were Southern prisoners, who had accepted this opportunity offered them of escaping from captivity.

When organised, the expedition numbered, all told, two thousand seven hundred men, the majority cavalry, two guns, and two companies of Pawnee scouts under Major North. The whole was under the command of an Englishman named Colonel Brown, a Confederate prisoner on parole.

We had very few waggons at the Fort, and had to carry our commissariat on three hundred pack-mules. By the time we had covered the short distance to Medicine Creek there was not enough forage for the night, as the mules had shied off their burthens *en route*. We discarded that mode of transit, and waited several days until three hundred waggons were got together. Making another move, we wended our way down to the Republican River.

The Sioux is the most powerful of all the Indian tribes on the continent of America. It has always been a warlike one, and has cost the United States Government a great deal of money and an immense amount of trouble.

I knew their camping grounds in summer and winter ; in fact, at any season of the year I knew exactly where to find them, on account of their always following the buffalo.

The knowledge of this fact was really the secret of my success when working with the United States troops. Not one of the generals who subsequently came out ever grasped this, and I was accordingly looked upon as a marvel of intelligence when, without the slightest indication of the whereabouts of the Indians, I would undertake to conduct the soldiers to where they were.

A guide on the frontier holds a very responsible position. It is not only his own life that is at stake, but the lives of the hundreds or thousands who are with him.

I have known cases where one slight error of judgment has resulted in the massacre of several hundred people. Results succeed events so rapidly in this kind of warfare that a guide must be always on the alert, and almost know by intuition the state of the surrounding country. The smallest sign, which to an uneducated eye would not be apparent, is a sufficient indication to an experienced guide of the close proximity of an enemy.

Every Indian who was killed in the West cost the Government about one million dollars. These were the figures arrived at by the authorities in Washington when they began to add up the little bill. This was due to the

T

difficulty of catching them, owing to the large area of country they had to scamper about in.

But to return to the command. We encamped on the Republican River, and waited patiently for any Indians who might come along and submit to be destroyed.

I was not paid to think, but only to do as I was told

so I did not venture to offer an opinion to Colonel Brown as to what course to pursue.

Before we had been out very long I realised that the expedition was a case of the blind leading the blind. My old horse knew far more about Indian warfare than the Colonel, or in fact any one in the command, with the exception of myself. Still it was no business of mine to speak. Every officer had an idea of his own, and each wanted it put into execution. I laughed in my sleeve and sat tight, waiting for events to develop themselves.

At length the Colonel became impatient, and was most anxious to get sight of an Indian. I knew very well that if he waited there for ten years he would never do it. They could sniff us out fifty miles off, and took good care to give us a wide berth.

Like a great many more, the Colonel, who by the way was Colonel of the 13th Missouri Volunteers, was desirous of gaining fresh laurels to return with, and accordingly, as the Indians would not come to him, he offered a reward of one thousand dollars out of his own pocket to any one who succeeded in finding an Indian encampment that he could attack.

This was too good a bonus to be ignored, so several parties went out to hunt up the wily redskin, but never returned; the Indians attacked and killed them.

At length the Colonel came to me and persuaded me to try and find a village, promising me anything I asked if I succeeded.

I said I required nothing if I succeeded, but if he would give me a Kentucky racehorse he had I thought I would be able to put him in the way of having some fun with the redskins.

The horse was duly handed over to me.

This horse the Colonel had ridden at the battle of Shilo, and the story in camp was, that on that occasion he had run away with his master, who did not get back to his regiment for three days.

The horse was a tall raw-boned one, and apparently as gentle as a gazelle. I was told that he was a bit of a flyer, and that was why I wanted him.

Poking one's nose into an Indian village and getting away quickly was not so easy a matter as most of the expeditionary force thought, especially after perhaps a thirty- or forty-mile ride, when the redskins, who were bound to dart out and give chase, would be mounted on fresh cattle.

I asked for volunteers to accompany me, and the only one who stepped forward was Lieutenant Beldon, of one of the cavalry regiments. With this officer and two Cherokee scouts I started.

Beldon was a good-looking, active young fellow of about twenty-five, and had a great deal of confidence in me. I had known him at the Fort for some time, and we had often been out shooting birds and small game.

We travelled along the banks of the river for five days, hiding during the day and travelling by night. Finding no trace of Indians, we at length grew brave, and determined the following day to go and reconnoitre up Short-Nose Creek. Before starting, however, we sent the half-breeds out to kill a fat buffalo for breakfast, thinking we might as well have a good feed and commence the day upon full stomachs.

After waiting a long time and getting pretty hungry,

THE FOE FOUND

whilst the Cherokees did not return, we became anxious and decided to go and see where they were.

I had not yet ridden the Colonel's Kentucky racer, but had taken him along as a spare mount. I thought I should like to try him this morning, so I saddled and rode him, leaving my other horse tethered in camp.

We went some distance before arriving at an elevated piece of ground, which we mounted to have a look round. I took out my field-glass, and at the moment some crows flew overhead. I said to Beldon:

"Our friends up there say Indians; maybe yes, maybe no."

As I spoke there was a report of firearms two or three times in rapid succession. Looking towards Short Nose creek, I saw the two half-breeds galloping towards us as fast as they could, every now and then looking back over their shoulders at a party of Indians following them.

Beldon and I stuck spurs to our horses and galloped towards them, covering a distance of fully three miles before we met. The Cherokees signalled us to stop, and Beldon stopped; but my breaks were out of order, or something had happened, for, pull as hard as I could, my steed paid no attention, and on we went. The brute had got his southern blood up, and had apparently not forgotten the battle of Shilo. Again I pulled, and bang went the bridle. I looked up and saw the Indians rushing towards me. They were at least fifty in number, and all Sioux and Cheyennes.

On seeing me tearing towards them they naturally thought the army was at hand, and that I was leading it. In an instant they turned and galloped away in the opposite direction.

I still went on at a break-neck pace as if I had been shot out of a gun. My chief object now was to stick on. At the same time I raised all the shouts and yells in different tones of voice I could manage.

Away went the Indians; every stride brought me nearer them, and a cold chill ran down my back. Fortunately for me, they had scattered as they turned, and apparently every man was looking out for himself.

We had covered about a mile in this way when I passed the first Indian. He swerved off to the right instantly. In a second or two I ran past the second, who did the same, and I found myself close to the third. Lifting my Spencer carbine, which I still had in my hand, I hit this chap a whack over the head and he rolled off his horse, which continued to gallop along beside me.

Drawing steadily ahead, I soon got clear of this animal and clean away from the remaining Indians, whose ponies were nowhere in the race with my thoroughbred.

A few shots came whizzing about my ears as I urged on my wild career, but after running about a couple of miles I was well out of range of these. We now reached the creek, and, dashing through it, plunged into the Indian village on the opposite side. I could not tell where I was going, for on either side of the stream was timber, which shut out the view. The Indians had cleared a long and narrow path, and down this I went.

My advent was so unexpected that I was through the village before the occupants had time to run out of their huts. The only person I saw was an old man, who suddenly jumped up in front of me, put his gun to his shoulder, and fired. I threw myself on the other side of my horse, and the bullet whizzed harmlessly by.

After clearing the village we sped on some little distance, and then came to a hill. We had now escaped all the Indians and were out of danger, so I thought it about time I had my spell of the fun. Mr. Kentucky didn't like the hill at all, and began to slow down perceptibly, but I plunged my spurs into him. Every time he showed signs of stopping I gave him a dig which made him jump about ten yards at a stride. In this way I kept him going until he fairly collapsed with exhaustion. I think he had forgotten the battle of Shilo by this time and was truly penitent, so I jumped off, and, taking the broken rein, tied it round his jaw as a makeshift.

I never saw a horse so completely subdued. We had cleared over five miles in an incredibly short space of time, and I don't know which felt the worse of the two, he or I. I was half inclined to blow his brains out for the trick he had played me, but for two reasons. One was that the report of my carbine would have brought the Indians to the spot, and the second was that when I began to load it I found nothing but the barrel left. I had broken off the stock on the head of the redskin I knocked over.

This was serious; so I thought we had better make tracks as speedily as possible. After giving my "beauty" a few minutes' rest I remounted, turned, and went down a cañon that crossed the creek about a mile above the village, thus making a flank movement, which eventually brought me back to the rear of the point where Beldon and the two half-breeds had taken up a position on a hill and were keeping the Indians at a distance.

The latter were still undecided as to where the army was, never dreaming for a moment that we were out there alone. Had they known it, we should soon have been made short work of.

When Beldon saw me he said: "Hullo, John! Is it you or your ghost?"

"Well," I said, "I reckon it's myself. It always is my luck to get into a hornet's nest, or something worse."

"What can you expect rushing madly into danger like that? You think you're bullet-proof, but one day you'll find you are not."

"You'll admit I am lucky, at any rate," I said, as a bullet buried itself in my saddle and made the racer give a bound which nearly threw me off.

At this moment the two half-breeds fired simultaneously, and then we saw two or three Indians lift a man on a pony and take him to the rear.

Then they charged halfway up the hill, turned, and

scampered round again, evidently too frightened to come straight on.

Every time they repeated this we met them with a volley which dropped several, and then a few of them rode off, evidently to secure reinforcements.

We now thought it about time to bolt, especially as our ammunition was running short, so we lost no time in getting back to our camp on our spare horses.

The two half-breeds had killed a buffalo cow for our breakfasts, and were in the act of skinning it when they were attacked.

There was no time to think about eating now, and we rode steadily on for the rest of the day and all the night.

The Indians were still following us, and we dared not stop, knowing that with their superior numbers they could easily kill us when our last shot was fired.

At length we reached a supply camp we had formed in a large cotton-wood copse, about six miles below Medicine Lake Creek. There we replenished our exhausted pouches and stayed two days, fighting the Indians the whole time. Then, destroying everything we could not take with us, we again pushed forward.

It was snowing heavily, blowing a gale, and so bitterly cold that we were almost frozen in our saddles. We kept on all the day, and at night reached Little Beaver Creek, where we found a pile of drift-wood, and set light to it to warm ourselves.

The Indians were firing into us from a hill above.

But we were desperate, and determined to get warm at any cost.

I had a piece of buffalo liver hanging at my saddle-girth, which was frozen so hard that we had to break it into pieces before we could get it loose.

This we cooked at the fire, two of us standing guard and firing at the Indians whilst the other two ate.

We reckoned that the enemy then mustered fifteen to our four. The others had given out from exhaustion.

When we finished we remounted our horses and rode on, the Indians still following and firing into us for about six miles, when they gave up the chase. I was very glad when they took themselves off, for with my broken carbine I should have stood a very poor chance if we had come to close quarters.

The following day we were startled to see a herd of buffalo galloping towards us, and amongst them one of the cavalry horses. By an adroit movement we turned the herd before they reached us, and as they rushed past we lassoed the horse and dragged him out of the crowd.

We arrived in camp, dead beat, a few hours later, and reported ourselves to the Colonel, who decided, as we had found no large village, to march up the Republican about eighty-five miles, then cross over to the Platte, and, coming down that, return to Fort Macpherson.

The horse we had captured belonged to a sergeant of the B Company of the 12th Missouri Cavalry, who had been sent out with three men to reconnoitre.

The party had been surprised in the early morning by the Indians, who had killed the three men. The sergeant, thrown from the horse, had hidden in a snowdrift, and some few days afterwards he made his way back to camp none the worse for his adventure.

CHAPTER XXIV.

MUTINY IN CAMP—ATTEMPT ON COLONEL BROWN'S LIFE—A SKIRMISH AT MEDICINE CREEK—RETURN OF THE EXPEDITION TO FORT MACPHERSON—GENERAL BRADLEY'S ARRIVAL—SCOUTING WITH HIS EXPEDITION—CATCHING A PONY—THE RESULT—ALARM—DANGER—VICTORY—ROW WITH LIEUTENANT WHALING—THE BROACHED KEG—RETURN TO HEAD-QUARTERS CAMP—REPORTED TO THE GENERAL.

WHEN the Colonel announced his intention of returning to Fort Macpherson viâ the Platte there was any amount of dissatisfaction in camp, amongst men and officers alike. The expedition was a hopeless one in many respects, and above all it ought never to have been sent out at that time of the year. It was not surprising, therefore, that at mess, the same night, after the Colonel had left, a resolution was passed by the officers that the orders should not be carried out.

The principal amongst the malcontents was my friend Lieutenant Beldon. He was particularly bitter against the Colonel for what he termed his selfishness in forcing the troops to undertake such a journey.

A SHELL UNDER THE BED

The following incident will serve to illustrate the strong feeling against the Colonel. We were encamped in a sandy bottom, and Lieutenant Beldon and some of his brother officers, seeing no way out of the difficulty but getting rid of the Colonel, placed a ten-pound shell under his bed, and laid a train of powder to where it could be ignited from outside. But the fuse did not ignite, and the next morning the Colonel was just as frisky as ever.

I knew nothing about this until months afterward. I could hardly believe Beldon would have been guilty of such a diabolical act, but two years later, when we were riding over the same spot, with his knife he dug the shell out of the sand. The shell is there to this day, as far as I know, and if Colonel Brown is still alive it will be an interesting souvenir for him to go and dig up.

Beldon was a smart officer, as brave a man as ever stepped, and a magnificent shot. He was always getting into trouble, however, and was finally shot by an Indian at Standing Rock Agency, on the Missouri River, whilst he was lying down to take a drink at a creek.

At length the moment arrived when the command was ordered to start for the Platte. Tents were struck, waggons loaded, everything in readiness, and the word to march given. Much to the Colonel's surprise, however, the troops refused to move. The artillery, who were Southerners, were ordered to fire upon the men; but the entire command was of one opinion, and the artillerists were told that if they fired a shot they would be seized and blown to pieces from the mouths of their own guns. They thought better of it, and caved in.

The upshot was that the Colonel had to give orders for the expedition to return to Fort Macpherson, then some eighty-five miles distant, and we started to do this stretch, as sullen a body of men as it is possible to conceive.

The principal cause of the ill-feeling was that the men were very badly clad; their feet and hands were for the most part frost-bitten, and they had little or nothing to eat, as the supply trains had not arrived for some time past.

On the third night of our journey we reached Medicine Creek, eighteen miles from the Fort, and encamped down in a bend of the stream with a high bluff behind it.

At about three in the morning a party of Indians, who had been following us, sneaked into camp and cut all our horses loose, whilst another party who had crept up the hill created a diversion by firing into us. The Pawnee scouts, however, managed to surround the cattle before they stampeded. We had a fight for half an hour, and, driving the Indians off, were left in peace.

This was the only honour and glory that fell to Colonel Brown's lot during the campaign. We arrived at the Fort the following day, and that evening I saw Colonel Brown receive a sound thrashing from a private soldier whom he had given permission to "lick" him if he could.

That seemed to wipe out all the grievances of the command, and the men received the Colonel back into their good graces again. This incident will show the military relations at that time existing between officers and men.

Shortly after our return the whole of these troops were recalled to Fort Leavenworth, where they were mustered out of the service and sent home.

My squaw all this time was with her brothers up north. There was a tacit understanding between us that when there was peace she lived with me, and when there was war, with her

people. I started her off before I joined the expedition, and had heard nothing of her since.

Nothing much beyond the ordinary routine was doing at the Fort during the spring and summer. Fighting was general all along the route, but nobody came out to organise things in any way until the autumn. Then General Bradley appeared, and set about getting an expedition together in a businesslike way. This numbered fifteen hundred men, and we set out from the Fort about the latter end of September, and remained out all the winter.

I again acted as chief guide, scout, and interpreter. First I took the expedition down to Thick Wood Creek, six miles south of the Forks of the Republican River, about ninety-six miles from Fort Macpherson. Here we had to wait for supplies and forage. Whilst we were waiting I used to take four men with me and go out hunting, to supply the General and his men with fresh

meat. The Indians were swarming in this district, and we had fights with them daily.

I was sent with a company of cavalry to patrol the country for some miles round the head-quarters camp and see that it was kept clear of redskins. One day whilst engaged in this work I got some distance ahead of the company, and, looking to the south side of the river, I saw grazing a few ponies and two large mules that had strayed from some expedition.

I thought I might as well catch a pony as not, and I

started after them. But when I got near enough to throw my lasso they bolted off, and I after them again.

I don't know how far we went. The chase was exciting, and I kept it up until my horse began to pant and blow like a porpoise. I thought it time to pull in, and, seeing a high mound before me, I rode up it and looked round for troops. I could see nothing of them; I had run about twelve miles from where I left them.

I dismounted, tethered my horse, and began to smoke whilst my steed was resting.

I suppose I had been stretched out on the ground watching the wreaths of smoke for ten minutes when I thought I saw something move on the top of a dry gulch a short distance off and quickly disappear.

I looked steadily for a few moments, but seeing nothing I concluded it was a bird, and I soon forgot all about it.

After some time my eyes fell upon the mound upon which I was lying, and my curiosity prompted me to get up and examine it more closely.

On the side I had left my horse the wind had blown out the sand, leaving a regular basin, the walls of which were at least twenty-five feet high. On the south side was a hog-back running down gradually to the base, and just wide enough for one horse at a time.

Whilst examining this remarkable place I looked up and saw three Indians watching me.

I stood for a moment paralysed, thinking what to do; my pipe dropped from my mouth and my hat began to rise on my head. I tried to push it down, but the hair was too stiff. I think every hair on my head was standing up straight.

Just then twenty-two more Indians came up from the ravine where they had hidden their horses.

I made up my mind that my time had come, although I knew that I was in one of the best forts in the world and had plenty of ammunition.

Pulling myself together, I set to work. First I put my horse where they could not see him. Then I took the saddle pockets off, and spread the cartridges on the ground where I could get at them readily.

When everything was ready I took my rifle and scrambled up to the point where I could see for miles around.

By this time the Indians had brought their horses in sight, and had pulled off their saddle blankets and leggings, ready to take my scalp.

I motioned to one of them to come up and have a talk, and he came within speaking distance and asked who I was and what I was doing.

I told him how I got there, and he asked me in Sioux where the soldiers were who had started with me that morning.

"They are a long way off, over there," I answered, pointing in the direction I had left them.

"Good," he replied; "we have been watching your movements for five days past, and have caught you at last. We have been trying to get hold of you for a long time. Do you see my men waiting there to scalp you?"

"Oh yes," I remarked cheerfully, "I see them. Are you Sioux or Cheyennes?"

"Cheyennes. We were in your camp on the Beaver when your brother-in-law 'Lone Wolf' interfered and saved your life. But he is not here now, Cha-sha-sha-o-pog-geo, to poke his nose into matters which do not concern him."

I was rather startled to hear him bring out my name so "pat." But I put on a bold, yet amiable front, and said:

"It makes my heart glad to think that my friend remembers me so well. He has made a very nice speech, but let me ask him one favour—that after killing me he will tell my squaw, 'Yellow Elk,' sister of 'Red Cloud,' where she can find my bones, as I know she'll like to bury them."

He replied: "You think to soften my heart by pleading for mercy through your squaw and her relations, but you'll never know whether I tell her or not."

"Very well, my friend," I answered, "since you are so sure of your game, come on. I'm ready for you. I have pulled some of your top-knots before now, and may pull yours yet."

He could not stand being chaffed any longer, so he shook his fist at me and returned to his companions, informing me he would be back soon and punish me for my insolence.

"Go away, you long and hungry devil!" I yelled at him. "You'll make good food for the vultures if you dare to darken the sight of my rifle, or my name is not Cha-sha-sha-o-pog-geo."

Three of the band now mounted their horses, made three circles round their comrades, and galloped towards me, the long fellow leading, on a big American horse he had stolen somewhere. He had nothing but a spear, with which he intended to pin me to the earth.

I allowed him to come as close to me as I thought discreet, and then, levelling my rifle, I sent a bullet through his horse's head; the horse crashed down on the top of him, breaking his spear. Trying to extricate himself, his back was turned to me. I took steady aim and fired. He fell back dead.

The others instantly went back to their comrades to report the success they had met with. Several now came creeping out to try and get their dead comrade away, hiding every few yards behind boulders of rock and any cover they could find.

They managed to get close to him, but, fearing to show themselves, they tried to lasso him and drag him from under the horse.

I now had plenty of fun with them, and every time I saw a head or a hand raised I fired at it.

Finding their efforts unsuccessful, they retired, held a council, and had a smoke. As result a man was posted on a neighbouring hill to pick me off with his rifle.

I saw him creep away from them, and kept my eye upon him until he took up his position, but to put him off his guard I appeared to be looking in another direction. But directly I got a good sight on him I turned suddenly and planted a ball right in his stomach, which effectually fixed him for the happy hunting grounds.

This resulted in another council and another smoke, terminating in three of them riding up to where the last man lay. As one dismounted I shot his horse, and then dropped the next horse, which had an Indian on its back. This made me feel quite cheerful, especially as I saw them pick themselves up and, jumping all three on to the remaining horse, gallop away out of range. I sent a couple of parting shots after them, but unfortunately they missed.

Still another consultation ensued, and they next tried to slip up under the mound and shoot arrows up at an angle of forty-five degrees, thinking to get at me that way; but I kept dodging from place to place, so that scheme would not work.

Whilst they were riding round the mound I shot another horse, which made four horses and two men *hors de combat.*

After keeping up these tactics for over half an hour they suddenly all rode off, leaving me master of the fort.

I was pretty thankful to see them go, and now, feeling as plucky as possible, scrambled up to the top of my mound and fired a few parting shots after them, but, so far as I know, did not hit any one.

I was now alone with the two dead Indians and the horses, but I am not afraid of corpses, especially when they are of my own making.

The first thing I did was to go and have a look at the long-legged devil. He was as dead as a doornail.

"You beauty," I thought, "you were going to lift my scalp, were you? Well, I'll take yours instead." So, giving my knife a whet across my buckskin shirt, I removed his hirsute appendage in the most approved fashion. Then I took the silver bridle from the American horse and went over to the hill to the other redskin.

This chap had evidently wriggled about a good deal before he died, and must have suffered some agony,

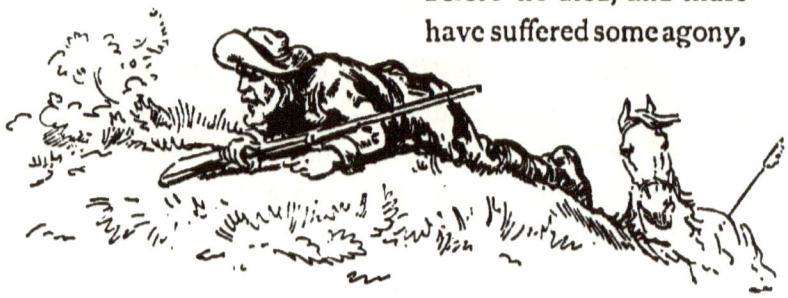

for his features were horribly distorted. I stripped him of his trophies and then went back to my fort.

I thought it about time for a smoke, so I filled up my pipe and continued the soliloquy in which I had been so rudely interrupted

After a while I thought I would go and have a look at my horse. I found him pawing the ground and champing his bit, as much as to say, "You are a pretty fine chap to leave me here like this. Why don't you take this arrow out of me?" One of the arrows they had fired into the air had lodged in his thigh, so I took it out, pulled the skin over the hole, and stopped the bleeding as well as I could. Then I tied my trophies to the saddle, mounted, and rode off in the opposite direction to that which the Indians had taken.

It was two o'clock in the morning before I found my company. Coming into camp, the sentry stopped me, and awoke the lieutenant, who came out in a towering rage and began swearing at me.

At that particular moment I should have preferred some coffee and hard tack to a lecture from a West Point cadet, and a row ensued in which the language was far from complimentary on either side. At first I tried to explain matters, but he would not listen, so I gave it up and paid him back in his own vernacular. This row between us lasted several days.

This gentleman's name was Lieutenant Whaling, of the Third Cavalry, and he was a " whiskey boozer." On leaving the head-quarters camp he brought with him a two-gallon keg of Commissary whiskey for medical purposes: the only use to which it was put, however, was to stimulate him in the use of bad language. This keg was kept in the ambulance box locked up, and he had the key.

The soldiers got mad at seeing him always taking a drink and never getting one themselves, so this night, after he had finished abusing me and turned in, some one broke open the box, drew the staple out of the keg, and all hands had a reviver. I had my share, and very welcome it was after my hard day's work. The empty keg was then placed in front of his tent, and on it was written in chalk : " With Care."

The following morning there was a tremendous row. He offered a reward of fifty dollars for information as to who took the whiskey, but of course no one knew. He had his revenge, however, on all the company before we got back, for he made the soldiers walk and carry their saddles on their backs all day, out of pure spite, in order to punish the man who broached the keg. The horses also he was always looking at, and if he could find anything to complain of, however trivial, the unlucky trooper had to dismount and carry his saddle. It has always been a marvel to me how it was he was not *accidentally* shot.

He threatened to tie me up behind the waggon and make me walk, but I told him plainly he had not the power to do so, and if he attempted it I should simply kill him and add a lock of his auburn hair to my belt. His reply was that he could have me put in irons, and tried by court-martial for misconduct and disrespect to an officer in the army.

I said that I respected his rank and the epaulettes

he wore, but had the greatest contempt for him personally; further, that I had no respect for a man who had none for himself.

This resulted in his telling me to consider myself under arrest: but I paid no attention to that.

We did not move camp that day, but before we started the next he got over his temper, apologised, and asked me to be friends with him.

I assented as long as he did not interfere with me and understood that my position empowered me to do as I liked after receiving my instructions from the General.

When we arrived in camp he asked General Bradley what sort of a man I was.

The General enquired why he asked the question.

He said while I was out with him I had threatened to kill and scalp him.

"What did you do to him," asked the General, "to make him use such language to you?"

He got in his account, whatever it was; but the General said I was a good man, that he liked me very much, and I was invaluable to them, as I knew the country better than the Indians themselves. Finally, that he would have me treated with respect by his officers. It was no use driving me, but by coaxing I would do anything that was required.

Mr. Lieutenant did not get much change out of this interview, and I noticed after it that he was always very polite to me.

CHAPTER XXV.

RESPONSIBILITIES OF A SCOUT—INDIAN CUNNING—SENT TO THE RICKAREE FORK—MASSACRE OF COLONEL FORSYTH'S SCOUTS—FOLLOWING THE INDIANS—RETURN TO GENERAL BRADLEY—A STRANGE VOICE—"SUPERSTITION"—NO. 280 SIDING—SHOT THROUGH THE THIGH—IN HOSPITAL—JENNIE'S ARRIVAL—MARRIED BY THE REVEREND JOHN ROBINSON—THIEVING SQUATTERS—A "RUN OUT" WITH BILL CODY—THE LOST HORSES—ALONE ON THE PRAIRIE—RESCUE BY SIX PALS—RETURN TO THE FORT.

HAVE made it a rule when guiding an army over the prairie, if the commanding officer asked me how far it was to wood and water, to give him an over-estimate rather than an under-estimate of the distance. This was because when men and animals are travelling over a strange country, hungry, tired, and thirsty, they are apt to imagine distances greater than they are.

In the district where we were the streams ran east and west, with about every twenty miles a larger stream of running water, clear as crystal, and full of fish. When camping we always endeavoured to get on one of these streams. There are also dividing ridges running between the streams, breaking up the country tremendously, and in these cañons and ravines head up together. It is consequently very difficult to move through such districts in waggons unless the guide knows the route well.

When I took the troops through in search of the Indians I had to be very careful, as the redskins would conceal themselves in the cañons and capture the supply trains before the escort knew where they were. Sometimes we had to drive trains all day, with our flank, two companies of soldiers, fighting the Indians as we marched along.

One night, when everything was quiet, a war party stole up to one of the sentries, killed him, then crept into the camp, cut loose a lot of horses and mules, fired into the tents, and made off with a number of the horses.

We had always to be on the alert; for the pluck and cunning of the Indians were almost inconceivable.

Another time, at nine o'clock in the evening, boot and saddle sounded, and every one tumbled out of his tent and scrambled on horseback.

The General sent for me, and said, "Nelson, I want you to take two companies of cavalry and go to the South Fork of the Rickaree. Do you know where it is?"

"I do, sir," I replied; "it's as nearly as possible a hundred miles from here."

"Yes," he said, "I know that. There's a party of soldiers there from the South besieged. One has escaped and brought me the news. I want you to go and save them. Get along as quickly as you can. I rely upon your discretion and bravery to rescue them all and bring them back to me in safety."

We started off westward, and rode all night as haid as we could, arriving about ten o'clock the following morning. The party consisted of Lieut.-Col. Forsyth and fifty picked scouts, who for seven days and nights had been without food, fighting for dear life the whole time.

The attacking force consisted of some 3,000 Indians, who had fortunately taken their departure just before we arrived.

The scene that presented itself was terrible. The scouts had retreated into a small cotton-wood grove, dismounted, and tied their horses to the trees. The Indians had killed all the horses first, and they were lying dead, still tied to the trees. The men had dug holes in the ground with their knives and crept into them, but, out of the fifty, forty were killed and wounded. There were dead white men, dead Indians innumerable, and dead horses all over the place.

Three other rescue parties arrived shortly after we did. We handed the rescued men over to one of these, collected as many soldiers from the others as we could get together, and started after the Indians.

After four days' travelling we came up pretty close

to them, and the commanding officer asked me how many I thought they numbered.

I examined the place of their last encampment, counting the fires where their tépees had been, estimated their number at not less than 4,000, and reported accordingly.

As we only mustered 250, all told, the officer thought the sooner we made tracks the better. He said he didn't want to find 4,000 men, which he reckoned was a larger party than the one he thought he had lost. So we returned to the head-quarters' camp, and reported the result of our mission to General Bradley.

The camp was moved about from one place to another, but no adventures worth chronicling occurred, and orders were at last given to return to Fort Macpherson.

One day, when we had nearly reached our destination, I was riding at the head of the cavalcade as usual, when I heard a voice say—

"Nelson, you are going to be shot."

I looked around, but could see no one. I pulled up my horse dead short.

We were in the middle of a plain at the time and no one was near us. Whilst I was standing there peering all around the General galloped up to me and said—

"Hallo, Nelson! What is it?"

"I don't know what it is, General," I replied, "but I heard a voice."

"What did it say?"

"'Nelson, you are going to be shot.'"

He burst into a roar of laughter, and said, "Oh, that's merely your superstition."

"Superstition or not, General," I answered, "with your permission I prefer to ride in the rear. I have had two or three warnings in my life, and have learnt not to challenge their accuracy."

"Very good," he replied, "go to the rear if you wish; I'll ride here, and we shall see if I am unlucky enough to get the shot intended for you."

We reached the fort safely, and the General was not shot, nor was I. He chaffed me a good deal about it, but I looked and felt serious. I could not get the idea out of my head, and it haunted me all that day.

At night I went down with a party of the boys to No. 280 Siding, a station on the Union Pacific Railway then building along the Californian route, and carried as far as Fort Macpherson. The line was on the north side of the river, which was crossed by means of a pontoon bridge.

I made my way to a saloon, which was pretty full of railway men, and after taking a drink or two and chatting with some of them went up to bed. I felt pretty tired, as we had ridden a long distance that day, and I made up my mind I would have a good long spell in a bed, for I had not slept in one for quite a long time.

I suppose I had been there about an hour when I heard a boy, a trumpeter belonging to my party, holloaing out for me. I got up and went down to see what they

were doing to him. He told me that one of the railway men had hit him on the head with a revolver. Seeing the man standing there, I said to him:

"Wait a moment, and I'll settle with you."

I returned to my room, fixed on my pistols, and said, coming down:

"You are a coward to hit that boy. If you want a quarrel, fight me."

He drew his pistol, and shot me through the thigh.

I drew mine, and had just got one of my pet "killing lines" on him when a fellow behind me hit my arm up and the bullet went through the ceiling.

I let off another shot with a similar result, and then my leg gave way and I fell.

They picked me up and took me in an ambulance to the Fort. There the doctors got hold of me and prodded about for the bullet, which after some days they managed to extract.

So much for my warning voice and the General's remark about superstition. I had rather more bed than I wanted this time, for they kept me on my back three months before they allowed me to move.

Another spasmodic peace was now patched up with the Indians at Laramie, but it was of short duration. It was entered into very much on the lines of its predecessors, so that some bands were fighting and others looking on.

The peace, however, enabled my squaw Jennie to come down south with a party of the Sioux and join me at the Fort. This time she had added to my responsibilities as a father and brought a baby son along with her, whom she presented to me as the heir to all the vast ranches of the Nelsons.

"All right," I said, "old girl; if you go on like that we shall want a whole prairie to support them."

However, I was very glad to have her back again, for she was able to look after me and do many little things for me.

The parson of the Fort had been having a good turn at me whilst I was in hospital, and had half convinced me that I was the wickedest man on the face of the earth. When Jennie came along he held up his hands in pious horror, and they went higher when he heard I had married her according to Indian custom and only given a horse for her.

His name was the Reverend John Robinson, a Methodist. He never left me alone, but got at me every day, saying that I ought to marry Jennie and make her an honest woman.

I said she was a darned sight more honest than any woman round the Fort, and that I would trust her anywhere and to do anything, from scalping a Pawnee to making a dough-nut; and as for marrying, I had married her according to the laws of the Sioux nation, and what more did he want?

He said we ought to be married according to the Church. I replied: "All right, if it will amuse you and not hurt me, you can fix it your own way, whenever you like. It's a farce any way, for 'Jennie' won't understand a word of it."

He came along a few days afterwards and fetched us in a waggon up to the chapel, where he said what he had to say and told me it was all right.

I interpreted it to "Jennie," who laughed, and thought what a funny old man he was.

I afterwards discovered it was no laughing matter as far as I was concerned, for it prevented me ever marrying a white woman. However, perhaps it was all for the best, for I doubt if any white woman would ever have lived with me. I was told I was never to call "Jennie" my squaw again. She was my wife now; and I took good care always to call her so when I was talking to the parson, who would invariably give me a lecture if I failed in that duty.

Gilman was the hay contractor, and the second cavalry were ordered out to guard his ranch. Whilst there, they built a fort underground, absolutely impregnable.

Roving bands of Indians were still on the warpath; but far worse than these were parties of disappointed miners coming back from Pike's Peak to the States.

They formed into bands, and broke open the ranches, taking whatever they wanted.

The Commander of the Fort formed a Company of Militia to ride up and down the road and watch these marauders. If they were caught robbing a ranch, upon arrival at the Fort they were placed under arrest, and kept there until they had paid treble for what they had stolen.

I have seen them come in with their trains loaded with canned fruit, whiskey, and even stoves, beds chairs, mowing machines, &c. The men who owned these waited at the Fort with their bills, which the miners were made to pay, if they had the money. Then the Commandant would order the goods they had stolen to be taken from them and stacked up upon the prairie, when they were handed back to their respective owners.

There was a scout at the Fort at this time named Bill Cody. I had known him since 1857, when he was driving teams along the route. He and I were very good friends, and a good deal of his knowledge of the country round he owed to me.

One day he came and inquired if I would accompany him on a little run out on the prairie. I was still unable to walk, but could sit on my horse without any inconvenience.

I assented, and we galloped off, riding nearly all day. I reckon we had covered fully seventy miles, when a deer sprang up right in front of us.

We both jumped off our horses, I on to my sound leg, and fired simultaneously.

The deer fell, but the crack of the rifles scared the horses, who bolted off like two streaks of greased lightning.

Cody ran after them for a few miles, but was obliged to give it up, and returned to where I was lying on the prairie, for I fell where I had jumped down, quite incapable of moving a step.

There was a little stream about five hundred yards off, and we decided that Cody should carry me there on his back.

I was a pretty good weight, but I clung on to him, and he covered the distance all right, after stopping a few times to take breath.

Arrived there, he deposited me safely on the ground, and then went out to bring in the deer.

After this he had to set to work and collect brushwood to make a fire. Then he cut up the deer, and I cooked a good square steak whilst he had a rest.

Our position was a most precarious one, and we had a long talk over what was best to be done. Small bands of Indians were roaming about all over the plains, and we both knew that without our horses we should stand a very poor chance if attacked by them.

Finally, Cody said there was nothing for it but for him to return to the Fort, get two fresh horses, and come back and fetch me.

I agreed to this as the only way out of the difficulty,

and we then sat and smoked until nightfall, when it was arranged he should leave me.

I shall never forget his last remark when he started off on his seventy-mile weary tramp.

"Good-bye, old chap: you hold the Fort until I come back."

I must confess I felt pretty miserable as I heard his footsteps die away. I lay for hours without moving, listening for the slightest sound, and clutching my gun whenever I heard a rustle, which, for all I knew, might either be an animal coming down to drink, or an Indian creeping up to kill me.

I kept my fire down as much as possible, so that the

glimmer should not be noticeable, and I kept myself wide awake by perpetually staring into the surrounding darkness.

About the middle of the night my leg began to pain me tremendously; the long ride during the day no doubt was the cause. Whether it was this alone, or the general strain on my nerves, I do not know, but I suddenly began to think what would become of me if Cody should be attacked and killed before he reached the Fort.

The thought sent me into a cold perspiration. I am not by any means a coward, and always look on the bright side of things, but somehow this notion got firmly into my head, and the long watches of the night were far from pleasant for me.

At length the morning broke, and what with pain and fatigue I fell asleep, and did not awake for several hours.

I now fed up my fire and had another turn at the deer, after which I crawled to the stream, and had a drink.

Most of the day I passed cooking and eating the deer. I don't think I ever gorged so much in my life. I tried experiments on every part, and altogether pronounced him very succulent and toothsome.

About evening my wood began to give out, and I became proportionately uncomfortable. It was now about time that Cody made his reappearance, and again the old idea seized me that something had happened to him.

The hours dragged on, and my last stick was consuming. Over it I was frizzling as fast as I could a piece of the deer, for I knew it was the last food I should get until help came, if it ever did, when in the stillness of the night I thought I heard a voice in the distance.

I listened attentively, and in a few minutes there came rolling distinctly over the prairie the word, "Nel—s-o-o-o-on."

It was not long before I had given a yell in return which might have been heard miles off.

This was answered by a shout that convinced me that more than Cody were on the search for me. After about twenty minutes hallooing and answering, they arrived, six of them, all pals of mine, who had jumped into their saddles and started out directly they heard the news.

Cody was too done up to accompany the party. He had covered the distance in an incredibly short space of time, and was thoroughly worn out. He had, however, given them the exact locality where to find me. In the darkness they had failed to strike it, and had been hunting around for quite a long time, until my first yell put them in the right direction.

We soon had the fire replenished now, and cooked up all the deer, which was particularly welcome to the party. The following morning we started back to the Fort; I on a spare mount they had brought for me.

I took good care not to venture upon any more runs out with Bill Cody until my leg was quite fixed up, for this escapade put me back several weeks, and I was obliged to go into hospital again.

A few days afterwards our horses came galloping up to the Fort as fresh as possible, with only a few fragments of their saddles left upon them. They had rubbed them off, and had had a fine old time of it out on the plains. How the Indians never got hold of them has always been a marvel to me.

CHAPTER XXVI.

DISCHARGED FROM HOSPITAL—GUARDING GILMAN'S RANCH—
HAYMAKING UNDER DIFFICULTIES—DEPARTURE OF THE GIL-
MANS—A TRIP TO NEBRASKA—DEATH OF THE FIRSTBORN—CAST
INTO PRISON — GENERAL DUNCAN'S EXPEDITION — THE LONE
SQUAW ON THE PLAINS—APPOINTED MASTER OF TRANSPORTS
AT OMAHA—RECOGNISED AS AN INDIAN BY THE GOVERNMENT
TREATY—BACK TO THE RESERVATION—TRADING WHISKEY FOR
HORSES WITH THE CLIFFORDS AND OTHERS—A FIGHT IN CAMP—
ESCAPE—THIRTY-TWO "PASS IN THEIR CHIPS"—RETURN TO THE
AGENCY.

AFTER I had been discharged from hospital I hung about the Fort for a few weeks until I felt thoroughly set up. Then I went to the Gilmans to see what they could do for me. The soldiers had returned from the outside ranch, and, as there was no one left to look after it, I was asked if I would. A fair amount of stock had been taken out there in anticipation of the Indians being driven right away from the road, but it seemed an almost hopeless task on the part of the military to drive them right way.

It was arranged that I should go out with my wife and the children and remain three months. At the expiration of that time the Commandant thought he would be able to drive the Indians out into the prairie and keep them there.

We packed up our traps and went out under a guard. The soldiers left us, only returning every now and then when they wanted anything.

I took possession of the Fort, which was about forty steps away from the ranch, and consisted of a circular room some twelve feet in diameter, excavated in the ground, with an underground passage from it running to the stables. A stockade surrounded it, absolutely impregnable, at least from attacks by Indians.

I had not been there very long before I had some visits from my red friends, who would creep up and try to carry the place by stealth.

I had a thousand rounds of ammunition, and my wife loaded my rifles whilst I blazed away. I killed several Indians and their horses whilst I was there.

Over and over again I have killed antelopes, through the chinks of the stockade, and run out to fetch them in.

One of my chief amusements was to ride out into the prairie and draw the Indians after me, then run into my hole and open fire on them.

After a time they would not come near me, but ride round in a circle, of which I was the centre, at about one thousand yards range, and whoop and yell, hoping to draw me out. But I never nibbled at that bait.

GETTING IN THE HAY

Finally, the Gilmans determined, as the ranch cost them more to keep up than it brought in, to pull it down, especially as, wood being scarce, they received a good offer from the railway people for it. Accordingly, a party of men came out from the siding under a military escort with a lot of waggons, and demolished and carried it into the Fort with all the remaining stock.

My wife and I took our departure at the same time, and when I returned I found myself looked upon as a sort of hero for having held out as long as I had.

When the hay season came on I superintended getting the crop in. I had to work on an island in the river a few miles from the Fort. We had four mowing machines, and used them under great difficulties.

The Indians annoyed us by getting into the long grass and taking pot shots at the men at work. I had to ride in front of the machines with a double-barrelled shot gun and a brace of six shooters, and I was a regular target for them. I often wonder now how it was I was not killed, for over and over again they have sprung up within a few paces, taken a pot shot at me, and bolted into the grass.

One day I jumped off my horse to have a skirmish with some of them who were having a lot of fun at my expense, when, just as I fired, my horse took fright and bolted. I felt so mad at his leaving me in the lurch, that I faced about and sent a bullet through his head, which effectually prevented his playing me any of those tricks again. The Gilmans behaved very badly over this. They made me pay for the horse.

I got away from the Indians all right. At any time they would rather face the devil than myself at close quarters.

After this crop was gathered in, the Gilmans sold out their stock at the Fort, and moved further away into Nebraska, where they bought a lot of land and built themselves a fine house out of the profits they had made. During the seven years they had been trading—I had been with them the whole time off and on—they had made over 200,000 dollars. I had materially aided in this, but I was not invited to participate in the division of the plunder.

A permanent treaty was made now (1868) with the principal fighting Indians, and certain localities or Reservations were set aside for them. There were still, however, a lot of marauding bands roaming about, making locomotion very dangerous.

I was invited by the Gilmans to accompany them for

a few months down to their new home and help them to get straight. As I had nothing better to do I assented, and sent my wife and children off to "Lone Wolf," who offered to take charge of them during my absence.

I was particularly fond of my little daughter, who was a charming little thing and very attached to me. That was the last I saw of her, for after my departure she grieved for me so much and cried so for days and days, that convulsions set in and she died. I did not know of this until my return in the spring of the following year.

When I did return to Fort Macpherson I found an expedition organised to drive the Indians into the Reservation which had been set aside for them at Whetstone Agency, Dakota.

A large number of them were following the buffalo down South, and could not be made to understand that it was incumbent upon them to keep their treaty obligations.

There were over two thousand of them at the Fort who were being fed at the Government expense, and amongst these a large proportion of the Ogallalas and Brûlés, with "Lone Wolf" and my wife. They were going up to the Reservation, and I wanted to accompany them, especially as I had accumulated a lot of stock, valued at over 3,800 dollars.

I made my preparations accordingly, and we were on the point of departure, when General Duncan, in charge of the expedition, sent for me and told me he wished me to accompany him as interpreter. I said I could not go, as I had made arrangements to look after my stock and take it up to the Reservation. He said I must go.

I replied that I begged to be excused.

"I insist upon your going," he said.

"Well, if you do that, General," I replied; "I shan't. and that's straight."

I do not know what passed between him and the Commandant, but the next thing was that I was arrested on a warrant of the latter and locked up in the guard-house.

There I was told I should remain until I assented, and, as every prospect was held out to me of remaining there for an indefinite period, I thought I had better give in without further bother; especially as the General came to me and said that the success of the expedition rested in a great degree upon my services as interpreter, and if I would consent to go he would guarantee the safe delivery of my stock at the Reservation.

Upon these conditions I consented. It was the worst day's work I ever did in my life, for when my wife arrived at the Reservation every one of my stock had been stolen, and I have never received a single cent compensation from the Government for them from that day to this.

The expedition consisted of five companies of cavalry and three hundred Pawnee scouts under Major North. My old friend, Bill Cody, was chief of the scouts and guides, and I was the second under him, with the rank and title of Chief Interpreter.

One day, after we had been out some time, we encamped down on Short Nose Creek. There Cody asked me to take two waggons, and go down and kill buffaloes enough for the command and bring them into camp.

Whilst we were talking a volley came from some fifty to sixty Indians who had secreted themselves in the bush. The rest of the command was on a hill to the rear, and the result was that we had a very narrow squeak for our lives.

The Pawnee scouts coming to the rescue, a running fight commenced and was continued for fifteen miles.

When the troops arrived upon the scene they heard a dog bark, and found that about two hundred yards from where we had been conversing an Indian village was pitched.

The enemy only had time to clear out with their squaws and children, leaving everything else they possessed behind.

Two days afterwards we found an old squaw on the prairie who was too decrepit to keep up with them, and they had left her to be devoured by the wolves. We ran the Indians round all the winter, eventually driving them into the Reservation, and then returned to the Fort, where we took the train and went down to Omaha.

I was there made master of transports, and had an offer to continue permanently in the service, but, finding I could not stand the restraint which my duties entailed,

I resigned and went up to the Reservation, where I found my wife all right and heard the news of the loss of my stock.

By the treaty that had been made I was recognised as one of the members of the Ogallala band of Indians, and entitled to all the rights and privileges that any other Indian enjoyed. My wife, children, and myself had a claim for land, farming implements, rations, goods, and in fact everything that the treaty guaranteed. I

may here state that I have never asked for anything myself; but in time the land will become very valuable, provided the Government do not steal it, which I think they will do sooner or later.

About three or four weeks at the Reservation nearly settled me. I began to pine for a more active occupation, and was meditating what form it should take when H. Clifford and M. H. Clifford, two brothers I knew, who had both married squaws, suggested a scheme.

The Indians had for some time past been stealing

horses from the whites, and now had a number of very fine animals. We could get a horse worth two hundred and fifty dollars for a gallon of tarantula juice, and the project was to go out and trade with them in this commodity.

Any qualms of conscience I may at one time have had, as to the iniquity of trading whiskey with redskins, had long since vanished. The mischief had already been done by others, and if they could not get it from one source they would from another. As this was now the principal commodity upon which trading negotiations were conducted, I thought I might just as well be in the swim as not.

There were some other white men at the Reservation anxious to join in the expedition, and as we thought the more the merrier we let them in. They were A. Roff, John Dodge, Toad Randal, J. Nesbit, and Johnny Come Lately, with myself and the Cliffords—eight in all.

It was a difficult matter to keep the Indians in the Reservation; they were running all over the place, and there were more out than in. We got a few waggons together, laid in a good stock of fire-water, and moved out into the open on the look-out for wandering parties. We ran across several of these, and did fairly well for some little time. The Indians would sell anything for whiskey, and parted readily with horses and mules, which had cost them nothing, for a few drinks.

At length we reached a big village which consisted of over five hundred lodges of Wajajas, Ogallalas, Brûlés, and Cheyennes. My brothers-in-law were then assisting me, for a consideration, to run the trade.

I had pitched my tépee close to "Lone Wolf's," and in it had placed a twenty-gallon keg of whiskey. The rest of my party had gone off to hunt up some Indians coming from the South, feeling safe in the knowledge that, with my interest and standing with the crowd, I should do a far better deal than if they were hanging around.

Things went on pretty satisfactorily for a few days, and most of the topers came in with their horses. These, as I traded them, I tethered outside my tépee.

At length a Cheyenne whom I did not know came in and asked for some whiskey.

I was lying down with my head against the cask at the time, and Lone Wolf was in the centre of the tépee, taking a drink and having a quiet smoke.

"Very good," said Lone Wolf, in reply to his inquiry; "go and get your horse, and you can have what it is worth."

He said he hadn't got a horse to trade with, and wanted whiskey without.

"Then you won't have any," said Lone Wolf.

"Won't I, though," he replied, and before I had time to realise what he was up to he had drawn his pistol and sent two bullets clean through the cask just a few inches above my head.

He thought, no doubt, to scare me into complying with his demand, but it did not work, for I stayed quite still and never moved a muscle.

"Lone Wolf" looked at him for a second or two, and then, bounding up, flew at him, grabbed his pistol away, and knocked him down with the butt-end of it.

The report brought in two or three others, who seized him and dragged him out of the tépee.

Whilst this was going on I stuck my fingers into the holes from which the whiskey was running out and drenching me. Soon the others came to my assistance, and we plugged them with pieces of stick.

The Cheyenne, directly he picked himself up, went off to his party, and made them come to demand satisfaction in a body, and insist that I should be handed over to them.

The Indians on my side told them to go away, as they did not want to have any disturbance.

This the Cheyennes refused to do, and finished the argument by firing a volley through the top of my lodge.

This was too much for my brothers-in-law, who went out and lassoed the man who commenced the disturbance.

About fifty of the Cheyennes now tried to get the man away, and an equal number of "Lone Wolf's" party were determined they should not.

In the struggle that ensued the lariat got twisted round the man's body, and both sides pulling at it resulted in the poor devil being dragged in half.

When this occurred the whole camp divided, and a regular hand-to-hand fight commenced.

Our party was the stronger of the two, and the battle waged furiously.

I saw nothing funny in being killed over a row which was none of my seeking, and accordingly crawled into the tépee, where I remained until the poles which were being persistently shot through fell upon me, and the whole place was becoming honeycombed with bullets.

Then my friends brought me a horse, told me to put on a blanket, mount, and ride for life.

I did so, but not without getting some holes shot through the blanket. After covering about three miles, I pulled up and waited until the firing had ceased. Then I made my way back quietly to camp.

When I arrived I found about half the village gone, and my friends gathered round the spot where my tépee had stood. This had all been torn down in the scrimmage, but the Cheyennes had been beaten off.

The first thing that attracted my attention was the head knocked out of my twenty-gallon keg, and the entire crowd drinking out of tin cups, buckets, dippers, in fact anything that would hold liquid.

I knew it was no use saying anything, so I looked cheerful under the depressing circumstances.

They told me I should find my brothers-in-law with the horses going towards the Platte. They had thought it better to get away with the stock, as they were afraid the Cheyennes would return and steal them.

I was advised to take the trail and follow them as quickly as possible, and say that the others would follow directly they had finished the whiskey.

I thought this about one of the coolest proposals I

ever heard ; but, knowing that in their frenzied state my life was not worth a moment's purchase immediately the spirit took effect, I galloped off as hard as I could pelt.

It was not until the following morning that I overtook " Lone Wolf," when I found that thirty-two of his band had "passed in their chips," and over forty-five were wounded.

I got back to the Reservation from that trip with thirty-seven head of horses and some nice buffalo robes. The Cliffords and the rest of the boys were not so fortunate, for they fell foul of the Cheyennes, lost all their whiskey, horses, and everything, and barely escaped with their lives.

CHAPTER XXVII.

BUFFALO HUNTING FOR THE CHICAGO MARKET WITH THE CLIFFORDS—HANK CLIFFORD GOES TO OMAHA FOR WHISKEY—TRADING WITH CHE-WAX-SAH—A DIFFERENCE OF OPINION—DEPARTURE—A FIENDISH REVENGE—THE PRAIRIE FIRE—ARRIVAL AT THE RENDEZVOUS—ARREST BY ORDER OF THE COMMANDANT—HANK CLIFFORD SENT TO GENERAL AUGUR—RELEASE—DEPARTURE FOR RED CLOUD AGENCY—MEETING WITH FRANK WHEELING, BRONCHO BILL, SLIM JIM, AND SELF-RAISING WILLIAM—A MARAUDING EXPEDITION—FOLLOWING A TRAIL—CAPTURE OF THREE HUNDRED HORSES—CHARACTERISTICS OF COMPANIONS—A CHEERFUL SURPRISE—FIGHTING AGAINST ODDS—FRANK SHOT IN THE SHOULDER—RE-CAPTURE OF THE HORSES BY THE ENEMY—DEJECTED RETURN TO THE FORT.

REVIVED by a few weeks' rest, I again began to pine for some active occupation. This time I bought a waggon with the proceeds of the sale of some of my horses, reserving four of the best to harness it. Hank Clifford, Mortimer Clifford, and Arthur Ruff, who had provided themselves each with a similar outfit, and I, engaged three teamsters, for whom we pooled together, and bought two more waggons, making six in all. We started for the south side of the Platte River.

We all took our squaws with us, and our object was to kill buffalo meat and consign it by rail to Chicago, where it fetched a very good price.

At a small station a few miles west of Fort Kearney we found a man who made a contract with us at six cents per pound delivered to him there. He took all risk of freight and of making his profit on the sale price.

When we reached the hunting grounds the buffalo were very plentiful, and every day we killed sufficient to load up our transport, which the teamsters drove off to the siding and delivered. In the first six weeks we made over 2,000 dollars between us, from which the number of animals we killed may be fairly estimated.

As the buffalo were dispersed by our continued attacks upon them, we separated and followed them individually, fixing a permanent camp and returning with our loads as we filled up.

We kept this up until the weather became too warm to consign any more meat, and then we sent Hank Clifford to Omaha to buy whiskey and groceries. With these we meant to trade with some of the roving Indians still kicking up their heels on the prairie.

Upon his return with the stock we all loaded up, and took different directions, agreeing to meet in two months at a given spot a few miles from Fort Macpherson.

Jennie and I went off to a village that I knew some

sixty miles distant, and opened trade with the band there. I was upon pretty friendly terms with them. We stayed some time and did a very good deal. We should have succeeded in disposing of all our stock to great advantage, but for the soldiers who were always chasing the Indians about to get them into the Reservation.

Up to the present, however, they had not found this village, which was very artfully located. That was why I had come to it.

One day word was brought us that the soldiers were coming along with the intention of killing them all.

I advised the chief, who was named Che-wax-sah, to sit tight, and that no harm would happen. But he got scared, broke up his camp, and started off. I wanted to go with them, but he would not allow me, saying that he believed I had put the soldiers on his track.

This I stoutly denied.

"Well," he said, "I don't believe you; so pack up your goods and clear out from us, or it will be the worse for you."

I was very indignant at being treated thus; but there was nothing for it but complying. So I loaded up my team, and made tracks as quickly as possible.

He was so bitter against me that I believe he would have killed me in camp had he dared. With the cunning and savagery of his race, however, he hit upon a far more diabolical scheme for getting rid of me and my wife.

I had gone some ten or twelve miles on my journey, when, hearing a noise behind me, I turned, and to my horror found that the red devils had set fire to the prairie.

The grass at that time of the year was very dry and dead, and the fire came sweeping down upon us as quickly as a horse could gallop.

Those who have never seen a prairie fire can form no idea of its magnitude and weirdness. Behind us was a stretch of flame miles in width, rushing on with a roar,

and ready in a few moments to engulf us and leave nothing but our calcined remains.

There was only one escape—to set fire to the grass around us, and so fight the fire that was burning against the wind.

I was almost dumfounded for an instant when I saw what was happening. There were seven kegs of powder in the waggon, and the outlook was far from comfortable.

Jennie, however, grasped the situation at a glance, and before I could tell her what to do had stooped down and set fire to the long grass in several places round us.

I rushed to the waggon and pulled the canvas down tight all round it. I then began whipping the fire out.

I pulled off my shirt, soaked it in water, and fought for dear life. Jennie, in the meanwhile, seized a water-keg and threw the contents over the waggon covers.

The oncoming scourge was jumping from thirty to forty feet every instant, and the heat was becoming intense. With a roar it reached our fire; then there was a sheet of flame and smoke that swept completely over the waggon, and then for several minutes I could see nothing.

I stuffed my wet shirt into my mouth and gasped for breath.

Those minutes seemed hours to me; at length I could stand it no longer, and rushed to where I had last seen my wife with her hands over her face trying to shut out the heat and smoke.

Suddenly my head came in contact with the waggon box, and I fell senseless.

When I regained consciousness I heard Jennie say, "We are saved, the fire has passed over. Get up and come here, you are too much in the smoke."

I tried to rise, but could not. My limbs were like lumps of lead. She came to me and poured some water over my head and face. This seemed to revive me, and with her assistance I managed to stand up.

My hair was all burnt off. Even my eye-brows had not escaped, and I was suffering great pain from burns generally.

Jennie was all right; she had emptied a keg of water over her, and drawing the shawl over her head had thrown herself flat on the ground.

It was some days before I was well enough to move, and a nice spectacle we presented when we did start. The horses were all singed, and I was a wild, weird-looking object that would have scared the crows away.

There was no necessity now to shoot game; the prairie round was strewn with small specimens of all kinds ready roasted for us.

I swore eternal vengeance on Che-wax-sah and his party; and kept my word, for when I got an opportunity I paid them back in their own coin, and well some of them remember the day and date.

We arrived at the rendezvous safely, and were the first there. After we had waited about a few weeks the others turned up, and we held a consultation as to our next move.

Whilst engaged in this—for we took several days over it—our deliberations were interrupted in rather an unexpected manner by the arrival of my friend Bill Cody with a party of soldiers. Their instructions were:

"Arrest John Nelson and outfit going with a party of Indians down South to hunt."

We protested that we were going to do nothing of the kind, and insisted upon being left unmolested. Cody, however, said that those were his instructions, and he had no alternative but to act upon them.

They had been issued by the commandant at the Fort, and we accordingly packed Hank Clifford off to inquire what he meant by such autocratic behaviour.

Upon arrival Clifford could get nothing out of him beyond that he meant to keep us prisoners, and he therefore went off to Omaha to see General Augur, who had

command of the district. We in the meanwhile remained where we were, with the soldiers mounting guard over us.

After a time Clifford returned, with an order commanding our instant release, and with a note to the commandant informing him that we were to be molested in no way, provided we did nothing to prevent the Indians being driven into the Reservation. The General further said that, so far as the buffalo were concerned, it would be a very good thing when we did kill them all, for then the Indians would leave the country.

We had a good deal of chaff with the soldiers over this, and commemorated our victory by a big drink from our remaining stock of whiskey. Then we pulled up stakes, and went west, up to the Red Cloud Agency at Fort Robinson, on White Earth River, in Dakota, about 250 miles from Fort Macpherson.

We arrived there without any further *contretemps*, and laid around playing poker and drinking whiskey for six months.

The restricted life up there after a time began to tell upon me. I felt that I must be off again ; but where to go and what to do I could not make up my mind.

Whilst in this undecided state I fell across Frank Wheeling (or Utah Frank, as he was called, owing to his position as chief of the Ute scouts), Broncho Bill, a well-known interpreter and squaw man, a man named Slim Jim, and another called Self-raising William. I never knew these two last men's other names ; I don't believe they ever had any. We were a merry party, and determined to go out and have some fun. We did not know quite how to set about it ; none of us had been doing anything for some time, and, as the old saying has it, " Peace troubled us." All we knew was that we wanted excitement, and the only way to get that was to fall foul of the Indians.

Finally, we agreed that the best way was to go out on a marauding expedition, make a raid on some Indian village, steal their horses, and, if necessary, take a few scalps, and then come back to the agency.

With this laudable object we armed and equipped ourselves for a month's raid. What was sauce for the goose was sauce for the gander. The Indians were always on that racket, and we did not see why they should have it entirely their own way.

Frank wanted to go north; but I said south, as I knew where to find the villages there. Accordingly, my plan was agreed to, and, leaving our squaws, we started off down into Kansas.

Game was very plentiful all the way, and we had a good time killing and feasting on as much as we wanted. Our hunting ground being reached, we scouted over the country for some days, travelling by night and hiding by day. On the south side of the south fork of the Solomon River we struck an Indian trail, which I estimated consisted of about sixty-five lodges, and, counting seven to a lodge, of about four hundred and fifty people. This we followed in a westerly direction for some sixty miles. I guessed there would be a village at the end of it, and my surmise proved correct.

Arriving within three miles of them, we secreted ourselves and our horses in the timber, from which we could watch their movements.

Several times whilst lying here two or three Indians passed within range of our guns. Frank and Slim Jim wanted to shoot them, but Broncho and myself held a different opinion. Our object was to capture some of their horses to repay us for having come so far. Besides, we knew that if we fired a shot the report would alarm the whole village, and we should have to fight the crowd, with the prospect of losing some of our topknots.

As far as we could gather, a function was going on in the camp, and every one seemed very busy there.

Out on the prairie, about two miles distant, the horses were running loose, grazing, and it made our mouths water to see how many there were of them. A council of war was held, and it was agreed that when night fell we should start out and lasso as many as we could, then return, and, travelling all night, get about thirty miles away before the Indians discovered their loss.

This programme we religiously carried out, and worked like niggers immediately the inmates of the village had turned in and everything was quiet.

We secured about three hundred head, and ran them as hard as we could tear due north towards the Platte River.

The scheme worked admirably, and all that night we were laughing and congratulating ourselves upon our good fortune. The following day, however, the colts began to lag behind. Unfortunately, we had got hold of mares and colts. When the latter began to break down we shot them, but this only had the effect of making the mares go back after them.

At length we made up our minds to stop awhile

and have a rest. So we selected a high hill, and put the horses on the north side out of sight.

We then had a picnic, Slim Jim acting as cook. I laid on the ground with my glass, watching for "black ducks."

When we had finished our meal we took a position on the hill whence we could see all round for miles.

The boys laid down for a nap, as they were all very tired. I, not feeling sleepy, undertook to watch. I could not help thinking out the characteristics of my companions as they lay there.

Broncho Bill would sleep, if he knew he would be scalped before he awoke. I think he was a descendant of the seven sleepers. When he was awake, though, he was particularly agile, and with his "fighting toggery" on, and his Irish blood up, an enemy to be avoided.

Frank Wheeling was a quiet and unassuming man who did not say much, but when he did speak it was worth listening to. A braver man than he never stepped.

Self-raising William reminded me very much of Hank Clifford; he knew everything, and everybody's business except his own. I often told him that he was a very smart man, and knew everything that he should not know, with the exception of one thing, and that was that he was a born fool.

As for "Slim Jim," he was born a thief, and two years afterwards was found hanging to the branch of a tree with a card pinned to his back, on which was written: "Checked through. Destination unknown. Died for want of breath."

Whilst ruminating in this way an hour or so passed, and, getting tired of perpetually peering through my glass, I laid it down by my side, and began to yawn. I don't know whether I dropped off to sleep or not, but, suddenly looking up the hill behind me, I saw a party of about thirty-five Indians calmly looking down upon our little camp.

In an instant I had fired my rifle at one of them; the bullet struck him in the side and he fell. Before the report had died away every man in our camp was on his feet, with the exception of Broncho, who sat up and roundly swore at the Indians for having disturbed him.

The Indians were a party belonging to the village we had left. They had been over to the Platte River, burning ranches, killing and stealing, and on their way home had come up in our rear, where they fell across the horses, which they had no difficulty in recognising as their own.

The first thing they had done was to collect these, and then climb up the hill to see what was the cause of their being so far away from the village.

The meeting on both sides was a cheerful surprise, as may be imagined. In an instant we were all running for our horses, which were tethered close at hand.

Broncho came walking leisurely down the hill. I said:

z

"Hurry up, Broncho, and let's get out of this."

Just then the enemy commenced firing at us, whilst some of them drove off the horses.

We formed into line and charged up the hill, driving them off it and down the other side.

Frank said to Broncho: "There goes your horse," pointing to a cream-coloured one, upon which an Indian

had sprung, and which Broncho had reserved as his own special racer.

"You darned old redskin," Broncho replied, "you shall never have him." And, raising his rifle, down went the Indian with a bullet through his head.

Another Indian had turned, and was getting a bee line on us, when Frank took a sight at him in return. Before he could pull the trigger a ball came from the left and struck him in the shoulder.

I saw his arm drop by his side, and riding up to him, inquired if he was hurt.

"Yes," he replied; "I guess I am."

I told him to go down the hill, and sent Slim Jim along with him.

Broncho, Self-raising William, and myself now had another charge, in which we killed two or three and routed the remainder. They bolted, and took cover in some timber, and there made a stand.

Finding we could not dislodge them, and seeing that all attempts to follow and recapture the horses would be futile, we returned to where we had left Frank and Slim Jim.

The former was now very bad, and we did not know what to do with him. I went again up the hill and dug some roots, which I cut up and placed on the wound. These stopped the bleeding and eased the pain.

We then struck out for the Fort, and made the best time we could in reaching it. Frank was there handed over to the doctors, who had a high old time with him for some weeks. As for ourselves, we were all very glad to think that we had got back with our scalps on. We had no time to secure those of the Indians we had killed, with the exception of one, of which I was the proud possessor. Frank, Broncho, and myself have been mad to this day to think that the Indians got their horses back. It was just our luck, after having gone so far and getting the prizes within our grasp, to lose them as we did

CHAPTER XXVIII.

SQUATTING ON MEDICINE CREEK—BUILDING THE FIRST RANCH—A NEW SPECULATION—COLLAPSE OF THE PROJECT—"SAVE US FROM OUR FRIENDS"—BUFFALO MEAT FOR THE SOLDIERS—CONVERSION OF PLEASANT VALLEY INTO FRONTIER COUNTY—THE JACK BRATT & CO. SWINDLE—PULLING UP STAKES FOR PINE RIDGE—TRADING WITH THE INDIANS ON THE RESERVATION—DIFFERENCES WITH DR. SEVILLE—THE J. W. DEAR TRADES-UNION—"WANTED FOR ILLICIT TRADING"—THE RAID ON THE VILLAGE—"HUNTING FOR JOHN NELSON"—THE DEPUTATION TO GENERAL MACKENZIE—A NARROW SQUEAK FOR THREE BEARS—PEACE WITH THE GENERAL—SEVILLE AND DEAR KICKED OFF THE RESERVATION—AN INDIAN FAMINE—RASCALITY OF GOVERNMENT OFFICIALS—AN INTIMATION TO CLEAR OUT.

MY next move was with the Cliffords and Arthur Ruff down to Fort Macpherson. A few miles south of the Fort was Medicine Creek, previously mentioned. This was a favourite spot of mine, and I had long wished to pitch my tent there.

We moved out, and I ran up the first log hut that ever adorned its shores. Hank Clifford followed, and then Arthur Ruff started one

The place soon became known as "Pleasant Valley," and the rendezvous of all the hunters in the vicinity.

It was in the midst of a good hunting country, where game of all kinds was very plentiful, and its fame spread far and near, sportsmen coming out even from England. For all arrivals my place, which was a sort of hotel, was the headquarters, and this brought me plenty of general business.

People soon came out, when they found we were so comfortably located, and before six months were over huts began to spring up all along the creek.

I thought of embarking in a new speculation to raise buffalo on my ranch, and so save the trouble of hunting them. I bought some Texas cows which were good milkers, and went out on the prairie and captured two buffalo calves. I caught also two otters, two coons, two elks, two antelopes, two deer, and four wolves; in fact, I started a regular menagerie. Some of the animals I kept for pleasure, the others for gain.

A party of my wife's relatives came out to visit us, and brought their families, their horses, dogs—everything. This was rather a big order for me, but I was bound to show them every hospitality. They had no sugar, coffee flour, or bacon, and I had to furnish them with these. I did not mind providing them with the food, but the way they threw it about and wasted it made me mad.

The Indian boys were the plague of my life. They averaged from four to ten years of age, and the young demons would go with their bows and arrows to the corral where my stock was, run the calves, elk, and deer round the yard, and then shoot arrows into them.

I returned from hunting one day just in time to catch them making a "surround." About a dozen were straddled on sticks to represent horses, and were running my calves round and round, shooting arrows into them, just as they had seen their fathers in legitimate hunting. My own boy was the ringleader. They had been having their fun some time before I arrived, for two calves were dead, and the rest of the animals died quickly.

I only managed to save one calf of the lot, and this I kept until he was a year old, when he became so spiteful, and fought the

children so, that I had to turn him loose. That was the end of my attempt to raise buffalo.

I next entered into a contract at the Fort to supply the troops with buffalo meat at my old price—six cents per pound. The contractor got ten to twelve cents for it. I used to take my waggon out, kill the animals, load up about 3,000 pounds, and trot off to the Fort. In this way I made money quickly and easily. I, however, never kept it long, for as soon as I was paid I used to rush into the store, have a good pull at some tarantula juice, and then go off and play poker.

In those days money was very plentiful, and no one thought of playing less than five dollars ante. Sometimes I would have my pockets full, and in less than two or three hours be skinned out of every cent.

Whilst in Pleasant Valley we organised the district into a county, and it was called Frontier County, the name by which it is still known. We had a surveyor, who was suddenly appointed justice of the peace, and as he could not hold two offices I slipped into his position, and surveyed the whole of the county. I was allowed a deputy, whom I made do all the detail work.

An incident occurred whilst we were there that created a considerable stir, and will serve to illustrate the way in which the Indians were swindled.

We were there altogether three winters. The second was an exceptionally hard one. Amongst the many ranchers who had come out was a firm named Jack Bratt & Co., who had bought a large tract of land from the Government, and established an extensive cattle ranch extending miles around the settlement.

During the winter they lost about 2,500 head of stock, frozen to death on the prairie. I put in a lot of work skinning them at forty cents apiece, and in this way made over 200 dollars.

These people hit upon an ingenious expedient to make the Government pay for their losses.

Spotted Tail was still wandering about with the

remnant of his band. Up to the present they had avoided being driven into the Reservation, and as he was pretty hard pushed Bratt got hold of him, and in consideration of a horse persuaded him to sign a document to the effect that his band, being pressed for food during the winter, had killed and eaten thirty of the ranch cattle.

As a matter of fact they had not touched one; but, anxious to get the horse, Spotted Tail readily fell into the trap.

To the figures thirty Bratt & Co. added two ciphers, and put in their claim for 3,000 to the Government. They received compensation at the rate of thirty dollars per head—in all, 90,000 dollars.

No one knew anything about this down our way until the Government agents at Red Cloud Agency deducted the 90,000 dollars from the Sioux tribute. Then the murder was out, and there was a terrible commotion in the country with the Indians.

The upshot of it was that Spotted Tail took action in the courts. I and the Cliffords, with several others, gave evidence proving the forgery, and Bratt & Co. were called upon to refund the entire amount. In doing this they were effectually "busted," and had to clear out of the country. This is but one example of the many frauds that have been perpetrated upon the Indians from time to time.

Soon after this was settled, so many people came out that I could stand it no longer, so, leaving the Cliffords there, I pulled up stakes and moved once more up to

Pine Ridge and the Red Cloud Agency. I had two more additions to my family by this time.

My next venture was buying goods on my own account and trading with the Indians on the Reservation. This created a great deal of jealousy with the traders licensed by the Government; but they could not stop me, as I was a recognised Indian. Still they did everything in their power to annoy me, and reported me to the Government agent, Dr. Seville. He ordered me off the Reservation, but I refused to go.

Red Cloud Agency proper covers a space of about three acres, fenced in with a stockade sixteen feet high.

One day I made up my mind to get even with the agent, so I planted myself at the entrance gate with a club, waiting for him to come out.

When he appeared, however, I did not strike him, but I said:

" Dr. Seville, I've been waiting for you two hours for the purpose of having a settlement with you. I give you the option of letting me alone and allowing me to carry on my business peaceably and unmolested, or receiving the soundest thrashing you have ever had."

He said, " Nelson, you are trading against orders, and as Government agent here I forbid your doing so."

" I require no orders," I replied. " I am a recognised Indian, and a party to the treaty with the Government, and there is no clause in that treaty which prevents our trading amongst ourselves. Accordingly, since there is no law to prevent me, I intend to continue as I have done, and defy you or any one else to interfere with me."

This almost took his breath away. He looked at me a moment and then at my club, which I was nervously twisting about in my hand, and said that if I would agree he would refer the matter to Washington for decision.

"Very well," I replied; "we will leave it that way, and I will continue as heretofore until the reply arrives."

One of the principal traders at the agency was a man named J. W. Dear, and he stood in with Seville, both of them robbing the Indians and feathering their own nests.

I was a thorn in their sides because I traded upon decent terms, whereas the others all worked under a sort of trades-union, so that prices were kept up to a standard that was ruin to the Indians, who had to submit to the extortion or go without the necessaries of life.

The Reservation itself covered an area larger than the whole of England, and the Black Hills ran right through it. About 11,000 Indians were at Red Cloud, and 9,000 at Rosebud Agency, some ninety miles distant.

On the Missouri at Standing Rock, and at the Cheyenne Agencies, there were about the same number. There were five agencies in all, and about 50,000 Indians had been driven in.

Nearly all the Sioux were there by this time, and amongst them my brothers-in-law, Lone Wolf and Torn

Blanket. My wife lived with these latter at a camp about three miles from the agency.

My other brother-in-law, Red Cloud, who was chief of the Sioux nation, and after whom the agency was named, lived just outside the agency, and I passed most of my time with him.

The way I carried on my business was to take my waggons and potter about the Reservation, dealing with all whom I came across.

I had made a longer journey than usual up into the Black Hills, and had returned to the camp where my wife was, when Dear and Seville, hearing of my arrival, hit upon the following plan to effectually rid themselves of me.

Whiskey was prohibited from being sold to the Indians upon any pretence whatever, and a trader found offending in this way was under a penalty of 500 dollars fine and from two to five years' imprisonment, in proportion to the gravity of the offence.

This law was applied not only to the Reservation, but to every town, city, or village throughout the United States.

The second night after my arrival, the village was surprised by a party of soldiers surrounding it, and the officer in charge entered with a warrant for my arrest, and demanded that I should be handed over to him.

One of my brothers-in-law came and told me what was going on. Disguising myself as an Indian, I slipped a blanket over my head, joined the crowd, and went to hear what I had done to be " wanted " so suddenly.

The information laid against me, and upon which the warrant had been granted, was that I had been reported for selling the prohibited liquor—and that was all we could gather.

My brothers-in-law declared I had only just returned from the hills, and had no whiskey at all, that not a drop had been brought into the camp by me or by anybody else, and that the information was a fabrication.

The officer replied that whether that was so or not he could not decide. His orders were to arrest me, and when he had done so the matter could be settled at the agency.

The soldiers accordingly proceeded to search the camp, and, looking everywhere, could not find me.

I was so well disguised that I chatted in Indian with the interpreter, a white man named Billy Garnett. We hunted together all over the place to find the culprit, and subsequently I had a chat with the officer as to what had become of him. I swore I had seen him arrive in camp two days previously, that he had only stayed a very short time, and had gone off again.

The Indians became so mad at the indignity thrust upon them, that they wanted to kill the troops, and armed themselves for the purpose. I could only prevent a massacre from taking place by saying that if they did anything of the kind I should instantly give myself up.

Lone Wolf went into my tépee, and, seizing my Winchester repeater, let off about a dozen shots into the air. The troops, seeing the threatening attitude of the Indians, thought it better to retire and fall back upon the agency.

When they had gone I jumped on my horse, and made tracks to a village about twenty miles distant.

The following day my brothers-in-law and a large number of the Ogallalas went in a body to Fort Robinson, and demanded an explanation from General Mackenzie, the officer in command. He told them that the information had been laid by "Three Bears," a chief of a small band of the Ogallalas who lived close to the agency.

Some of the party instantly bolted off, seized him, and brought him before the General, where he confessed that he had told a lie, and had been bribed to do so by my enemies, the traders.

Hearing this, the General immediately apologised, and wrote a letter to me withdrawing all aspersions upon my character, and inviting me to come and see him—this he sent by "Lone Wolf."

Three Bears had the narrowest squeak for his life, and, but for a guard the General placed over him, he would have been lynched on the spot.

This piece of villainy on the part of my enemies really did me a lot of good, for nothing would induce the Ogallalas to trade with any of them after that, and the result was that I practically had a monopoly of their custom.

I received the General's letter the following day, and rode up to Fort Robinson, where I was very kindly received. The General said he could plainly see that it was an attempt to get me off the Reservation, and he would not countenance it. Further, that if anything else occurred, and I was annoyed in any way, I was to come to him, and he would protect me. I thanked him very much for his kindness, and told him that after all the good services I had rendered the Government I should not be likely to do anything illegal and calculated to upset all the good ends we had been working for.

He said he could hardly credit that I could have done such a thing, and had a hearty laugh when I told him the fun I had in helping the soldiers to look for myself.

We parted excellent friends, and never again had any cause to meet to explain matters. In fact, whenever the General wanted advice he sent for me, and I was very pleased to assist him to the best of my ability.

I determined, however, that I would yet be level with Dr. Seville, so I procured some samples of his flour, tea, coffee, sugar, and other stores, and sent them to Washington.

This settled him; he was instantly recalled, and another man sent out to fill his position. Dear's licence also was revoked, and another sutler appointed in his place.

"Everything comes to him who waits," and my turn came when I saw these two rascals kicked bag and baggage out of Red Cloud Agency.

As an instance of the villainies these men perpetrated, we were left for three months without beef, all there was to eat being a quantity of barrels containing pork *bones from which all the meat had been removed.* As a result, a famine set in, and the Indians had to kill their dogs to live.

The Government all the time were ignorant of what was going on. A large sum was annually voted to supply the Indians with food, but it passed through various hands, until we got only the bones I have mentioned.

Even when beef did come along it was in the form of all the decrepit, diseased, and dying cattle that could be obtained in America. Anything was good enough for "redskins," and they had it.

Over and over again I have seen the Indians kill these animals when they were served out to them, take the skin, and trade it at the Government store for biscuits, leaving the meat for the carrion and dogs, *as it was not fit for human food.*

The new agent soon fell into his predecessor's little ways, and things became just as bad as ever. The temptation to make money was too great for any of them. All they had to do was to pinch, starve, swindle, and cheat the Indians, and did it readily enough.

I and all the other white men on the agency complained again and again, and sent in affidavits to Washington; but they never got beyond the Indian Department, where the swindling first started. The only reply we received was to mind our own business and not interfere in matters which did not concern us. I thought it was about time to clear out after this polite intimation, and accordingly I lit my pipe and sat down, as was my wont, to have a long think and a smoke over my next project.

CHAPTER XXIX.

A TRADING SPEC TO DEADWOOD—OBJECTION OF SITTING BULL TO MINING IN THE BLACK HILLS—GENERAL CROOK ACTS AS MEDIATOR—A GENERAL EXODUS ORDERED—ESTABLISHMENT OF THE RECORD OFFICE—A WINTER IN SIDNEY—RETURN IN THE SPRING—THE LOST CLAIM—APPOINTMENT AS CHIEF OF THE SIDNEY POLICE—NOTES ON OUTLAWS—LYNCHING OF "FLY-SPECKLED BILLY"—ADVANTAGES OF PRACTICAL LAW—DOC MIDDLETON KILLS A SOLDIER—"RUSTLERS" AND DESPERADOES—A STREET FIGHT WITH THE MILITARY—A RESOLUTION TO QUIT—JOINING CLIFFORD AND RUFF ON THE RUNNING WATER—THE RANCH POST OFFICE—"JENNIE" SENT TO PINE RIDGE.

THE gold fever had at this time broken out in the Black Hills, and I decided to try my luck there. Several other men on the Reservation were of the same opinion, so we determined to form a combination and start freighting.

I had a six-horse team, which I loaded up with spades, picks, soap, provisions—everything useful I could get hold of.

We went up to Deadwood, then a small mining town or collection of log shanties, about 165 miles from Red Cloud Agency.

People were flocking there from all parts of America, and the hills around were alive with miners hard at work.

The gold in the district was mostly quartz, but at the time I speak of the work was chiefly carried on in the gulches. I knew there was gold there, for I had not forgotten the lump the Indian had found some years previously when I was out with the Wajajas.

I sold out my stock at a handsome profit, returned to Red Cloud, and from there to Sidney, Nebraska, eighty-five miles farther on, for a fresh supply of goods.

At Sidney I rented a house, put my wife and family in, and returned with my freight to Deadwood, now 240 miles distant.

I made this journey with my teams backwards and forwards seven times, and managed to clear over 250 dollars a trip.

The Black Hills, as I have said, were in the middle of the Indian Reservation, running almost right through it, and as the whites came pouring in after the gold the Indians saw their chance of remaining in undisturbed possession of the country allotted them under the Treaty of 1868 disappearing.

Sitting Bull and his tribe, who were up in the Hills, made representations to Washington; receiving no satisfactory reply, they decided to drive the whites out, and accordingly attacked them at every opportunity.

At length the miners could only get about a couple of hours' work out of the twenty-four; they had to fight the rest of the time. Matters became so serious that the Government sent out General Crook with a number of soldiers to protect the whites and get them out of the country.

The miners were now between two fires—with the Indians after them on the one hand, and the soldiers driving them out on the other.

The General promised they all should return the following spring if they went away quietly now. Upon this understanding he got them all together, and took them off the Reservation in whatever direction they wished to go.

Deadwood was now deserted. Every one went to Custer City, a small settlement about midway between the former and Red Cloud.

Whilst this went on, I was busy bringing up parties of miners on the quiet; for the General would no sooner clear them out of their claims than, like magic, others appeared in them. The new-comers paid me well to run them up.

At length the old man tumbled to my little game, and lay in wait for me at Custer, where I arrived with a party of over three hundred.

He promptly sent us to the right-about, and intimated to me that, if he caught me at that little game again, he would make things unpleasant.

It was no use kicking, so we had to join the crowd and go back. Before leaving, however, a block-house was built at Custer, and in it a record office established, where a register of all claims was deposited, with four men to look after it. I had a claim on Spring Creek, some few miles west of the city, and this I inscribed in the book with all necessary formalities.

General Crook had brought some geologists with him to prospect on behalf of the Government and report on the mineral wealth of the hills. When this work was done we all cleared out and left the Indians in peace.

During the winter the geologists sent in their report. This proving most satisfactory induced the Government to make a treaty with the Indians, by which the latter, in consideration of a certain sum of money, gave up possession of the Black Hills and guaranteed the safety of certain roads up to them.

As a matter of United States history, and a sample of the justice that has been meted out to the Indians, I may here state that this consideration-money, or any portion of it, has not been paid up to the present time.

In due course notice was given that all might return in the following spring, and the 1st of May was the day appointed when an appearance was to be put in, and claims taken up. Failing the appearance, the claim was at the disposal of any one who chose to take it.

I was at Sidney at the time, and I hitched up my waggons, and made all speed to Custer.

Just as my luck would have it, one of my teams broke down on the way, and I arrived a day after time: the result was that some other fellow got my claim. This was the more annoying to me, as it was afterwards sold for 35,000 dollars, and became known as the Red Bird claim.

I felt so disgusted at my loss that I sold out my stock of provisions and tools for anything they would fetch, and, shaking the dust of Custer City from my boots, made my way home to Sidney again.

I now embarked on an entirely new career. Being a householder, and an eminently respectable member of society,

I was offered the post of chief of the police, and accepted it without a moment's hesitation. My force consisted of seven men, of various sizes and shapes. They had plenty to do, as the town was full of cow-punchers, mule-whackers, soldiers, and all sorts and conditions of men.

Sidney also was the starting-place for the Black

Hills, so that a pretty diversified collection of people, always changing, was to be found there.

At night the fun would commence when the saloons were filled; the proceedings generally terminated in a row between the civilians and the soldiers. A funeral as a rule occurred afterwards, somebody always being ready to furnish the corpse.

I have always flattered myself that I was the right man in the right place during the tenure of my office in Sidney. Things were very different then from what they are now, and the *modus operandi* of dealing with persons who came within the clutches of the law short and decisive.

Wild and reckless through life, deprived of the privileges most men enjoy, I had a sort of sympathy with some of the men, in spite of the trouble they caused me. I often thought that recklessness such as mine was the key to the misery of many of the cut-throats and thieves who favoured the town with their presence.

Living as I had lived on the plains, for reasons other than theirs, I had often come in contact with many bad characters who deserved a better fate. As a rule they were men who came originally from the East, and men who had committed crimes greater or less, and had made themselves scarce.

Once out West, they quickly went from bad to worse; the wild lawlessness of their surroundings was an inducement in itself to give free vent to all their bad passions.

Many I had known were men of considerable education and attainments, though it was only after I had roughed it with them for some time that these facts would come to light.

Beneath the rough exterior of the hunted outlaw one would not expect to meet with redeeming features, but in more cases than one I have found them.

I think I had either seen or known personally all the bad characters in the West up to the time of which I am writing. The number who had died with their boots on, that is, had been either shot or hanged, was very great.

When the towns became too hot to hold them they would skip out to the plains, and it was there that I had come across them. A white man is a white man under those circumstances whether he be a murderer or not, and, although I had my suspicions of many of them, it was only when they were caught and executed that I learnt the reason of their being whisked into eternity.

One of my greatest difficulties whilst at Sidney was preventing the lynching of my prisoners after I had taken them. This was the inhabitants' favourite method of disposing of any special case I had in my clutches.

We had a small jail made of logs and dobie bricks, and in this we would put the boys we caught. Frequently when we looked for them in the morning we found they had been at work with their knives, and by digging holes clean through the walls had escaped.

As a rule I didn't mind this, for they had the sense to clear out and never to come back again, and this saved me a lot of trouble.

Personally I was decidedly opposed to lynching, although I had seen a great deal of it, and upon more than one occasion taken a very active part in a happy dispatch.

Whilst on one of my late journeys up into the Black Hills, at a small mining town, I saw a fellow named Fly-speckled Bill lynched. He rode into the town and up to the log hut which was the only drinking saloon in the place. Seeing an old man standing there, he jumped off his horse and invited him to step inside and take a drink.

The old man declined, saying that he never drank whiskey. To which the reply was: "If you don't, I'll kill you."

"No, you won't," said the old man.

These were his last words, for Billy immediately pulled out his six-shooter and blew the old chap's brains out.

I was standing at the door of the blacksmith's shop adjoining the saloon, and had overheard the conversation between the two men. I never thought for a moment that Billy meant it seriously, but directly I saw him pull I took a back step into the smithy. Fortunately; or I should in all probability have had a bullet in my skull, for the second shot he fired passed through the old man's face and buried itself in the door-post as I quitted it.

I said to the blacksmith:

"Look here, Pard, I can't stand this. Here's that Fly-speckled Billy just shot an old man because he wouldn't drink with him. I should have been wiped out too if I hadn't taken a step inside this shanty. Here's the bullet in the door-post. See for yourselves. Is this to be tolerated or not? What say you?"

"No," was answered from the blacksmith and his mates, who saw nothing funny in being peppered whilst at work.

The noise of the shots had by this time brought several more people to the shanty to enquire what was up. When it was explained to them we all went in a body into the saloon.

There we grabbed Mr. Fly-speckled before he knew what we were up to, and in less than five minutes we had taken him to a telegraph-pole and sent him to settle scores with the old man and his Maker.

It was a sort of instantaneous court-martial. No one said what was going to be done—in fact, no one spoke. The general feeling was that he had to die, and that straight away.

In a case of this sort the murdering rascal was not fit to be at large. No one felt safe while he was around.

I never pulled a running rope more willingly in my life than I did in this case. I think Billy himself was the calmest and most collected of the lot. He made no resistance after we first grabbed him, and was still puffing at his cigar as we led him along. He watched the preparations without moving a muscle, and it was only as he was hoisted into mid-air that his cigar fell from his lips.

In Sidney, one day, I came across a party of the boys who had served a fellow in almost a similar way. This was also for murdering a man in cold blood. I arrived on the scene in my professional capacity just as the breath was out of his body, and was well laughed at by the crowd for not being in time to stop their fun. "One-minute-too-late-Nelson" they used to call me after that.

There was one advantage about this expeditious method. No legal machinery was requisite to set it in motion, and there was no chance of a reprieve arriving after sentence had once been pronounced.

In opening up a new country practical law has its advantages, and just on the confines of civilisation it would be impossible to get along without it.

On one occasion, at the Dancing Hall in Sidney, a citizen killed a soldier, and afterwards became one of the most noted desperadoes in the country. I was in the place at the time, and, seeing the fight, tried to stop it; the soldier was dead, however, before I could give any practical assistance.

The citizen's name was Doc Middleton, and I could not blame him in any way for what he had done. The soldiers were always bullying the people in the most outrageous manner, and taking every opportunity of insulting them:

This particular soldier had knocked Middleton down three times for no reason whatever, and then the latter shot him.

It so happened that Middleton, who was a quiet, peaceable fellow, and a freighter, was a friend of mine, and I told him to skip out of the town as quickly as he could, giving him the chance of doing so whilst I went to pick up the soldier. Of course, by the time I had fumbled the latter about and pronounced him dead, Doc had got clean away, and I had to make a terrible fuss with those present for having allowed him to escape.

The soldiers chased him from place to place, eventually getting him into a cañon one day; but, strange to say, he kept the whole company that was sent after him at bay. He killed several, wounded others, and eventually got away from them.

Finally he was betrayed by some of his friends, and sentenced to five years' imprisonment—a lenient view being taken of his case because of the persecution to which he had been subjected.

After serving his time he became as good a citizen as he was before, and the last I heard of him was as sheriff of Sheridan County, and report said that when there was a hard case to be taken Doc Middleton was the man. Middleton's case was not the only one of this description that occurred during these troublous times in Sidney. Very few men would stand the abuse of the Government officials, and I must confess that I could not blame most of the people for what they did.

These men, however, must not be confounded with another class of desperadoes—*i.e.* those who would not work and were what is termed "Rustlers" or house thieves. For these individuals I had no pity at all, and always did everything in my power to rid the country of them. Most of them are still serving their time in prison, and as to the rest I know where their bones lie bleaching on the plains.

This class of man is rapidly becoming extinct. Things are very different now from what they were twenty years ago. The old trails are filled up, and, as horse-stealing has ceased to be a virtue, the boys now "go it on the square."

The soldiers, after the murder of their comrade by Middleton, became more vindictive than ever against the citizens, and fired at them on the slightest provocation; the result was, I was at work day and night patching up disputes between them.

One night a cowboy came to me, and reported that the military were out and fighting with the people at the farther end of the town.

I got my gun, and accompanied my informant to the place where the disturbance was.

When the soldiers saw me coming they fired a

volley at me, one of the bullets passing through my clothes and grazing my ribs just in the region of the heart.

I felt faint for a moment, but the cowboy hit me a smack on the back and told me to pull myself together. I did, and he and I, throwing ourselves flat on the ground, kept up a continuous rain of shots from our repeaters until we cleared the street.

I then sent off one of the civilians to the commanding officer with a message, and he sent out a company to arrest all his men who were out with their rifles. They had no difficulty in finding nine we had wounded; the others managed to sneak in, doubtless with the assistance of their companions, and no other arrests were made.

I went off to a doctor to have my side strapped up, and when I got home, thought the matter over, and arrived at the conclusion that keeping the peace in Sidney was a job beyond my capacity, and the sooner I cleared out before I was assassinated, the better.

I had arrested a good many "hard cases," apart from rowing with the soldiers, and both sides had sworn vengeance on me. Accordingly I wound up my affairs, resigned my position, and went out to join Hank Clifford and Arthur Ruff, who had started a ranch on the Running Water River, about ninety miles distant.

I took my wife and family with me, and we arrived there safely. The ranch was a sort of hotel and restaurant on the high road, and the Deadwood stagecoach always stopped at it to change horses and grub the passengers. In addition, we kept the post-office, which gave us a position of some importance along the route.

My wife helped to look after the domestic arrangements of the hotel, and I attended to the post business. All round we did a very good business, and everything went swimmingly for about twelve months, when the women began to quarrel amongst themselves. I then sent my wife and the children down to Pine Ridge, a new agency that had been established about seventy-five miles east of Red Cloud.

The agencies were always being moved about, for no reason whatever, beyond the giving employment to some contractor who stood in with the agent. This meant the appropriation of some of the Government tribute set aside for the sustenance of the Indians, and a proportionate division of the spoil amongst the plunderers.

CHAPTER XXX.

THE CHEYENNES ON THE WAR-PATH—REJOINING THE GOVERNMENT SERVICE—EXPEDITION TO THE SAND HILLS—WATER EVERYWHERE, BUT NOT A DROP TO DRINK—SAVED BY THE SNAKE RIVER—FRANK WHEELING CARRIES A DISPATCH, AND TRUDGES TWENTY-FIVE MILES ON FOOT—DEATH OF ANOTHER CHILD—ERECTION OF PINE RIDGE AGENCY—TEACHING THE INDIANS TO DRIVE—REPRIMANDED FOR THRASHING A REDSKIN—MR. AGENT MACGILLICUDDY—APPOINTMENT AS CHIEF OF INDIAN POLICE—ERECTING A TELEGRAPH LINE—THE AGENT'S PECULATIONS—ROBBERY OF 200,000 DOLLARS A YEAR—PRESIDENT CLEVELAND TO THE RESCUE—A FEW WORDS ON THE INDIANS—A FEW MORE ON MYSELF—PREDESTINATION—AT LAST A "GLOBE TROTTER"—A LIST OF OFFICERS FOUGHT UNDER.

SOON after my wife's departure news came that the Cheyennes, dissatisfied with the way things were conducted at their agency, had gone on the war-path, and were passing up through Kansas and Nebraska, thickly settled States, killing, plundering, and burning everything in their path. They were bound for the Black Hills, and heading straight for the Red Cloud agency. The soldiers were following them up, but had failed to overtake them.

This information rather upset us, as may be imagined, especially as the crowd had to pass our ranch *en route*. A consultation was held, and it was resolved that I should post off to Fort Robinson, taking the women along with me, and offer my services to the Government, and that Clifford and Ruff should clear up things at the ranch and follow in a few days.

Arrived at the Fort, I was instantly engaged as scout and guide, and there met my old friend Frank Wheeling, who held a similar position. In about a week Clifford and Ruff turned up, and we all found ourselves engaged to drive the murdering crew out of the country.

Three squadrons of cavalry were all the soldiers available, and with these we started off towards the sandhills to meet the on-coming scourge. The country there is very difficult to travel through, and water that is fit to drink very scarce.

We had been out three days and nights, and after the first day had not had a drink. The mules drawing the waggons gave out, and we had to cut them loose, leaving the waggons to take care of themselves.

I knew the district very well, and if I had been left alone would have taken the troops day by day to where drinking-water was; but every one had a say, and I let them have their own way, as they would not listen to me.

At length things became serious, and it was imperative that water should be found at once. Hank Clifford wanted to go south, Frank Wheeling east, and I north. I knew I was right, and told the commanding officer so. A consultation was held, and the result was that it was decided that my advice should not be taken.

I did not see anything funny in dying for want of a drink. My tongue was lolling out of my mouth, and my horse was suffering as much as I was. So I rode up to the commanding officer and told him that if he liked to follow me he could ; if not, I should go alone.

As he did not condescend to answer me, I trotted off by myself.

I had ridden about three miles, and, finding a hill in front of me, I rode up it to see what direction my companions had taken. To my surprise I found them following me as fast as they were able, and motioning me to return to them.

I accordingly rode down and awaited them, when the commanding officer came up and said to me :

" Nelson, are you sure of finding water ? "

" I am, sir," I replied.

" About what o'clock ? "

" At one o'clock, sir, if my horse does not give out;" it was then 10 A.M.

" Very well, lead on. We'll follow you."

So I led the way, and about 12.30 struck the Snake River. It was a sight I shall never forget, the way both men and horses dragged up to and literally threw themselves into the stream. For about five minutes not a sound was heard. All were drinking.

We had nothing to eat, as everything was in the waggons. A party was accordingly sent back to procure whatever rations could be carried on the mules' backs, the waggons being left to follow.

The officers had taken care of themselves and let us starve. Frank Wheeling was lucky enough to steal an officer's rations out of his saddle-bag whilst he was not looking, and, giving me a sign, we went off quickly and divided the spoil, and

had a good laugh.

The following day we made a forced march on to the Running Water, where we found a cattle ranch, bought a steer, and had a feast.

Whilst there we received a dispatch from Fort Robinson to say that the Brûlés had also gone on the war-path, killed every one at the agency, and were coming up through the country where we then were.

We had now been travelling several days and nights without stopping, and were tired out. It was, however, necessary to get a dispatch into Fort Robinson, and Frank Wheeling was sent with it.

He arrived at his destination safely, and started back with the answer. About twenty-five miles from where we were camped he gave up, and lay down to have a few minutes' rest, holding his horse by the reins. The animal broke away, however, and returned to the Fort, leaving Frank to do the twenty-five miles on foot.

When he did get in, he brought orders for the command to return at once. We marched back, not covered with much glory, but having run a greater risk of losing our lives than if we had come plump upon the enemy. Upon arriving at the Fort we found that during our absence the Cheyennes had been captured by the Sioux, who had been enlisted in the Government service for the purpose and sent after the marauders, upon the time-honoured principle of "setting a thief to catch a thief." We found both bodies of Indians at the Fort, and also learned that the report about the Brûlé rising was false.

I was very glad, for I could hardly think that my old friends would willingly have taken up arms against the Government after their experiences of the past.

The expedition was paid off, and the soldiers went into quarters. I stayed on for a few days, when suddenly I received a message that one of my children had died at Pine Ridge, and I hurried down there. When I arrived I found it was my third daughter, three years old. She was already buried.

As the Government were now prepared to transfer the stores and warehouses of the Red Cloud Agency to Pine Ridge, I engaged to assist the officials in the erection of the various buildings, and drove a team from one to the other, transporting the necessary plant.

Upon the completion of this work and the full establishment of the agency it was decided to issue waggons and harness to the Indians, in order that they might be initiated into some of the benefits of civilisation; but they were to find their own horses.

A large consignment of waggons and harness had been sent to a station on the Missouri River, and I was engaged to go down and superintend their distribution.

The first I drew numbered six hundred waggons and six hundred sets of harness, and my duties were to instruct the Indians in the way to harness the horses and use the waggons. They had never possessed either before.

The fun soon commenced. I thought I should have gone mad in trying to show them how to put the harness on the horses. Sometimes they would have it over their heads and at others underneath them; anywhere but where it ought to have been. The Indian ponies also had never been in harness before, and that tended to enliven the proceedings.

At length we made a start for the Reservation: some got along pretty well, others did not try to move, and the Indians did not know how to make them. The first day we covered less than three miles.

Amongst the crowd was an old Indian who would not do anything he was told. He had a good team of horses, but they would always stop going uphill. As a result the whole caravan had to wait until I went along with a bull-whip and frisked them up. This the Indian could have done just as well as I; but no, he would sit on the waggon and look at his team, never attempting to move them along, although he knew a couple of miles of waggons were at a standstill behind him.

At first I tried to explain to him that he must talk to his animals and coax them along, and, if that had no effect, switch them up with his whip. It was no good, however, and I had to ride up the line at least a dozen times to set him on the move. There was no necessity for any one to tell me where the stoppage was. I knew before I started.

At length I got into a towering rage, and rode up to his team as usual with my whip, fully determined to give them something they would remember this time, when the old redskin informed me he would not allow his horses to be whipped. I replied that I would whip him if he did not keep his team moving and do as he was told. As he then cheeked me, I thought it incumbent upon me, in the interests of the others, to administer to him a little wholesome chastisement, which I accordingly did, and we had no more stoppages after that.

When we reached the agency, however, he reported me, and I was brought before the agent and severely reprimanded. This annoyed me excessively, and I refused to take charge of any more trips of that description. I told the agent that he had better try his own patience at giving driving lessons to his *protégés*; I had had enough of it, and had never been so insulted in my life as to be reprimanded for thrashing a redskin.

I was master of the situation over this, for he tried himself and sent other people down to the Missouri, but they all failed to teach the Indians anything. Between them they broke up more waggons than they got to the Reservation, and in the end the agent was recalled and a new one sent out.

Mr. Macgillicuddy was the new arrival, and I soon made his acquaintance. The first thing he asked me to do was to get in cord-wood if he supplied me with the Indian teams, all lying useless since I had given up practising as teacher of driving to the agency. I assented, and brought in twenty-four cords at two and a half dollars a cord.

Macgillicuddy had appointed his brother as chief of the Government store, and the fellow wanted to keep in with me, as I was useful to him in various ways, so I went to him with the money I had received and purchased rations. He gave me enough of the Government stuff to stock a large ranch, and I went off rejoicing. I had enough to keep my own and several other families all through the winter, and I wondered at the time what this excessive liberality meant, but I learnt afterwards that it was to purchase my silence about various matters which came under my observation.

My next appointment was as chief of the Indian police, and my duties were to look after horse thieves, whiskey smugglers, &c. The whites were perpetually stealing the Indians' horses, running them down into the settlements, selling them, and then returning for more.

I had to scour the country for miles round, collect these stolen ponies from the settlers, and bring them back to the Reservation. I kept at this for some time. About the year 1879 I was appointed waggon-master of some ox and mule teams to lumber up telegraph-poles for the line about to be constructed from the Missouri River to the agency, and from there to Camp Sheridan.

This work was done under the direction of Mr. Macgillicuddy, and he gave me a section of forty-two miles to complete on my own account, providing me with Indians and half-breeds to assist. I drew forty dollars a month for this, and finished my part of the line as well as, if not better than, any along the road. I do know that my poles were firmly planted, which is more than can be said of most of the others, as subsequent events have proved.

Following this I took another wood contract, out of which I made a little, but for what I charged two and a half dollars a cord Mr. Macgillicuddy debited the Government ten dollars, and for the hay which I got in at ten dollars a ton he charged twenty dollars.

I didn't tumble to this for a long time, nor to the

fact that all the stores he was selling from the commissariat were Government property intended for the Indians, which he was retailing to the settlers and any one who came along, putting the Indians on half rations to make up for it.

Finally the bomb exploded, and he was sent for to go to Washington and explain matters. While there he did explain—to his confederates in the Indian commission, who stood in with him—and to our great surprise he returned master of the situation.

This so riled the Indians that they kept writing to the Government, with the result that a special commissioner was sent out, who investigated the books and reported that everything was in order. This was not surprising, inasmuch as Macgillicuddy had bought over the commissioner.

We were determined not to be done, however, and kept on our letters, backing them up with over two hundred affidavits, and this brought out an extra special commissioner, who was up to a trick or two, and would not be bought over.

We went to him in a body and presented him with two hundred and fifty affidavits more to take back with him. Yet the Government did not remove the agent. They dared not, for he said openly that, if he fell, he would drag his confederates in office down with him.

This went on for a few years, and he then tried to run the whole of the affidaviters off the Reservation. He succeeded in getting rid of a lot of them, but I was bullet-headed and would not budge.

At length, when President Cleveland came into power, he was removed, and it was found that during

the six years he had been acting as agent he had made over two hundred thousand dollars a year!

I have given this as an instance of the gross injustice that has all along been perpetrated on the Indians. To-day there are men in America who are rolling in the wealth they have stolen from these poor creatures.

The best friend the Indian nation ever had is President Cleveland, and to him the honour is due of having at last meted out justice to a race which, whatever their faults, were masters of the continent before a white man ever set foot on it.

The time is not far distant when the Sioux will become the same as white people, and fifty years hence there will not be a single "full blood" on the Reservation. This is apparently a sad ending to a great nation, but it is one that the march of civilisation must necessarily bring with it. For many years of my life I have been contributing to this, and it is doubtless the best and only termination that can be expected.

For myself, I must confess that I have done little or no good. Many men with the opportunities and advantages I have had in the West would at my time of life have been living at ease on well-stocked ranches, or possibly have been the owners of townships now worth a little fortune.

But self-gain has never been an object with me. I have trodden a country over which I could look and say honestly, "This is all mine." Go where I liked, I could have selected my own location from the finest pasturage to the most auriferous of soil, and yet I do not possess one yard of land in the whole of the United States. The only freehold I shall doubtless ever claim will be the six feet in which I shall, ere long, be stretched.

I do not say this in any carping spirit, for I confess

that it is my own fault, and if I am not a rich man at the present moment I have only myself to blame.

I believe in predestination. Whatever a man's occupation or station may be in this life, provided his heart is in the right place, he can get on and make friends. I have trudged round for sixty-two years, and have put my theory to a practical test, so I can speak with some degree of authority. I would, however, have it understood that, as I have seen the error of my ways, I by no means advocate the following of them by others.

During all the years I had been away I had heard or seen nothing of any of my relatives or friends. One of my great regrets through life has been that I never saw either my father or my mother after running away from Charleston. I have brothers and sisters, I believe, who are still living there, but none of them has up to the present expressed any desire to take me into the family circle as one of themselves. An Indian wife and half-breed children are not connections that many Southerners would care to recognise, and since I am what I am, we are perhaps better apart.

I believe my uncle's sons are still well-to-do people in Missouri. They ought to be, for when the old man died I am told he cut up for quite a decent sum.

Since leaving the Reservation at Pine Ridge, in my old age I have taken to "globe trotting." When and where my travels will end I know not. The restless spirit of my youth is still strong within me, and whilst I have health and strength to be on the move I shall continue to move.

The picture of Cha-sha-sha-o-pog-geo sitting at his cabin door with a long pipe in his mouth, his silvery hair hanging in ringlets over his shoulders, whilst his great-grandchildren play at his feet, is not yet painted even in my imagination. There is no knowing what may occur, and even this unromantic termination of my career is within the bounds of possibility.

I regret I am unable to make the finale of these

pages more exciting, but, with the best intentions in the world, I have to recognise the important (perhaps to myself) fact that I am still alive. I have merely intended this record of my experiences to be descriptive of the opening up and advancement of a new country, and as such I trust it has fulfilled its purpose. There are many more men in the world who could give equally interesting reminiscences. Mine are embraced in a, comparatively speaking, limited area, but I have found it sufficiently large for my purpose. In conclusion, I venture to hope that the reader will have found the record of my doings, within its limits, of equally interesting dimensions.

For the benefit of any who may be interested I give below a list of the officers in the United States army under whom I have served as scout, guide, and interpreter :

General Bradley	Captain O'Brien	Lieutenant Hayes
,, Duncan	,, Murphy, 5th Cavalry	,, Hoskins
,, Augur	,, Egan, 2nd ,,	,, Hall
,, Carr	,, Mix, 2nd ,,	,, Riley
,, Emeray	,, Taylor, 5th ,,	,, Bates
,, Smith	,, Brown, 5th ,,	,, Beldon
Colonel Brown	,, Thompson	,, Forbush
Major O'Brien	,, Lyle 5th ,,	

Harrington

This seems
of balderda[sh]
the narrati[ve]
sixties and
did not go
Sioux being
Mormons in
There was n[o]
did not run
operated by
tale of the
Rawhide was
ever started

Arlington Originally

T's seems to be mostly reassuring; as a
husband. Not enough to aid in the
narrative. Spotted Tail is a famous
sixties and seventies, I believe; nor th[e]
did not go in for beaver trapping as man[y]
Sioux being almost entirely fur bearer[s]
Laramie in 1847 in all liklihood, however [I]
There was no Great diversity in 1847.
I1 I not run caravans east of the mountain[s]
operated by Smit[h], St. Vrain, and the Am[erican]
Calo of the renaming of the Republican river[?]
Bewnice was known as such but this mor[ning] his
over starved occupy Utah. Fort Laramie wa[s]
1853, but for me he is correct in sayin[g]
Mormon war and the Mountain Massacre occur[ed]
was 1859). Dots did Lost in Life toward
the Ash Hollow fight. His account of the
fitness is more balanced[?]. The Utah Exp[edition]
Port Laramon[?] ahead of Johnston, and m[ust]
beyond Fort Kearnel before he .. to for[t]
John doubt on the assertion that Johnson
the troops before they left Fort Leavenw[orth]
of the march of the troops to Salt Lake i[n]
Mountain Meadows Massacre was not 80 mil[es]
some 200 miles south of there. It is cor[rect]
snatted the bonds of Virginia. The Arm[y in?]
California--and on fact a U. S. Garrison o[f]
over a dozen children survivors of the ma[ssacre]
returned to .. Lee was caught not some fiv[e]
after the massacre.

If this gore us up to p. 190, and I thin[k]
error shows some the families who the --

www.ingramcontent.com/pod-product-compliance
Lightning Source LLC
Chambersburg PA
CBHW030428300426